THE
ARMS DEAL
IN YOUR
POCKET

A popular government without popular information, or the means of acquiring it, is but a prologue to a farce or a tragedy, or perhaps both. Knowledge will forever govern ignorance, and a people who mean to be their own governors must arm themselves with the power which knowledge gives.

James Madison, 4 August 1822

PAUL HOLDEN

THE
ARMS DEAL
IN YOUR
POCKET

JONATHAN BALL PUBLISHERS

For Mia

First published in 2008 in paperback by
JONATHAN BALL PUBLISHERS (PTY) LTD
PO Box 33977
Jeppestown
2043

Reprinted twice in 2008
Reprinted twice in 2009

ISBN 978-1-86842-313-2

Set in 9,5/13pt ITC Stone Serif
Editing by Frances Perryer, Johannesburg
Cover design by Lucky Fish, Durban
Design and reproduction of text by Triple M Design, Johannesburg
Printed and bound by CTP Book Printers, Cape

CONTENTS

Foreword   vii

Preface   xv

Acronyms and Abbreviations   xiii

1 'Pure Butter': Selling Arms in the New South Africa   1

2 Was the Arms Deal a Good Deal?   14

3 The Cover-Up   33

4 The First Casualty: Tony Yengeni   68

5 'Death of a Salesman': Joe Modise   87

6 Agent RS452 and the Resignation of
   Bulelani Ngcuka   112

7 The Case against Schabir Shaik   131

8 The Case against Jacob Zuma   179

9 Unfinished Business and Unanswered Questions   228

Appendices

Appendix A Who's Who and What's What in
    the Arms Deal   263

Appendix B The Only Arms Deal Timeline You'll
    Ever Need   283

Appendix C More Companies Than You Can Shaik
    a Stick At   316

Notes   321

Recommended Reading   355

FOREWORD

ANDREW FEINSTEIN

The Arms Deal and its cover-up continue to cast a vast, dark shadow over South African public life.

The ANC President, Jacob Zuma, has been charged with fraud and corruption in relation to the deal and will contest the next election as the ANC's candidate for President with his trial on these charges hanging over him.

President Thabo Mbeki's legacy will forever be tarnished by his central role in the deal and his determined undermining of a thorough and unfettered investigation into it (in addition to the far greater crimes of his unabashed and deadly Aids denialism and his support for the criminal regime of Robert Mugabe).

The Arms Deal and its cover-up were the moment at which the ANC and the South African government lost their moral compass, when the country's political leadership was prepared to undermine the institutions of our democracy – for which they and many others had fought – to protect themselves and the party. It was the point at which, in the words of Edward Said, they were prepared to 'repeat untruths until they have the force of truth'.

In late 2008, as a direct consequence of the Arms Deal and

its cover-up, the state and the ruling party seem constantly willing to undermine the rule of law to serve their interests. Leaders of the ANC and its allies claim they will kill to ensure that Jacob Zuma becomes President, referring one assumes to the corruption trial which could thwart his ambitions. The current Speaker of Parliament, Baleka Mbete – also the ANC's national chairperson and chair of the party's 'Political Committee' – closed down the Travelgate prosecutions, which resulted in senior MPs being prevented from facing the legal consequences of that sordid chapter in the life of our democratic Parliament. The President suspended the Director of Public Prosecutions who dared to issue a warrant for the arrest of the Commissioner of Police, who had been implicated in corruption and perverting the course of justice. As a consequence of a massive public outcry, he then appointed Frene Ginwala, an ANC loyalist who, as the former Speaker of Parliament, added to the chorus of ANC voices that excluded Judge Willem Heath from investigating the Arms Deal (despite a recommendation from Scopa), to judge whether his actions were warranted.

These and other similar actions have created not just a crisis of governance in South Africa, but a moral crisis that threatens to destroy the very tenets of our democracy.

Paul Holden has written a succinct, informative and devastating handbook to the Arms Deal, the root of this crisis. He has deftly identified and explained the key aspects of the deal – the illogicality of many of the purchasing decisions, the allegations of corruption, the under-utilisation of the equipment bought, the cover-up and, most importantly, the crucial questions that remain unanswered.

I would recommend this handbook to anyone concerned about the future of South Africa's democracy. And having read this disturbing indictment I would encourage you to join the call for a full, unfettered judicial and expert enquiry into the deal and its cover-up so that the South African public will, finally, know the full truth of this shameful episode in our democratic history. And then the perpetrators of this deal should face the full force of the law.

It is only in this way that South Africa will be able to move forward and recapture the spirit of 1994 with an accountable government that focuses, not on the defence and protection of its leaders, but on the real issues facing us: the plight of the millions of our people who live in poverty, the almost six million who are living with HIV or AIDS, and the scourge of violent crime.

PREFACE

The Arms Deal is a complicated beast. It has generated a huge amount of press (over 10 000 newspaper articles at last count) and been marked by a series of revelations that, while remarkable, have been difficult to put into proper context.

One of the major difficulties in understanding the Arms Deal and all its shocks is that it covers the best part of 18 years. If you were born in the year of Mandela's release and you look forward to casting your first vote in the 2009 election, the Arms Deal has been in the background all your life. No wonder people struggle to remember exactly what went on when and why.

Another major problem is the language in which the Arms Deal has been presented and discussed. The weapons themselves are shrouded in technical terms beyond the ken of the layman. Then there is the multitude of people and organisations involved, which can get somewhat confusing.

That is why this book was written. To make things easier to understand, we start where it makes sense to start: at the very beginning. The chapters are ordered chronologically, so that you can follow the story as it unfolded on the ground, and, by the end of the book, reach the temporary end of the story that continues to unravel and reveal itself.

Every chapter, too, has an 'info box'. This box previews the contents of each chapter, with a short timeline of the key dates to remember. If this is not enough and you feel yourself starting to get lost, turn to the Appendices at the back. Here you will find an extended timeline that tells the story as it unfolded on the ground. You will also find a list of all the people and organisations mentioned throughout the book, each with a short biography or description.

Writing a book of this nature presents its own particular problems. One is that the story continues to unfold. While the Arms Deal has rumbled on for the best part of 18 years, there is no sign that some of the major narrative strands will be tied up neatly in the near future. As such, the decision had to be made to enforce a cut-off point at which the writing would stop: you can spend the rest of your life, it seems, waiting for certain strands to be resolved.

The cut-off point chosen for this book was 24 August 2008. As a result, anything that has emerged since then has not, of necessity, been covered in this book. However, you are urged to turn to the section entitled 'Recommended reading' so that you can, at the very least, continue to follow all the ins-and-outs, wrangling, accusations, counter-accusations and revelations as they emerge.

I have been given unstinting assistance in writing this challenging book. I'd like to thank all those that have helped me to get my facts straight and assisted to tighten up the narrative, including my editor, Frances Perryer; the eagle-eyed Mark Gevisser; the tireless Andrew Feinstein; the ever-rigorous Gavin Woods; the composed Claire Wright; the constantly genial Francine Blum and Jeremy Boraine; designer/typesetter Kevin Shenton; and my coterie of cheer-leading loved ones, including my father, Richard; my brothers Mark and Jeremy; Sophie, Evan, Tymon, Marion and Judith. My biggest debt, however, is to Mia: it is your encouragement and unfailing love that has made this book possible. The book is dedicated to you in honour of your patience, respect, encouragement and remarkable tolerance for Arms Deal-related pillow talk.

Welcome to the Arms Deal.

Paul Holden
Johannesburg
25 August 2008

ACRONYMS AND ABBREVIATIONS

ADS: African Defence Systems

ALFA: Advanced Light Fighter Aircraft (the Gripen)

ANC: African National Congress

Cosatu: Congress of South African Trade Unions

DASA: DaimlerChrysler Aerospace

DESO: Defence Export Services Organisation (UK)

DIP: Defence Industrial Participation

DSO: Directorate of Special Operations (see Scorpions)

EADS: European Aeronautic Defence and Space

ECAAR: Economists Allied For Arms Reduction

GEAR: Growth, Employment and Redistribution Plan

GFC: German Frigate Consortium

GSC: German Submarine Consortium

ID: Independent Democrats

JCEMI: Joint Standing Committee on Ethics and Members Interests (Parliament)

JIT: Joint Investigating Team (also known as the 'Three Agencies')

JSC: Judicial Services Commission

LIFT: Lead-in Fighter Trainer (the Hawk)

LUH: Light Utility Helicopter

NDPP: National Director of Public Prosecutions

NIP: National Industrial Participation

NPA: National Prosecuting Authority

NWC: National Working Committee (ANC)

PAC: Pan Africanist Congress

RDP: Reconstruction and Development Programme

SAAF: South African Air Force

SACP: South African Communist Party

SAN: South African Navy

SANDF: South African National Defence Force

SAPS: South African Police Service

Scopa: Standing Committee on Public Accounts (Parliament)

SDP: Strategic Defence Procurement

SFO: Serious Fraud Office (UK)

SIU: Special Investigating Unit (also known as the Heath Unit)

CHAPTER 1

'PURE BUTTER': SELLING ARMS IN THE NEW SOUTH AFRICA

WHAT'S IN THIS CHAPTER?

- The state of the military at the end of apartheid.
- The first moves towards buying military matériel on a large scale: the corvettes.
- Protests against the corvettes.
- How we decided on the Arms Deal: the Defence White Paper and Defence Review.
- How the Arms Deal was sold to the South African public.

KEY DATES FOR THIS CHAPTER

- **1989–1992** The SADF suffers severe budget and staff cuts.
- **1993** It is announced that the SA Navy is looking to purchase four new warships, the corvettes.
- **LATE 1993** Foreign arms companies begin inundating the SANDF with enquiries.
- **1994** After SA's first democratic election, Joe Modise is appointed Minister of Defence. He authorises the navy to begin tendering for new corvettes.
- **FEBRUARY 1995** The SA Navy announces that it has narrowed down the tenders for corvettes to the Bazan shipyard in Spain and the Yarrow shipyard in Scotland.
- **JUNE 1995** The corvette deal is scrapped after intense public criticism. Any new purchases will only be made after a substantial review of the SANDF's military requirements.
- **1996** The Defence White Paper is presented to Parliament, arguing for the adoption of the 'core-force' concept. The recommendations of the White Paper are to be included in the SANDF's Defence Review.
- **JUNE–AUGUST 1997** Both Cabinet and Parliament approve the first phase of the Defence Review.
- **LATE 1997** Thabo Mbeki announces that the government has invited tenders from foreign arms companies.

Under apartheid, the military establishment was often seen as a behemoth with the means to wreak havoc throughout Southern Africa at the push of a button. Armed troop carriers rumbled through the townships attempting to put a lid on the war taking place on the streets of South Africa's poorest neighbourhoods. The ability of the army to cross the South African border and attack ANC safe houses terrified anti-apartheid operatives and the states bordering the country. The raid on Gaborone on 14 June 1985, which saw the South African Defence Force (SADF) cross the Botswana border to attack a private home thought to house ANC guerrillas, emphasised the apparent omnipotence of apartheid's armed forces.

But appearances were deceptive. The SADF had a soft underbelly. With a focus on land-based encounters in the townships and abroad, funds had been funnelled to support the army.[1] In addition, the UN arms embargo against South Africa, although often broken by various shady operators, effectively prevented the SADF from modernising two branches of its forces: the Air Force and the Navy. As a result, by 1990, both were in terrible condition, stocked with hopelessly outdated equipment. During its war in Angola, the South African Air Force (SAAF), flying French Mirage fighters, was devastated by the Cuban army's much more effective Russian MIG-23s.[2]

The Navy was even worse off. Its various ships, bought before the eruption of the township revolt, were approaching obsolescence. To service these aging hulks, it was forced to search 'the scrap heaps of the world' for parts, as one Navy chief put it.[3] Its three submarines were due to be taken out of active service by 2005, while its strike craft, large frigates, were due to be retired in 2000.[4] Some didn't even make it that far: the SAS President Pretorius, the last of the Navy's three

3

frigates in its 'President' class, was sunk after being stripped of useful parts, while the *SAS Rijger*, a seaward defence boat, was sold at a cut-price rate of R13 500 to a Hout Bay tour operator who was planning to use it for pleasure cruises.[5]

The Navy's problems were compounded by budget cuts in 1990. During apartheid, the Navy had a budget that averaged 17 per cent of a total defence budget that was 15 per cent of the state's entire expenditure. By 1992, however, it was only awarded 8 per cent of a defence budget that made up 9 per cent of the national budget. The Navy was forced to rationalise and fired over 2 000 sailors.[6] A plan to build four corvettes (fast attack ships slightly smaller than frigates) to replace the Navy's crusty frigates was scrapped in August 1991 because of budgetary constraints.[7] In 1992, Chief of the Navy, Vice-Admiral Lambert 'Woody' Woodburne, resigned, lashing out at the 'ridiculous' funding cuts that threatened a 'prime national asset'.[8]

'Do people really understand the value of a navy?' Woodburne mused in a 1992 interview.[9] Apparently not. Although the Navy argued that it needed to protect South Africa's harbours from attack, and its fisheries from poachers, the idea that it could be replaced by an inexpensive coastal patrol gained ground. In early 1993, the Parliamentary Floor Committee investigated maritime policy and argued that the country's sea needs would best be served by closing down the Navy and transferring all existing equipment to a national coast guard.[10] It was a logical decision: four corvette warships would cost roughly R425m each, while five fast patrol boats, which could do the job of protecting fisheries better, would cost R35m each.[11] And, with Nelson Mandela at the helm of the world's newest best friend, who would really want to attack us?

With the Navy forced into a corner, a new strategy was required: it would have to sell itself better. Vice-Admiral Robert Simpson-Anderson, who replaced Woodburne as head of the Navy, commented in a 1993 interview that 'it's very difficult to quantify the value of a Navy, to show in financial terms and value of investments which [have] been made.'[12]

As it became clear that South Africa was finally moving towards democracy the Navy received the lobbying support of the international armaments industry. In March1993, Vice-Admiral Robert Simpson-Anderson announced that he was looking to buy four new corvettes.[13] By September, it was reported that the Navy and Air Force were being 'inundated with queries regarding potential new equipment from many countries, particularly Europe and the Far East, and this is expected to intensify once the arms embargo is formally lifted'.[14]

Foreign navies literally raced to be the first to visit the new South Africa: the French proudly announced that they would attempt to trump a British naval visit to Simonstown by a couple of days in January 1994.[15] Intense pressure was put on the new government by visiting dignitaries. In September 1994, UK Prime Minister John Major came to South Africa, armed with a letter to Mandela lobbying for new arms contracts.[16] By 1995 Pretoria was 'fast becoming one of the world's premier arms trade centres with weapons deals involving millions of rands taking place behind closed doors … Pretoria has been swamped by foreign guests in uniform all visiting the South African National Defence Force – and keen to grab a slice of the lucrative arms market.'[17] Undoubtedly the fervour with which Pretoria was wooed by weapons sellers owed a lot, at the time, to the mini-depression that had occurred in the arms industry after the fall of the Berlin Wall.

It was good timing for the Navy. And the new Defence

chiefs seemed to stand behind Vice-Admiral Simpson-Anderson: in 1994, Joe Modise, now the Minister of Defence, agreed to allow the Navy to submit requests for tenders for the new corvettes. Tenders flooded in and by 1995, the Navy had whittled down the bidders to two options: the Bazan shipyard in Spain and the Yarrow shipyard in Scotland. It seemed like a done deal: the Navy, five years after firing 2 000 sailors, was set to buy four new corvettes for R1.69bn. In reality, there were two separate products purchased. First, the government bought the ship platform, which is a fancy way of saying the boat itself. Second, it bought a combat suite to be installed into the ship platform. The combat suite was the weapons and defence system of the corvette. R1bn was to be spent outside the country, as foreign companies were to supply the ship platforms.[18]

The sight of anti-apartheid stalwarts standing arm-in-arm with the new South African National Defence Force (SANDF) in the decision was surreal: 'the rapidity of the conversion of old guerrillas like Defence Minister Joe Modise and his Deputy, Ronnie Kasrils, to the benefits of big weaponry must count as a modern miracle', a *Sunday Times* editorial read.[19] Even more surreal was the idea that, barely a year after taking office, the ANC's first major purchase would be weapons, not houses. As Tony Yengeni, the ANC's future Chief Whip and Chairman of Parliament's Joint Standing Committee on Defence, commented: 'the levels of poverty in the country are so high that most victims of poverty cannot comprehend that a new democratic Parliament can endorse spending a substantial amount on corvettes'.[20] And with good cause, as William Gumede noted: 'The party came to power pledging drastic cuts to the defence spending that characterised the apartheid era, in favour of social services.'[21]

The South African Students Congress, one of the largest

student organisations in South Africa's universities, was appalled by the announcement and led a march of hundreds of students to the Union Buildings in Pretoria to petition the new Education Minister, Professor Sibusiso Bengu. They argued that the funds that would be spent on the corvettes would better be spent on establishing a loan and bursary scheme for university students, a scheme that would cost the same as the corvettes to establish.[22] Within the new ANC Cabinet the corvette decision sailed into some less-than-impressed ministers. Both Jay Naidoo (Minister without Portfolio tasked with leading the Reconstruction and Development Programme) and Trevor Manuel (Minister of Finance) reportedly questioned the deal.[23] Cosatu wondered whether the country wouldn't be better served by investing the funds in social welfare, or, at least, getting South African ship builders to make the corvettes.[24]

The decision to buy the corvettes received a bashing in the mainstream media. A *Sowetan* editorial opined: 'We cannot agree that, being a country which is faced with the huge task of improving the living conditions of its people, we should divert such large sums to buying expensive boats for the Navy. We have to agree with the SA Council of Churches that the real enemies of the country are hunger, poverty and homelessness. Fighting these should be a priority above all others.'[25] An editorial in the *Cape Times* pointedly wondered, 'Can the expenditure of at least R1,7 billion on naval ships, in peacetime, be justified while millions of South Africans still live in squalor with minimal access to the most basic facilities? At a pinch the Navy can manage a little while longer with the strike craft and other vessels it already has, but there can be no greater urgency than housing the homeless.'[26]

The 'newest hawk'[27] in the defence department, Ronnie

7

Kasrils, quickly went on the lobbying offensive. A failure to equip the Navy was a desperate dereliction of duty, he explained to a Cabinet sub-committee hearing on the decision: 'Defence is our sovereignty, our democracy, the peace we strive for. And that, colleagues, means that we have got to deal with possible threats, maybe not today or tomorrow, but five, ten or twenty years on.'[28] Even though South Africa faced no imminent threat, at danger was its 2600 km coastline, prey to malicious poachers, and its vital trading ports, as Kasrils attempted to make clear in a 1995 interview. 'Our trade is totally dependent on imports and exports; 80 per cent in terms of value and 95 per cent in terms of volume goes through the ports. So we're an island economy ... for our wealth, our economy, we have to understand how dependent we are on the sea. If our ports were mined or blockaded, we'd have a major economic crisis ... There's no war threat around the corner, but, in three years' time, if the situation turns ugly, we'll pay through the nose and have a battle against time to make up capability. War doesn't wait for you to get yourself organised.'[29]

The defence industry took a more seductive approach. When there was no war around the corner, it was difficult to argue for new weapons. Instead, it was argued that the corvette deal would actually make South Africa money. This would be achieved by offsets, also known as counter-trade. Offsets are agreements on the part of arms suppliers to invest money in the South African economy in return for receiving tenders. Offsets in the corvette deal, it was estimated, would lead to between R3bn and R7.6bn in new economic activity in the country.[30] The British tender, through the Yarrow shipyard, promised work for 25 000 people and 10 000 houses.[31] The Spanish tender, through the Bazan shipyard, offered a 'menu' of 18 offset options, which included the offer to fund a new fleet of hake fishing boats, even though, it was later discovered, the proposal would only be viable if the hake stocks in the country were substantially over-fished.[32] Antonio Sanchez-Camara, president of the Bazan shipyard, predicted that 'billions of rands will stream into South Africa as a result of the deal'.[33]

Armscor, the South African armaments giant, made a vocal case in the media, selling the corvette deal as an industrial participation package more than a weapons purchase. Managing director Tielman de Waal argued that the deal would lead to a net inflow of R2bn into the country and would help the government meet its RDP obligations: 'Normally, foreign procurement entails a net outflow of reserves, negative impact on our trade balance, and an increase in our defence burden. However, the counter trade aspect has added a new dimension to foreign acquisition. Subject to the defence budget and cabinet approval, the acquisition of the corvettes meets convincingly the needs of both the RDP and defence and it is pure butter!'[34] Krish Naidoo, corporate communications director at Armscor, wrote that the corvette deal 'successfully straddles the gap between state security and protection of the populace. It will also create employment and resources by protecting our marine environment. Furthermore, it will boost the RDP through countertrade inherent in the corvette deal.'[35]

Behind the scenes, a more complicated picture was emerging. Thabo Mbeki, newly appointed as the Deputy President of the country, reportedly travelled to Germany at the beginning of 1995 and told the German Foreign Minister that 'the race is still open'.[36] Infuriating the Spanish and UK bidders, the corvette tender was reopened as the government, now taking fuller control of a deal initiated by the old SADF, sought more favourable terms and bigger counter-trade offers. The government was seen as dilly-dallying: 'The manner in which the purchase of corvettes had been handled was a "chronicle of confusion and lost opportunities" which had left the SA Navy and government compromised and embarrassed,' wrote the influential business mouthpiece, the *Financial Mail*, quoting Democratic Party spokesperson James Selfe.[37]

The final decision on whether to purchase the corvettes was to be made by Cabinet. As a result of the public outcry and the particularly haphazard manner in which the purchase was pursued, it decided, in June 1995, that the corvette deal would have to be scrapped. Instead, the country would look at buying arms only once a Defence Review had been completed outlining a rigorous defence policy for the years to come.

A Defence White Paper was completed and presented to Parliament in 1996, followed by a final Defence Review, which was presented in phases to Cabinet and Parliament in 1997 and 1998. The White Paper, which informed the later Defence Review, struck an ambiguous note. Much as Kasrils had argued with regard to the corvettes, the White Paper acknowledged that there was no military threat to South Africa. But, in such an unstable world, could we really afford to be caught unprepared?

> ... in the South African context there is pressure to reduce defence spending substantially. There is an urgent requirement to divert financial resources to the RDP in order to meet basic socio-economic needs. A failure to meet these needs will generate conflict and instability. There is no conventional military threat in the short- to medium term ... The non-military threats emanating from instability and underdevelopment in Southern Africa should

be tackled primarily through political and socio-econom-
ic measures …

The SANDF has to maintain a long-term capability to
fulfil its primary function. It is not possible to create such
a capability from a low level of preparedness if the need
suddenly arises. It is therefore imperative to retain a sustainable core force and to upgrade, and where necessary,
replace obsolete equipment.[38]

The Defence Review was more strident. It argued that the
lull in South Africa's military conflicts gave the country the
space to 'right-size' the military according to a 'core-force'
concept. According to core-force design, the military would
cut staff but modernise its weaponry, so that it could more
efficiently fulfil its duties as a regional peacekeeper.[39] It argued that there was an urgent need to purchase new *matériel*
for the Navy and Air Force, and submitted a wish-list of purchases that included 4 corvettes, 4 submarines, 4 maritime
helicopters, 28 fighter planes, 40 utility helicopters and 54
battle tanks.[40]

The reality was that, even though the Defence Department
mouthed the slogans of the RDP, it was always committed to
new arms acquisitions. Indeed, in May 1997, a month before
the Defence Review was submitted to Cabinet for approval,
it was reported that both Kasrils and Modise had approached
Thabo Mbeki to try and convince him of the need to purchase the weapons. This was reportedly done after Trevor
Manuel, in charge of government finances, had been un-
willing to budge on the request. Kasrils confirmed that there
were 'tense negotiations' between Modise and Manuel.[41]

Again, the lobbying seems to have worked. The Cabinet
approved the first phase of the Defence Review on 18 June
1997, and it was presented before Parliament in August of

the same year, where it received the same stamp of approval. Speaking in Parliament, Kasrils waxed poetical as he lauded the Defence Review and its new shopping list as the road to Renaissance:

> This house stands on the threshold of a bold new age.
> You have the power to define our nation's destiny.
> Your decision will affect generations to come.
> Your endorsement of this historic Defence Review will invigorate the Renaissance.
> And your support will put us in the vanguard of Africa.[42]

In the same speech, Kasrils held out the seductive carrot of counter-trade, while taking a sidelong jab at the one minister who could stop the whole process:

> There will be substantial off-set agreements so that, for instance, South African steel and other local components and equipment will be used in production. There will be major off-set or counter-trade agreements, so that for every rand spent abroad, the same amount will be invested in South Africa.
> Such packages will be of enormous benefits to our GEAR Strategy. It will bring in investment and create jobs. Therefore Defence acquisition will be Trade and Industry led. Far from being a drain on our resources, it will provide a tremendous boost to our economy and Treasury.
> It will delight the Minister of Finance.[43]

Cabinet and parliamentary approval of the *Defence Review* meant that, once again, the SANDF could start shopping around for *matériel*. Towards the end of 1997, Thabo Mbeki, part of the Cabinet sub-committee tasked with undertaking the acquisitions, announced that invitations to tender would be released by the end of the year. The aim: to purchase R12bn worth of equipment.[44]

The Arms Deal had begun.

CHAPTER 2

WAS THE ARMS DEAL A GOOD DEAL?

- How we bought what we bought.
- What we bought and what it does.
- How the Arms Deal was sold: offsets and their problems.
- What did the Arms Deal cost and what else could we have got for the same amount?
- Did we need all of this stuff?

KEY DATES FOR THIS CHAPTER

- NOVEMBER 1998 Thabo Mbeki announces that Cabinet has chosen the preferred suppliers – the main companies who will be supplying the arms to South Africa.
- AUGUST 1999 The final affordability assessment on the Arms Deal is presented to Cabinet, which warns of the financial risks inherent in the Arms Deal.
- 3 DECEMBER 1999 Government signs the contracts and loan agreements that finalise the Arms Deal.
- 11 OCTOBER 2000 Scopa holds its first hearings into the Arms Deal. Chippy Shaik and Jayendra Naidoo admit that arms companies will only face a 10 per cent penalty if they fail to deliver on offsets. They also admit that the cost of the deal has escalated to R43.8bn.
- SEPTEMBER 2006 Defence Minister Lekota admits in Parliament that offsets have only created 13 000 jobs as opposed to the 65 000 jobs promised.
- 2008 According to the 2008 budget, South Africa has spent R43.09bn on the Arms Deal to date, with a further R4.3bn to be spent by 2011.

HOW DID WE BUY WHAT WE BOUGHT?

Following the approval of the Defence Review in Parliament, government quickly got down to the business of selecting and buying the desired military hardware. In charge of the process was a Cabinet sub-committee on acquisitions. The members of the sub-committee were Thabo Mbeki (Deputy President), Alec Erwin (Minister of Trade and Industry), Trevor Manuel (Minister of Finance), Stella Sigcau (Minister of Public Enterprise) and Joe Modise (Minister of Defence).[1]

Buying the arms was supposed to be a relatively straightforward process, governed by Armscor's own practices regarding arms acquisitions (Armscor is a South African government-owned arms manufacturer). The Cabinet sub-committee issued a series of invitations to tender. These invited various arms companies around the world to submit information about the arms they had to offer, including technical specifications and cost of the goods that would be provided, detailed information as to what offsets would be offered as part of the package, and what financing terms the arms company or its home country could provide.

These tenders would be provided to the government, which would then evaluate them in a series of different sub-committees, each one looking at a different piece of equipment. On these sub-committees were representatives of Armscor, the Department of Defence and its Secretariat, the Department of Trade and Industry and the Department of Finance.[2] After these sub-committees had completed their assessment, this would be referred to the Arms Acquisition Council, which was the last level of approval before the potential purchase and its terms were presented to Cabinet. The Arms Acquisition Council would then evaluate the proposals submitted by the various sub-committees, and provide final approval of the Acquisition Plan. The Acquisition Plan was a 'mandatory document that indicates a commitment to acquire the product concerned at a specified price. It thus commits the budget of the Department of Defence to a particular expenditure.'[3] The Arms Acquisition Council would then provide the Acquisition Plan to either the Cabinet sub-committee on Defence or directly to Cabinet, which would then make the final decision on the purchase.[4] This rigorous process was intended to ensure that South Africa received the best weapons at the best available price, and to limit potential corruption in the arms acquisition process, as Joe Modise promised in 1999: 'I want to assure you that the bids have gone through a fine tooth comb to ensure an ethical outcome.'[5]

In November 1998, Thabo Mbeki, heading the Cabinet sub-committee tasked with overseeing the whole process, announced that the government had selected its list of preferred suppliers, and that the arms acquisitions were to go ahead. This was the first time that a firm figure was presented as to the cost of the purchases: it had previously been estimated at between R12 and R15bn, but was now estimated at R30bn, which was variously described as 'huge' and a 'bonanza'.[6] After the Cabinet sub-committee announced its list of preferred suppliers, the negotiations were handed over to a series of further sub-committees to iron out the terms of the agreement with the preferred suppliers. In this process, the government would attempt to negotiate a package that would supply South Africa with the best return on money spent. This process was completed by 3 December 1999, when the government signed the final purchasing agreements, and Trevor Manuel signed the loan agreements that would pay for the equipment.[7]

WHAT DID WE BUY?

The final agreements signed on 3 December 1999 bought the SANDF a considerable amount of equipment, most of which was to re-equip the aging Navy and Air Force. This is what we bought, what it was estimated to cost at the time, and where it came from:

TABLE 1 What we bought, where it came from and how much it cost[8]			
EQUIPMENT	QUANTITY	CONTRACTOR/SUPPLIER	PRICE IN RMILLION (1999)
Corvettes (Meko A200)	4	German Frigate Consortium (Germany) providing the ship platform; Thomson-CSF (France) and African Defence Systems (South Africa) providing the combat suite	R6 917
Submarines (Class 209 1400 MOD)	3	German Submarine Consortium (Germany)	R5 354
Advanced Light Fighter Aircraft (The Gripen)	28	SAAB and British Aerospace as a joint British-Swedish Consortium (UK/Sweden)	Part of R15 772 total
Lead-in Fighter Trainer Aircraft (The Hawk)	24	British Aerospace (UK)	Part of R15 772 total
Light Utility Helicopter (Agusta A109M)	30	Agusta (Italy)	R1 949
Total cost			R29 992

WHAT DOES ALL THIS STUFF DO?

The corvettes: Ronnie Kasrils quaintly described corvettes as the 'bakkies of the sea'.[9] Measuring 121 metres, they are smaller than the frigates that the Navy previously used. They are equipped with a sophisticated weapons system, which makes up 40 per cent of their total cost. The corvettes are supposed to be the workhorses of the Navy, providing the capacity for search-and-rescue operations, maritime patrols with an eye on law enforcement, and a helicopter launching-pad, which substantially increases surveillance range. The corvettes also have 'blue sea' capacity (the ability to sail in parts of the ocean far away from the shore), which means that they can sail as far south as Marion Island.[10]

The submarines: Purchased to replace South Africa's Daphne submarines, on the assumption, Terry Crawford-Browne has noted, that submarines makes small navies important.[11] Thus deterring foreign powers from attacking the country, the submarines are also intended to provide a stealthy way of protecting South Africa's coastal trade, by being able to spy on illegal activity and feed this information to surface ships, and to provide support in peace-keeping operations.[12]

The Gripen: A 'multi-role combat aircraft', according to its official website, which also calls it 'the wings of your nation'.[13] This nippy supersonic attack fighter has replaced the Cheetah C and Cheetah D fighters that were on the SAAF's inventory. It can be used to provide armed cover and support for land-based attacks, reconnaissance, air-borne dog-fights and airspace control.[14] Built as a joint initiative by Britain and Sweden, it is also used by the air forces of Sweden, the Czech Republic, Hungary and Thailand.

The Hawk: Built by British Aerospace, the Hawk provides trainees with flight experience before they move on to the supersonic Gripens. It can also do limited search and rescue missions, reconnaissance and patrolling.[15] It replaces the Impala trainers used by the SAAF, and was chosen over the cheaper Italian Aeromacchi MB339. The selection of the Hawk attracted considerable criticism. Even the UK's Royal Air Force (RAF), which uses the Hawk, found that the Aeromacchi was 'far and away better than anything the RAF currently possesses.'[16]

The helicopters: The Light-Utility Helicopters were bought from Agusta in Italy to replace the SAAF's 40-year-old French Alouette helicopters. They can accommodate up to eight people, and can also be used to carry up to two stretchers. They are intended to be used for search and rescue operations, medical and humanitarian assistance, helping with police patrols and patrolling South Africa's borders.[17]

WHAT ABOUT THOSE OFFSETS, THEN?

When the Arms Deal package was announced, one of the major incentives offered to ensure its approval was the amount of money that South Africa would get in return for signing the contracts. As we saw in the last chapter, Ronnie Kasrils promised that the deal would 'delight the Minister of Finance'.[18] The reason for this was the offsets that came bundled with the signing of the packages. These commitments made on the part of arms contractors to literally offset the cost of purchasing from them would be fulfilled in numerous ways: arms companies could directly invest in the country, thereby promoting new economic growth (this is also known, in the counter-trade industry, as 'buyback'); or they could agree to purchase other goods from South Africa to balance the country's terms of trade (known as a 'counter-purchase').

As criticism of the Arms Deal has gathered pace, the government has been more reticent in singing the praises of the offset agreements. But, back when the contracts were signed, they were presented as one of the main reasons to go ahead with the deal. Even before the final contracts were signed, the government announced with considerable fanfare that the Arms Deal would lead to investment in the country worth between R104bn and R110bn, and the creation of roughly 65 000 jobs. Indeed, Joe Modise, in his last budget speech to the country six months before the final deal was signed, went out of his way to spell out the miraculous windfall that the offsets presented, and how they would be structured:

> Re-equipping the defence force is being done in such a way as to add value to our economy. In return for our expenditure, our economy will benefit by
>
> • an estimated 110 billion rands of new investment and industrial participation programmes;
> • and the creation of approximately 65 000 jobs.
>
> The sceptics have suggested this is wishful thinking.[19]

Offsets weren't just the icing on the cake of a great deal. They were often presented as incontrovertible proof that the Arms Deal made sense. Andrew Feinstein, in an interview with the BBC in 2003, noted that the offset programmes

> ... were extremely important for two reasons. One, they were absolutely critical in the process of persuading Parliament and the South African public that this deal was worth doing. Secondly, they were crucial in persuading various ministers, particularly the Ministers of Finance

and Trade and Industry in South Africa that the deal was worth doing, because they initially were opposed to the deal for cost and other reasons in Cabinet, and the presentation of the offset proposals were instrumental in changing their minds.[20]

Leon Engelbrecht, a defence industry expert, argued that 'the South African government has never sought to justify the programme on the merits of the equipment to be purchased or the existence of some military threat to the country... Instead, they rationalized the purchases with reference to the anticipated offset R29 billion spent on arms would generate in investment and trade.'[21]

But offsets are not the economic panacea that they first seemed. In fact, they are a particularly controversial way of engaging in trade, and are usually prohibited by the World Trade Organisation (WTO), except in relation to developing countries.[22] Even then, there are strict rules governing how offsets are used in trade. According to the WTO Agreement on Government Procurement:

> Entities shall not, in the qualification and selection of suppliers, products or services, or in the evaluation of tenders and award of contracts, impose, seek or consider offsets.
>
> Nevertheless, having regard to general policy considerations, including those relating to development, a developing country may at the time of accession negotiate conditions for the use of offsets, such as requirements for the incorporation of domestic content. Such requirements shall be used only for qualification to participate in the procurement process and not as criteria for awarding contracts.[23]

In layman's terms, this means that a developing country's government may require that an arms company includes offsets in its tender offers in order to be considered. But offsets may not be used as the basis for such a decision: they cannot be a deal breaker. This makes more sense if you consider that, if a country signed a deal purely on the basis of an offset agreement and not on the necessity of the goods purchased, it would be tantamount to legal bribery.

International experience seems to suggest that the large majority of arms industry related offset programmes end in ignominy. Mark Gevisser, biographer of Thabo Mbeki, notes that international experience has shown that offset 'promises are unenforceable and inevitably broken' while doing 'little more, in the end, than inflate the purchase price of the goods'.[24] Indeed, academic literature has argued that, in many cases, arms companies increase the price of the goods they sell in order to cover any penalties they might pay: 'the costs incurred by arms companies as a result of the offset deals are simply passed on to the recipient ... the level of job creation and technology transfer over and above that which would have occurred without offsets is generally minimal'.[25]

Did the arms companies stick to their offset agreements? The Standing Committee on Public Accounts (Scopa), a Parliamentary oversight body that questioned the validity of the deal, was surprised to find out in October 2000 that they didn't even have to. On 11 October 2000, Scopa, led by Gavin Woods of the IFP, Andrew Feinstein and Laloo Chiba, both of the ANC, questioned Chippy Shaik and Jayendra Naidoo about the deal in a public hearing. Naidoo and Shaik were key players in the acquisitions process: Shaik was the chief of acquisitions for the Department of Defence, while Naidoo was the chief negotiator for the government.[26] Their testimony revealed that, in fact, the arms suppliers only faced a penalty of 10 per cent of the purchase price if they defaulted on their offset agreements; an amount that was considerably less than the offset agreements as a whole.[27] If they felt like it, the arms companies could refuse to meet their offset commitments, and only pay a R3bn penalty: roughly 3 per cent of the R104bn to R110bn that had been promised to Parliament and the public on the announcement of the deal.

Kasrils's rosy promise that offsets would 'delight the Minister of Finance' began to look shakier after Naidoo and Shaik, in the same hearing, attempted to downplay their importance to the Arms Deal. 'I think too much emphasis is being put on the fact that the Department of Defence acquires equipment because of [offsets],' Shaik warned.[28] Naidoo made an even more startling admission when he admitted that 'it is a highly questionable proposition that offsets will generate economic development. Our exercise was to recoup some of the expenditure on the armaments approved by government. The acquisitions were not meant to generate a massive economic boom, but would be economically neutral.'[29]

Whether offsets have materialised is a difficult question to answer. Public scrutiny was disallowed, as Terry Crawford-Browne noted: 'The public was (and is) expressly forbidden details of the offset programmes in terms of "commercial confidentiality clauses", which violates Section 217 of the Constitution.'[30] Conflicting information has been provided by the government, making it hard to put together a complete picture of the process. Another obstacle is that the offset deals have not been independently audited, and all information is based entirely on government pronouncements. In September 2006, Minister of Defence Mosiuoa Lekota admitted that only 13 000 of the 65 000 jobs promised had been created.[31] When the first 'milestone' (points by which the arms companies were supposed to have achieved certain targets) was reached in 2003–2004, three of the arms contractors had defaulted on their offset commitments: Ferrostaal by R4bn, BAe/Saab by R840m and Thales (formerly Thomsons) by R262m.[32] More recently, however, the Department of Trade and Industry has claimed that offsets have resulted in R9bn worth of investments and created 50 000 jobs.[33] Armscor, in its 2007 annual report, argued that most of the contractors were actually ahead of schedule in meeting their offset targets, and had contributed R11.4bn in returned investments.[34]

Critics have responded fiercely to these reports. Andrew Feinstein argued that 'this does not change my view that offsets are economic nonsense. If there are sustainable economic investments to be made … they do not require the state to spend billions on weapons.'[35] Terry Crawford-Browne, responding to the report that the frigate deal offsets had led to R850m investment, has contended that 'since we spent R10bn on frigates we don't need, R850m is a very poor return on that investment.'[36]

WHAT IT COST – AND WHAT WE COULD HAVE HAD INSTEAD

The Arms Deal, at the time, was the largest foreign acquisition ever undertaken by the South African government. But getting a straight answer as to what it cost has proven difficult. As noted above, when it was first publicly announced, it was said to cost roughly R29.9bn. During the same Scopa meeting in which Jayendra Naidoo and Chippy Shaik admitted that offsets might not materialise, it also emerged that the cost of the deal had grown to R43.8bn.[37] Scopa was shocked when it was also admitted that this amount didn't even include the financing costs of the deal: what the government would be paying in VAT, export duties and interest on the loans that the country had taken out to make the purchases.[38] Consternation greeted the estimate in 2003 that the deal had grown in cost to R52.3bn, excluding financing costs.[39] Explaining the apparent lack of disclosure on the financing costs of the deal, Shaik shifted the responsibility onto another department: 'Financing arrangements are a matter between the department of finance and overseas banks.'[40]

The reality is that, while the deal was ongoing, it was difficult for the government to accurately estimate the costs. This is because the deal was structured in a complicated way. Portions of the deal were to be paid to local suppliers in rands only. A much larger portion, roughly 85 per cent, was to be paid back in foreign currency; the currency that was used to pay for certain pieces of equipment depended on which country's home government underwrote the original loan agreements. This meant that, as the rand depreciated, or appreciated, the cost of the deal would rise and fall. Admittedly, the rand has largely fallen: from the R6.25 to the US dollar that was used as the basis for the estimate of the deal,[41] to the roughly R8 that it is has hovered around since the beginning of 2008.

The most recent estimate of the cost of the Arms Deal is provided by the 2008 National Budget. According to the Budget, the Arms Deal, without financing charges and interest payments, will have cost R47.4bn by the time the final payment is made in 2011.[42] In other words, since the deal was announced in December 1999, the total cost to the

South African taxpayer has increased by over 50 per cent. In addition, the recent international credit crunch and the resulting rapid depreciation of the rand are still anticipated to increase the remaining costs of the deal.

At a time when South Africa was implementing its Growth, Employment and Redistribution[43] policy of fiscal austerity, it came as a surprise to commentators that the government would commit itself to the Arms Deal. Perhaps it would have been understandable if the government had not been fully aware that the cost of the deal could escalate. However, prior to the signing of the Arms Deal, the Cabinet was presented with a thorough Affordability Report on the deal drawn up by the Department of Finance. The Report warned the government that, because of the huge sums involved and the rand's volatility, it was an incredibly risky idea to agree to the deal:

> The proposed armaments procurements are distinguished from other government procurements by four key characteristics. The sums involved are extremely large; they involve fixed contractual commitments extending over long periods with high breakage costs; they are heavily import-biased; and their costs are offset by a set of associated activities (the NIPs) which cannot be guaranteed.
>
> These characteristics create a set of important and unique risks for government. The analysis of these risks suggests that as the expenditure level increases these risks escalate significantly. In fact even expenditure of R16.5 billion may create a situation in which government could be confronted by mounting economic, fiscal and financial difficulties at some future point. Ultimately the decision about expenditure levels really constitutes a decision about government's appetite for risk.[44]

It seemed that money was no object, as the Joint Investigation Report into the Arms Deal illustrated. The Report found that the Minister of Defence, Joe Modise, had initialled the contracts to purchase the three submarines before the Affordability Report had even been presented.[45]

Another key concern of the Affordability Report was that, by spending this amount on the Arms Deal, other areas of South African society would be ignored, or, at the very least, suffer from less funding: payments on the Arms Deal would 'crowd out' other pressing social demands. But Thabo Mbeki, Chair of the Cabinet sub-committee overseeing the purchases, obviously did not agree. Speaking in Sweden in November 1998, he made the argument that 'the idea that the money you are using to acquire defence equipment is necessarily money that is being diverted from housing is emotionally appealing, but it is wrong'.[46] It was a difficult point to sell, especially as only a month previously, South Africa's Health Minister, Nkosazana Dlamini-Zuma, had rejected the idea of providing ARVs to pregnant mothers as the programme was too expensive to even contemplate.[47] Five years later, the Report of the Joint Health and Treasury Task Team found that providing ARVs to everybody who would need them by 2008 would cost R5.7bn a year (10 per cent of the estimated cost of the Arms Deal at the time), and would 'defer' the deaths of 1 721 329 people as well as the orphaning of 860 000 children.[48]

In fact, the South African government has spent considerably more each year on the Arms Deal than the R500m a year suggested by Modise in 1999. Indeed, the Arms Deal, from 1999/2000 to 2007/2008, took up a greater chunk of the National Budget than low-cost housing, aids policy or bursaries for tertiary students, with an estimated R4.3bn still to be spent by 2011 (remember, as well, that these figures

TABLE 2 What we actually paid for the Arms Deal compared to other social expenditure[49]

FINANCIAL YEAR ENDING (IN R BILLION)	2000	2001	2002	2003	2004	2005	2006	2007	2008	TOTAL
Strategic defence procurement (Arms Deal)	2.901	4.223	6.342	5.864	4.502	6.331	4.537	4.515	3.882	**43.097**
HIV/Aids, Aids and STI strategic health programme	N/A	0.181	0.265	0.459	0.7662	1.107	1.511	1.953	2.473	**8.7152**
National student financial aid scheme	0.390	0.443	0.449	0.500	0.545	0.583	0.864	0.926	1.332	**6.032**
Grants to housing funds (for construction of low-cost housing)	2.970	2.997	3.225	3.800	4.246	4.473	4.843	6.677	8.342	**41.573**

exclude the financing costs of the deal and might still increase substantially as the rand struggles during the international credit crunch).

What else could we have bought for the same amount in 1999? The simple answer is: quite a lot. In real 1999 terms, the same amount of money would have bought or paid for one of the following:

- **1 993 333 RDP houses at R15 000 each** (this was the subsidy amount offered for an RDP house in 1999), roughly 300 000 fewer than would be needed to clear the country's housing backlog as it stood in November 2007.[50]
- **The salaries of 474 603 educators** for a year at an average annual salary of R63 000 (over double the number of educators employed by government in 1999).
- **The salaries of 590 909 members of the police and correctional services** for a year at an average annual salary of R50 600 (triple the number of police and correctional services employees employed by the government in 1999).
- **The salaries of 590 909 nurses** for a year at an average annual salary of R63 000 (nine times the 75 000 nurses employed by the government in 1999).
- **The salaries of 381 864 medical doctors** for a year at an average annual salary of R78 300 (a staggering 29 times the 13 000 doctors employed in 1999).[51]
- **A power-station the size of Lethabo**, which produces 3 558 MW, more than the total electricity demands of a city the size of Johannesburg, or roughly 16 per cent over what we would need to avoid our current spate of 'load-shedding'.[52]

These figures also raise questions about the effectiveness of the Arms Deal as a job-creating exercise. Working from the estimate of R29.9bn for the total cost of the package, which would produce 65 000 jobs, it would have cost the South African taxpayer R460 000 per job created – almost six times the average annual salary of a medical doctor in 1999.

In 2008, it was announced that the country would spend more money on renewing the equipment for South Africa's land-based forces. No figure for this has yet been provided, but the way it has been reported has raised a vital question: did we really need this stuff? One of the major reasons given for the Arms Deal was that it would help South Africa meet its regional peacekeeping obligations. According to the 2008 budget, landward forces are the 'backbone of South Africa's peace and stability initiative on the continent'.[53] But, over the last ten years we've bought everything except weapons and *matériel* for our 'landward forces'. As Mark Gevisser has written: 'what good will those Meko frigates do, after all, keeping the peace in Darfur or in the landlocked Great Lakes region? And the Gripen and Hawk fighter-jets acquired from BAe are far better suited to conventional military activity than peace-keeping functions.'[54]

That the arms we bought don't suit our needs was belatedly confirmed by Major-General Otto Schur, the Defence Department's chief director of acquisitions. In replying to questions posed by Scopa in 2007, Schur noted that the SAAF was planning to cut down on the use of the Gripens and Hawks because of a lack of need:

> The current need for combat aircraft and combat aircraft support for joint operations is very low because there is no real conventional threat. For that reason, the air force is focusing mainly on transport capabilities (both helicopter and fixed wing) as well as the training of new pilots to feed into the squadrons to prepare for future op-

erations ... Instead of 200 hours a year per aircraft, we may only achieve 100 hours per aircraft. We will not use them as often because there is no need in the short term. Until such time as the physical risk to national security escalates, where it requires a larger investment in combat systems, this is a wilful decision to reduce the investment in that environment.[55]

Similar noises were made with regard to the use of our newly purchased submarines in December 2007; according to top defence experts, South Africa's Navy could not afford to pay enough to attract the skilled staff necessary to operate all the submarines purchased (partially because of the fact that the Arms Deal took such a big chunk out of the defence budget). As a result, there was the possibility that we would end up mothballing two of the three submarines we had acquired.[56]

Of even more concern than having bought *matériel* we don't need, *Business Day* has argued, is the idea that we still have to deal with arms companies for some time to come: 'the skin crawls at the prospect of having to entertain these parasitical arms pedlars any longer in our midst. They are an affront to honest business.'[57]

CHAPTER 3

THE
COVER-UP

WHAT'S IN THIS CHAPTER?

- How the investigation into the Arms Deal began – the Auditor-General and Patricia de Lille.
- The Scopa investigation and how it was sidelined.
- The exclusion of Judge Willem Heath from the Arms Deal investigation.
- The findings of the Joint Investigation Report.
- Details of how the Joint Investigation Report was edited by the Executive before its release.

KEY DATES FOR THIS CHAPTER

- NOVEMBER 1998 The Auditor-General identifies the Arms Deal as high-risk from an audit point of view.
- SEPTEMBER 1999 Patricia de Lille presents Parliament with her now famous 'dossier', which contains allegations of extensive corruption in the Arms Deal.
- NOVEMBER 1999 An 'audit steering committee', which includes Chippy Shaik, is formed to 'steer' the Auditor-General in his investigation of the Arms Deal.
- 15 AUGUST 2000 Shauket Fakie, the Auditor-General, releases the first official report into the Arms Deal and argues for the need for further investigation after finding evidence that acquisition procedures had not been followed to the letter.
- 11 OCTOBER 2000 Scopa (led by Gavin Woods, with Andrew Feinstein head of the ANC Study Group), holds its first public hearings into the Arms Deal. Chippy Shaik and Jayendra Naidoo are extensively questioned, and their answers shock the Scopa panel.

- **30 OCTOBER 2000** Scopa releases its '14th Report' into the Arms Deal, which argues for a super-investigating team be formed to investigate the Arms Deal. The Report specifically requests that the Heath Unit be included in the investigation.

- **12 JANUARY 2001** Four government ministers host a press conference in which they claim that Scopa and the Auditor-General did not properly understand the Arms Deal.

- **19 JANUARY 2001** Thabo Mbeki writes to Judge Willem Heath to tell him that he will not receive a presidential proclamation to investigate the Arms Deal. Mbeki also appears on public TV to explain the decision. On the same day, Jacob Zuma sends a 'hostile' letter to Gavin Woods in which he explains why Heath has been excluded from the investigating team.

- **8 JUNE 2001** The ANC moves a motion of confidence in the Speaker of Parliament, Frene Ginwala, in the wake of the furore around Scopa. The motion is passed using the ANC's majority, but Andrew Feinstein abstains from voting.

- **12 JUNE 2001** Scopa announces that it is 'too busy' to investigate the Arms Deal.

- **AUGUST 2001** Andrew Feinstein resigns from Parliament in reaction to the way Scopa's investigation into the Arms Deal has been sidelined by the ANC government.

- **NOVEMBER 2001** The Joint Investigation Report is presented to Parliament, but opposition MPs walk out in protest at an alleged cover-up. The Report, nevertheless, strongly questions the role of Joe Modise in the selection of BAe's Hawk trainer jet and finds that Chippy Shaik failed to

recuse himself from meetings where tenders involving
African Defence Systems, a company in which his
brother Schabir had a stake, are discussed.

- FEBRUARY 2002 Gavin Woods resigns from Scopa in
  protest at the way the ANC is using its majority in the
  committee to prevent it working properly.
- 2003 Richard Young wins a court case against the
  Auditor-General forcing the AG to provide all
  the documents used in the drafting of the Joint
  Investigation Report to Young. The documents
  show that the Report was heavily edited to clear the
  government of any wrongdoing.

In November 2001, Parliament was host to a spectacle. The
Joint Investigation Team, made up of the Auditor-General's
Office, the National Prosecution Authority (NPA) and the
Public Protector, presented its final report into claims of irregularities in the Arms Deal. After two years of public wrangling and dissension, the Joint Investigation Team (also referred to as 'The Three Agencies') was supposed to provide
the final word on the Arms Deal: with unparalleled access to
sensitive information, the report that was submitted would
hopefully sort out, once and for all, what exactly happened
during the arms acquisition process and whether there was
any evidence of corruption in the Arms Deal.

But even before the Joint Report was presented to Parliament it was being slammed by opposition parties. The Democratic Alliance dismissed the parliamentary presentation as
a 'glorified press conference', while the United Democratic

Movement hammered the report as a 'celebrated palace verdict'. Both of these parties walked out of Parliament during the presentation made by the Joint Investigation Team.
Other opposition parties may not have walked out, but
they, too, were distressed by the final report: the New National Party claimed that they were 'not satisfied with the
final product', while Patricia de Lille, representing the Pan
Africanist Congress, claimed that the report had been 'sanitised'.[1] Seven years after the ANC had taken power with a
firm commitment to human rights, freedom and accountability, it was now being slated as a 'Big Brother' party desperately attempting to cover up its Arms Deal tracks, destroying
democracy in the process.

THE INVESTIGATION BEGINS

The investigation into the Arms Deal began even before the
final contracts were signed. In November 1998, the Deputy
Auditor-General, Shauket Fakie, identified the Arms Deal as
a high-risk proposition from an audit point-of-view.[2] The
number of negotiations, and their relative secrecy, meant
that the Arms Deal could possibly be prone to corruption
or mismanagement. Fakie, whose job it was to run a fine
tooth comb over public finances to ensure that they were
being used responsibly, wrote to government to request permission to investigate the deal. When the Auditor-General's
Office received no reply, Fakie, with the authority of Henry Kleuver (the head of the Auditor-General's Office at the
time), sent two further letters to the office of Thabo Mbeki
in May and August 1999. Finally, Mbeki's office responded,
referring the matter to the Department of Defence. On 20

September, after receiving this referral, Fakie wrote to the new Minister of Defence, Mosiuoa Lekota, asking to meet urgently: 'The office of the auditor general has received information pertaining to the current media speculation of bribes that were paid by foreign institutions to senior officials regarding certain tenders.'[3]

This time, the government was more likely to respond quickly. Eleven days before Fakie wrote to Lekota, Patricia de Lille, the fiery PAC MP, had made a shocking announcement to Parliament. She had come into possession of a 10-page briefing document signed by 'concerned ANC MPs'. The document was a bombshell: it raised questions about the offsets and whether they would be properly delivered, and, more importantly, fingered a series of high-level politicians in corrupt activity. Amongst those fingered in the document were Chippy Shaik, Jayendra Naidoo (not to be confused with the 'other' Jay Naidoo, the former Minister Without Portfolio and head of the RDP) and Tony Yengeni. The report was forthright: 'South African companies, interested groups, senior government officials and members of parliament who are involved in the Arms Deal are corrupting the democratic process in South Africa'.[4] During her speech to Parliament, De Lille refused to name those implicated in corruption, or release the real identities of the 'concerned ANC MPs'. Nevertheless, she demanded, as the document had, that a judicial commission of enquiry be established to investigate the Arms Deal and any potential corruption.[5]

Rocked by the allegations, the ANC government took two different approaches to the revelations. In public, the De Lille dossier, as it became known, was dismissed by Defence Minister Lekota as a 'shabby attempt to undermine what has been a process conducted with utmost propriety, integrity, transparency and accountability through a cowardly combination of misinformation, innuendo and personal smear'.[6] Behind closed doors, however, Lekota agreed that an investigation needed to take place. Responding to Fakie's request for the Auditor-General's Office to pursue an investigation, Lekota, now rocked by the De Lille scandal, gave the AG *carte blanche* to pursue the investigation: 'Approval is hereby given to the auditor-general, or his designated representatives, to have access to all documents pertaining to the government-to-government packages for audit purposes. The chairman of Armscor and the acting secretary of defence have been informed of my decision.'[7]

Only days after Fakie was given free rein to investigate the Arms Deal, the Cabinet sub-committee in charge of the acquisitions, headed by Thabo Mbeki, laid down their own line. Claiming that Lekota wasn't fully in the loop about the sub-committee's decisions, Brigadier General Keith Snowball wrote to Fakie explaining to him that only the sub-committee could give the Auditor-General approval to investigate the acquisitions process. This, Snowball claimed, was a decision that had been made when Fakie's May 1999 request had been received by the committee (but never answered). Instead, the investigation could only go ahead if Fakie cleared his 'terms of reference' for his investigation with the sub-committee. Attached was a new letter from Lekota, which stated that 'approval is in principal [*sic*] given to the auditor general or his designated representatives to have access to all documents pertaining to the strategic defence package for audit purposes subject to the auditor general detailing the terms of reference for such a financial audit ... These terms of reference must be discussed with all the relevant ministers before the final approval can be given.'[8]

The law that required the Auditor-General to clear his terms of reference was the Auditor-General's Act of 1995, which incorporated the Defence Special Account Act of 1974. The latter had been passed by the apartheid-era government for a very specific purpose. It allowed the government to censure any report submitted by the Auditor-General that was to the 'detriment of the public interest'. [9] In reality, it allowed the apartheid government to break arms sanctions placed on the government by excising whatever it felt necessary from an auditor-general's report. In other words, the new ANC government would do exactly what the apartheid government did: use legislation that contradicted the Constitution's dictate that 'no person or organ of state may interfere with the functioning of these institutions' to censor the report of an independent government institution.[10]

In order to direct the investigation an 'audit steering committee' was formed at the end of November 1999. On the 'steering committee' were representatives of the Auditor-General's Office and members of the original Arms Deal sub-committee, including Chippy Shaik, later found by the Auditor-General to have flouted conflict-of-interest rules, and Vanan Pillay, who was later fired by the Department of Trade and Industry for accepting a R55 000 discount on a Mercedes-Benz sold by one of the Arms Deal contenders.[11]

On 15 August 2000, Fakie, now heading the Auditor-General's Office after the departure of Henry Kleuver, released the first official report into the Arms Deal. The report, in its own measured way, raised serious concerns about the entire deal. In discussing the acquisition of the Hawk, for example, the Auditor-General argued that the practice of choosing the Hawk did not meet standard regulations on acquisitions. The Hawk was chosen even though it was more expensive and less technically competent than the cheaper Italian Aeromacchi aircraft. Joe Modise, as head of the Department of Defence, had argued that the choice should not be affected by cost. The largest purchase in the entire Arms Deal, therefore, should be determined by looking at a 'non-costed' option instead. This was, according to Fakie, 'a material deviation from the originally adopted value system … The DoD in reply to the finding was of the opinion that amongst others, the shortlisting of contenders during the technical evaluation using only the costed option would un-fairly favour the bidder who was the ultimate winner in any military value/cost-competitive evaluation, even before the solicitations of offers took place.'[12] In more prosaic terms, the government had decided to buy the Hawk regardless of cost and technical requirements, thus flouting the rules that governed procurement.

Fakie also questioned whether or not offsets would be forthcoming, and argued that the penalties imposed for non-delivery were inadequate: 'the guarantees were on average approximately 10% of the contract price. I am of the opin-ion that the guarantees, in case of non-performance, may be inadequate to ensure delivery of the NIP [offset] commit-ments. This could undermine one of the major objectives of the strategic defence packages which was the counter-trade element of the armaments package deal.'[13] Even more damning was his reading of possible conflict of interest in the deal: 'Based on the findings, I am of the opinion that the aspects of independence, fairness and impartiality could have been addressed more significantly. Although the role players were subjected to a security clearance, the poten-tial conflict of interest that could have existed was not ad-equately addressed by this process. This aspect could have been addressed more significantly by way of obtaining dec-larations prior to the strategic offers process.'[14]

Fakie argued that his review was far from complete. This was because there were, according to repeated government statements, two phases in the signing of the acquisition package. The first was the primary contracts. These were the contracts that were directly signed between the South African government and the Arms Deal companies. The second part of the deal was the sub-contracts, also referred to as the secondary contracts. The secondary contracts were signed by the Arms Deal companies with further companies, both South African and international, to provide individual elements of the arms acquired. So, for example, the South African government signed a contract with British Aerospace to provide the Hawks (a primary contract); British Aerospace then signed further contracts with South African companies for the provision of certain elements of the arms they were delivering, such as weapons systems (a secondary contract).

Fakie's review only looked at the primary contracting elements of the deal and did not engage with the secondary contracts at all. However, as Fakie concluded in his review, the secondary contracts were subject to severe allegations of corruption, and had to be investigated.[15]

While Fakie was undertaking his investigation, other agencies began to take an interest in the Arms Deal. The Special Investigating Unit headed by Judge Willem Heath had already received documents from Patricia de Lille, and had begun a preliminary investigation. In February 2000, the Office for Serious Economic Offences (which later became the Directorate of Special Operations, also known as the Scorpions[16]) admitted that it, too, was beginning a preliminary investigation into the Arms Deal.[17] Both of these agencies had broader investigative powers than the Auditor-General's Office, including the right to request personal bank statements and to request documents that fell outside the purview of the Department of Defence.[18] Similarly, when Fakie presented his August 2000 report, Selby Baqwa, the head of the Public Protector's Office (a sort of public administration ombudsman tasked with overseeing the prudent running of public affairs), announced that he too was engaged in a preliminary investigation of the Arms Deal.[19] What was lacking, however, was formal co-ordination between the investigating teams. This was soon to change.

ENTER SCOPA

As a matter of course, the Auditor-General's Report landed in the pigeon-hole of Andrew Feinstein, a member of the Standing Committee on Public Accounts (Scopa). Scopa was a Parliamentary watchdog committee that oversaw public expenditure and conduct and undertook remedial action if it found that an arm of the government had misspent public funds. It was a remarkably efficient unit, uncovering problems in public expenditure such as Winnie Madikizela-Mandela's abuse of state-owned cars, and even recommending the dismissal of the Commissioner of Correctional Services when he failed to provide adequate accounts to the Auditor-General.[20] Scopa was usually led by a member of an opposition party. In this case, it was led by Gavin Woods, an IFP MP, who Feinstein has described as 'intense ... with a weathered face lined by a straggly beard and moustache.'[21] Feinstein was the head of the ANC Study Group, which formed the ANC component that served on Scopa. The ANC Study Group included a mixture of ANC veterans such as Laloo Chiba, with fresher ANC faces, such as Serake Leeuw and Bruce Kannemeyer. Feinstein's position entailed liaising with the ANC's leadership on key issues while also acting as the main contact point with Gavin Woods. Together, they met to establish the *modus operandi* of Scopa and direct its conduct.

Immediately on reading Fakie's report, Feinstein, Woods and the rest of the Scopa team realised that the matter had to be investigated further. The ANC Study Group held two separate meetings to discuss Fakie's report, and supported further investigation. Gavin Woods, too, was keen to see the matter pursued further. Feinstein, at the insistence of Vincent Smith, 'a little known Gauteng MP whose abrasive manner sat uneasily in the committee',[22] briefed the leader of Government Business in Parliament, Deputy President Jacob Zuma, about Scopa's intention to pursue the matter. Zuma, during the briefing, was apparently supportive of the investigation. The same, however, could not be said of the ANC's Chief Whip, Tony Yengeni. Scopa had decided that the best way forward would be to convene a public hearing on the acquisitions process, which would see Scopa questioning both Chippy Shaik and Jayendra Naidoo. According to Feinstein, when Tony Yengeni caught wind of the upcoming public hearing, he suggested to the Scopa team that 'this is a big matter ... I don't think a public hearing is a good idea. This matter should be dealt with internally.'[23]

But Yengeni's argument came too late, as he raised the matter only minutes before the public hearing. In front of assembled media and non-governmental representatives, Scopa questioned Naidoo and Chippy Shaik extensively. The hearings were a public relations disaster for the arms acquisition team. As mentioned in the previous chapter, Naidoo and Shaik were forced to admit that the offset component of the deal was unlikely to come to fruition and that the cost of the deal had escalated dramatically, rising from R30bn to R43.6bn since its signing only a year previously. The decision to undertake the purchase of the Hawks from

British Aerospace, described above, also came under close scrutiny. After extensive questioning, it emerged that 'for 17 per cent greater technical value (which was not required by the Air Force) the Ministers had decided on 72 per cent greater cost!'[24]

Also on the agenda were the claims of conflict of interest levelled at Chippy Shaik. Central to the concerns was Chippy's alleged role in assisting his brother, Schabir, to get a slice of the Arms Deal pie. Schabir Shaik was the representative for African Defence Systems (ADS), which had submitted a tender to be the company to supply the information management system for the combat suite of the corvettes to be bought (the combat suite controlled the weapons systems of the corvette, acting like the 'brain' of the ship, while the information management system provided the means by which all the computers that made up the combat suite transferred information between each other and coordinated defensive manoeuvres.[25]) One other company was in the running: C^2I^2, headed by Dr Richard Young. Scopa was concerned about the fact that allegations had been made that Chippy Shaik had failed to recuse himself from meetings about the selection of the company to provide the information management system, thus creating a direct conflict of interest: Chippy, it was argued, might have swung the argument in favour of his brother.

During the hearings, Chippy was adamant: he had definitely recused himself from any meetings that involved discussions around the combat suites, and would provide minutes to prove it.[26] It later emerged, however, that he had failed to recuse himself from the meetings and had, in some instances, participated actively in discussions about purchase of the combat suite. In addition, the price of Young's system had been increased under suspicious circumstances.

Although C²I² was the favoured combat suite of the Navy
(a later report showed that the Navy had provided no fewer
than 15 technical points for why the product offered by C²I²
was a better system[27]), the acquisitions team, which included Chippy Shaik, had added an additional R40m to the cost
of the C²I² tender. This additional cost was referred to as a
'risk premium', which was the cost that would be incurred
by the primary contractor, in this case Thomson-CSF, if C²I²
failed to deliver on its tender. In addition, evidence later
emerged that C²I²'s proposal had been handed to ADS, allowing them to submit a quote below that offered by C²I².[28]
As will be shown in detail later, Chippy's testimony regarding the combat suites at Scopa was, in other words, misleading.[29]

After the hearings, Scopa believed that they had only
started to scratch the surface of improprieties in the Arms
Deal. They felt that the Department of Defence and Chippy
Shaik had been evasive on certain issues. After discussing
the matter within Scopa, it was decided to investigate further. Andrew Feinstein and Gavin Woods teamed up to find
out more. After the hearings, which received considerable
publicity, they were approached by numerous individuals
with information on the Arms Deal. Some of this turned
out to be bogus, while some seemed to hint at a broader set
of misdemeanours in the arms acquisition process. A key
source of information for Scopa was Dr Richard Young of
C²I². Woods and Feinstein travelled to meet Young, and, although perturbed by concerns over his agenda, were won
over by the documents provided, showing that the selection
of ADS over C²I² involved some underhanded practices.[30]

What became clear from these preliminary investigations
was that there was a definite need for a full-fledged and coordinated investigation into the Arms Deal. As such, Scopa

drafted a report to be presented to Parliament. Included in a stack of end-of-day Committee reports, the Scopa report, known as the 14th Report, was passed unanimously by Parliament. After assessing the various areas of concern encountered by Scopa in its initial investigations, the 14th Report argued for the need for an expert forensic investigation:

After the National Assembly had referred the Auditor-General's report to this Committee, the Committee received a large amount of unsolicited evidence, of varying plausibility, from a number of different sources. Amongst the numerous allegations and assertions were those which reflected common ground to a significant degree. It is on the basis of this, and the Committee's perception of the other issues raised in this Report, as well as the need to prove or disprove once and for all the allegations which cause damage to perceptions of the government, that the Committee recommends an independent and expert forensic investigation …

In noting the complex and cross-cutting nature of the areas to be investigated, the Committee feels that the investigation would be best served by combining a number of areas of investigative expertise and a number of differing areas of legal competence and authority. It therefore recommends that an exploratory meeting, convened by the Committee, be held within two weeks of the tabling of this Report in National Assembly. The Auditor-General, the Heath Special Investigating Unit, the Public Protector, the Investigating Directorate of Serious Economic Offences and any other appropriate investigative body should be invited, so that the best combination of skills, legal mandates and resources can be found for such an investigation.'[31]

GOVERNMENT RESPONDS

But what they suggested had ruffled some feathers, and the government quickly went into defensive overdrive. On 12 January 2001, in response to the findings of Scopa and the Auditor-General, Trevor Manuel (Minister of Finance), Mosi-uoa Lekota (Minister of Defence), Alec Erwin (Minister of Trade and Industry) and Jeff Radebe (Minister of Public Enterprise) held a press conference at the Johannesburg International Airport. The press conference was startling for its quite brutal attack on the findings of Scopa and the Auditor-General:

> [The Cabinet] takes serious issue with the ill-informed conclusions drawn from the Auditor-General's Review and the Scopa Report. These fail to understand the most elementary features of the defence acquisition process. It is our view that the Review and the Report were too cursory to do justice to this matter and have called into question the integrity of government without justification ...
>
> We also find it strange that so many people in our country have been driven into a virtual frenzy by mere allegations of wrongdoing, without a single shred of evidence of actual wrong doing being produced ...
>
> The Government will go ahead to implement the defence acquisition to meet its constitutional obligations to the country and to the National Defence Force.
>
> The Government remains committed to cooperate in any legitimate investigation into any elements of the defence acquisition process, but will not allow itself to be diverted to participate in what amounts to mere fishing expeditions.[32]

Claiming that neither Scopa nor the Auditor-General fully

understood the Arms Deal was a remarkable statement, especially considering that the Cabinet sub-committee had, in fact, 'steered' the Auditor-General's initial investigation into the Arms Deal.

The next target of the government's fight back was Judge Willem Heath. Heath headed the Special Investigating Unit (SIU), and it was recommended by Scopa that he be included in any investigation into the Arms Deal scandal. The inclusion of Heath was important as Heath's unit had wide-ranging powers that no other investigating body possessed. These powers included the legal right to impel individuals to testify even if what they said implicated themselves (they couldn't 'take the fifth', to use American terminology), and, perhaps most importantly, the legal right to annul any contract found to be illegal and recover the funds already spent on that contract.[33]

Heath's Unit could only be deployed by special proclamation of the President of South Africa.[34] Heath, already interested in the Arms Deal, submitted a formal request for the right to investigate directly after Scopa's report was presented.[35] Heath was a high-profile public figure with an uncompromising approach to corruption and a strong independent streak; the *Mail & Guardian* had referred to him as a 'firebrand judge'.[36] However, the government was unimpressed with his approach, viewing him as difficult and high-handed, and tried as hard as possible to make sure that he got nowhere near the Arms Deal. Immediately after Heath applied for a formal probe, ANC spokesman Smuts Ngonyama explained on national radio that 'the view of the ANC is that we don't want Heath to be part of this probe. He has used the information he has obtained to lambaste the government and blackmail the government by saying that unless you put me to work, there is a cover up. Why must the government feel paralysed by the Patricia de Lilles and Douglas Gibsons of this world, hobnobbing with Judge Heath?'[37]

Matters came to a head on 19 January 2001, when Thabo Mbeki sent a lengthy letter to Judge Heath rejecting his application for the right to investigate the Arms Deal. It was no stiff, formal letter. Heath had rejected Mbeki's request for the Unit to hand over the evidence in its possession to government, for fear of a cover-up. Mbeki ripped into Heath, his application for a probe and his refusal to hand over documents, and argued that Heath was desperately attempting to find work that was not rightfully his:

> Finally, and most important, Judge Heath, I am led to believe that you know that you do not have even prima facie evidence that, in law, any person or persons committed a criminal offence in connection with the matter under discussion.
>
> Indeed, members of your unit have been operating under the misapprehension that you, in person, when last we met, informed me that there was no basis for the issuance of a proclamation authorising you to investigate any recovery of state assets in connection with the defence acquisition.
>
> This would have been the correct thing for you to do, which you did not do. Instead, you embarked on an unseemly campaign to 'tout' for work, with a level of desparation [sic] I am still trying to understand.
>
> Given all the circumstances detailed above, as recommended to me by the Minister of Justice, I have decided not to issue a proclamation for the Special Investigation Unit to investigate the strategic arms acquisition programme.[38]

To get the message across even more firmly, Mbeki appeared on TV to explain his decision not to include Heath. It was a bizarre performance. Mbeki presented a series of organograms, ostensibly developed by Heath, which allegedly showed that both Mbeki and Mandela were involved in Arms Deal corruption. In fact, the organogram was developed by the editor of *Noseweek* as an intellectual exercise, and had not been drawn up by Heath at all.[39] Mbeki also used the platform to attack the findings of Scopa and the Auditor-General, and even claimed that there existed salaried bodies who were attempting to sabotage the Arms Deal in nefarious ways:

> The conclusions drawn by the Auditor-General and Scopa are wrong. In good measure, this has happened because neither the Auditor-General nor Scopa spoke to the people who took the decisions about the defence acquisition, namely, the Cabinet and a Cabinet sub-committee that was chaired by me as Deputy President of the Republic ...
>
> The Minister of Justice then contacted Judge Heath directly, once more to provide us with information to issue the Proclamation he has been calling for.
>
> It is also clear that we cannot allow the situation to continue where an organ appointed by and accountable to the Executive refuses to accept the authority of the Executive. This situation of ungovernability will not be allowed to continue ...
>
> Our country and all our people have been subjected to a sustained campaign that has sought to discredit our Government and the country itself by making unfounded and unsubstantiated allegations of corruption. Among other things, this campaign has sought to force us to do

illegal things, to break important contractual obligations, to accuse major international companies of corrupt practice and to damage our image globally, arguing that if we did these things, we would, inter alia, strengthen international investor confidence in South Africa ...

We know that various entities have been hired to sustain the campaign to create a negative climate about our country and government. I would like to assure you that the campaign will not succeed.[40]

Mbeki developed a three-fold legal argument for the exclusion of Heath. First, he argued that Heath's Unit had no *prima facie* evidence of corruption in the Arms Deal. Second, he had approached two legal advisors, Advocates Lubbe and Kahn (Directors of Public Prosecutions in the Western Cape), to get their opinion on the inclusion of Heath. Mbeki claimed that Lubbe and Kahn had written that there was no legal need to include Heath in the Arms Deal probe. Third, Mbeki argued that the Constitutional Court had just declared that it was unconstitutional for a judge, in this case Heath, to head the SIU, precluding it from taking part in the investigation.

All of these arguments were essentially spurious. First, it was usually not expected for a Unit to have *prima facie* evidence before it had even begun an investigation: investigations usually produce evidence *after* they had done their investigating. It was also arguable that there was sufficient *prima facie* evidence based on the Auditor-General's preliminary report alone. Second, the Constitutional Court had, indeed, demanded that Judge Heath be relieved of his position as head of his Unit. However, the Constitutional Court had given a year for this to happen, and did not recommend that the SIU as a whole be disbanded. Mbeki could easily have given the Unit the right to investigate under a different head, or on the understanding that it would have a new head within a year. Lastly, Khan and Lubbe had actually stated the exact opposite. In a letter to the Minister of Justice, Penuell Maduna, they had argued:

> there are sufficient grounds in terms of the Special Investigating Units and Special Tribunals Act, No 74 of 1996, for a Special Investigating Unit to conduct an investigation, and, in our opinion, such an investigation is warranted.[41]

The response of the media to Heath's exclusion was immediate and forthright. Xolela Mangcu, a highly respected political analyst, argued that 'Mbeki's decision to exclude the unit and publicly accuse the AG and Scopa of wrong-doing subverts the separation of powers and undermines the instruments of accountability in so fragile a democracy'.[42] *Business Day* similarly commented that 'when Parliament's standing committee on public accounts recommended a multi-agency inquiry into the arms procurement deal in October last year, and offered to facilitate such a collaboration, Idasa suggested the case might prove to be a litmus test of democratic accountability in the new SA. Sadly, it appears that the government is bent on failing the test.'[43]

'THE DEATH OF SCOPA'

With Heath out of the way, the ANC leadership turned its attention to Scopa. According to Andrew Feinstein, the support that the ANC Study Group had received from key leadership figures such as Jacob Zuma and Frene Ginwala quickly evaporated after they released the 14th Report. In early November, just over a week after Scopa had published the report, the ANC Study Group was brought before the ANC's Governance Committee, which had recently been established to provide 'political leadership' to the ANC in Parliament.[44] In attendance were Jacob Zuma and Essop Pahad, among other ANC heavyweights.

According to Andrew Feinstein, far from being a simple briefing session, the meeting was a tireless harangue against the actions of Scopa. Ntsiki Mashimbye (chair of Parliament's Defence Committee) started the meeting by criticising Scopa for having only a vague understanding of the Arms Deal. According to Feinstein, after he explained the evidence that Scopa had in its possession, Pahad launched into a 'ferocious diatribe', accusingly asking 'who do you think you are, questioning the integrity of the government, the Ministers and the President?'[45] When Pahad had departed, Jacob Zuma spoke up for the first time. He argued that, while Scopa had been fulfilling its constitutional role, it had operated in a leadership vacuum. This would no longer be the case.[46]

As pressure on the government mounted to include Heath in the Arms Deal investigation, the ANC leadership tried to force Scopa to retract its earlier demand for Heath to be included in the probe. Frene Ginwala released a statement in December in which she argued that Scopa had, in fact, only *recommended* that Heath be included. Ginwala noted that she was 'not aware of any resolution by Parliament or the National Assembly instructing the president to issue any proclamation regarding the work of the Heath Commission'[47] – in other words, the fact that Scopa's report had been unanimously accepted by Parliament did not mean that the government was compelled to include Heath in the investigation.

In a letter written by Ginwala to Zuma in January 2001, she went even further, and argued that a parliamentary recommendation did not necessarily have to be accepted by the Executive: 'it is within the competence of the Legislature after due consideration of the legal and procedural requirements, to make a recommendation to the Executive on areas within its jurisdiction, which the Executive may choose to accept or reject. Parliament's authority is persuasive. The Legislature cannot instruct the Executive, except to the extent that legislation it enacts defines and sets the legal framework within which the Executive undertakes its constitutional responsibilities.'[48] Ginwala's letters had, in effect, given the Executive ample cover for not including Heath in the investigation into the Arms Deal.

The ANC leadership still wasn't finished with Scopa. On 19 January 2001, the same day that Heath's application to be included in the arms probe was rejected, Gavin Woods received a stinging letter signed by Jacob Zuma in response to Wood's forthright request for the inclusion of Heath in the Arms Deal probe.[49] The letter written to Gavin Woods attacked Scopa's recommendation for the inclusion of Heath, and directly accused Scopa of being unfairly biased against the government:

> Scopa states that it is interested to carry out an investigation because our Government, foreign Governments and the prime contractors, major international companies, are prone to corruption and dishonesty.
>
> If this is in fact the starting point for Scopa, it seems that the investigation you seek is tantamount to a fishing expedition to find the corruption and dishonesty you assume must have occurred …
>
> Natural justice demands that you both substantiate the

allegation that the persons, governments and corporations we have mentioned are prone to corruption and dishonesty and provide even the most rudimentary or elementary evidence that any or all of these acted in a corrupt and dishonest manner.

I believe that it is a most serious matter indeed for our parliament or any section of it, to level charges of corruption against foreign governments and corporations without producing evidence to back up such allegations ...

The Government will also act vigorously to defend itself and the country against any malicious misinformation campaign intended to discredit the Government and destabilize the country.[50]

Under such intense pressure from the upper echelons, it came as little surprise that the ANC element of Scopa soon cracked. When the ANC Study Group met towards the end of January, they faced a barrage from Frene Ginwala and Naledi Pandor, the head of the National Council of Provinces. Ginwala argued that the Study Group should retract the demand for inclusion of Heath. Feinstein was put into an invidious position. Torn between loyalty to the ANC and his own convictions, he caved, along with the other members of the ANC Study Group. They quickly drafted an apologetic statement, and, to turn the knife further, demanded that Feinstein read it to the press. The resolution was simple, and exactly what the ANC leadership wanted: Scopa recommitted itself to the 14th Report, but now claimed that it had not actually specifically requested that Heath be included in the probe.[51]

Feinstein quickly realised what he had done. When he saw a distraught Gavin Woods directly after reading out the statement, he swiftly changed his mind. Together, they approached the media, and retracted Feinstein's previous statement: Scopa had, in fact, always wanted Heath to be included in the investigation.[52] As an act of courage, it was unsurpassed. But it signalled the end of Feinstein's career on Scopa. Days after Feinstein and Woods defended their position, Feinstein was removed from his position as the chairperson of the ANC Study Group and replaced by Geoff Doidge, seen as an ANC loyalist. It was an obvious attempt to regain Executive control over the formerly independent Scopa. This was made strikingly clear by Tony Yengeni, who explained to the media that 'some people have the notion that the public accounts committee members should act in a non-partisan manner. But, in our system, no ANC member has a free vote.'[53] The ANC would now use its majority to control Scopa carefully, preventing any repetition of the embarrassing non-partisan independence that the body had shown.

The official end to Feinstein's ANC career came in June 2001. In response to the furore around Scopa's 14th Report, the ANC moved a motion showing support for and appreciation of the Speaker; a motion that was carried by the ANC's majority. Feinstein registered his disillusionment by abstaining from the vote: 'for the first time in my seven and a half years as an ANC representative, I didn't vote with my comrades.'[54] Feinstein's abstention caught the attention of the ANC Chief Whip, who referred it to the ANC's Secretary-General, Kgalema Motlanthe. After an emotional meeting, Feinstein and Motlanthe agreed that the only solution to the crisis was for Feinstein to resign. On 23 August, Feinstein faxed his letter of resignation to the media: 'It is with sadness that I intend to resign from Parliament with effect from the end of August 2001. I have realised over the past few months that I can no longer play a meaningful role in

Parliament under the present political strictures.'[55]

With Feinstein sidelined, it was left to Gavin Woods to carry on the investigation. But he was hamstrung by the fact that the ANC was now using its majority in Scopa to prevent any further embarrassments. On 12 June, only four days after Feinstein had abstained from the Ginwala vote, ANC members on Scopa claimed that they were 'too busy' to continue investigating the Arms Deal. Individual members, such as Gavin Woods, could still investigate in their own capacity, but Scopa would no longer pursue the matter.[56]

In February the following year, Woods finally threw in the towel. After publishing two scathing reports on how Scopa had been neutered by the ANC leadership, he resigned from his position on Scopa, lamenting the fact that Scopa had lost 'its focus and with that a dramatic loss of productivity and of work standards. This translated directly into a serious loss of scrutiny and oversight and with it the early signs of government departments losing their respect for Scopa.'[57] Feinstein, responding to Wood's resignation, announced the 'death of Scopa': 'The last rites have been read. Unless the ANC can pull itself back from the brink and revert to the position it introduced with the advent of democracy by insulating Scopa from party politics and allowing the members of the committee to determine by consensus whether financial regulations have been transgressed, reports of Scopa's death will not have been premature.'[58]

THE JOINT INVESTIGATION REPORT

With Scopa and Heath excluded from the investigation, the job was left to the 'Three Agencies': the National Prosecuting

Authority (NPA), under the leadership of Bulelani Ngcuka; the Public Protector, led by Selby Baqwa; and the Auditor-General, represented by Shauket Fakie. The 'Three Agencies' spent over a year investigating the Arms Deal, and finally presented their findings, known as the 'Joint Investigation Report' to Parliament in November 2001.

The 400-page report was relatively comprehensive. Two people came under particularly intense scrutiny.

The first was Chippy Shaik. As described above, Chippy's brother, Schabir, was the director of African Defence Systems (ADS), which had won the right to supply the corvette information management system suite ahead of Richard Young's C^2I^2. Part of the reason why ADS had won the tender was that, during the tender process, the price of C^2I^2 had been inflated by a so-called 'risk premium'.[59] Some worried that this was done corruptly; that C^2I^2's tender had been misrepresented to ensure that ADS received the tender, and that Chippy Shaik had exercised undue influence over this section of the deal.

During the Scopa hearings, Chippy had frequently stated that he had declared his interest in this element of the deal, and had recused himself from the hearings. After looking at the minutes of the various meetings, the report rejected Chippy's explanation wholesale: 'There was a conflict of interest with regard to the position held and role played by the Chief of Acquisitions, Mr S [Chippy] Shaik, by virtue of his brother's interests in the Thomson Group and ADS, which he held through Nkobi Holdings. Mr Shaik, in his capacity of Chief of Acquisitions, declared his conflict of interest in December 1998, but continued to take part in the process that led to the ultimate awarding of contracts to the said companies. He did not recuse himself properly.'[60]

However, even though Chippy was shown to have failed

to recuse himself, the report still found that the selection of ADS's information management system was valid. This, it seemed, was the *modus operandi* of the report as a whole: there might have been some severe irregularities, but the government's contracting position was not flawed. Indeed, within the space of three paragraphs, the report seems to contradict itself directly (the reason for this became clear at a later stage, and will be discussed below). In discussing the addition of the risk premium that increased the price of C^2I^2's system, the report acknowledged that 'there is no evidence to indicate that a proper risk assessment of the IMS was made'. Even though the risk premium was added without a proper risk assessment being made, the report still cleared the decision: 'The investigation team is of the view that it cannot be found that the imposition of a risk premium on the IMS of C^2I^2 was unreasonable.'[61]

The second person fingered in the report was Joe Modise. Modise, as described earlier in this chapter, was deeply involved in the selection of British Aerospace's Hawk over the cheaper Italian Aeromacchi plane. During the initial selection process, the Hawk was eliminated in favour of the Aeromacchi. When Modise was informed of this elimination, he demanded to know why. When it was explained to him that the Aeromacchi was both cheaper and more technically proficient, he responded that the acquisition team needed to take a 'visionary' approach to the subject. He demanded that the Hawk and Aeromacchi planes be compared without cost involved in the criteria.[62] The Aeromacchi and Hawk were neck-and-neck when compared without cost, but the Hawk was still chosen, ostensibly because British Aerospace's offset offers were better than the Italians'.

The Joint Investigation Report, although perturbed to find that the largest section of the entire arms acquisition was decided without regard to cost, found that, in general, the selection of the Hawk was acceptable: 'The decision to recommend the Hawk/Gripen combination to Cabinet as the preferred selection for the LIFT/ALFA was taken by the Minister's Committee for strategic reasons, including the total benefit to the country in terms of countertrade investment and operational capabilities of the SANDF.'[63]

Modise's role in the selection of the Hawk was direct and material, but it might have been made with less salubrious reasons in mind than military need or cost to the taxpayer. Indeed, Modise, it was later shown, had acquired shares in Conlog before his retirement.[64] Conlog was a company that had been selected by British Aerospace as one of the companies to deliver its industrial participation programme: Modise was set, as a result, to make a fortune. But the Joint Investigation Report merely rapped Modise on the knuckles:

> It has come to the attention of the investigation teams that the former Minister of Defence was allegedly involved in a company that was to benefit from the SDP Procurement. The Minister concerned was actively involved in the procurement process before his retirement. Although no evidence of impropriety was found in this regard during the public and forensic phases of the investigation, such a situation seems extremely undesirable as it creates negative public perception about a process that might otherwise be in order.[65]

One concern raised by the report, and which received remarkably little press, was the government's oft-stated defence of the Arms Deal: that the government had no role in the selection of secondary contracts (such as ADS), and could not be held accountable for any corruption that emerged from this selection. For example, in July 2001, the Minister of Defence, Mosiuoa Lekota, argued that 'the primary contracts are between the government and the multinationals. When the multinationals have to fulfil their contracts they are now in a position to conclude sub-contracts. It does not involve government ... To expect the government to take responsibility for this would be stretching the matter too far. There is no evidence to suggest the government said you must conclude a contract with so-and-so.'[66]

But the Joint Investigation Report disputed this argument. The fact that Chippy Shaik *could* have had a conflict of interest in a deal that involved a subcontractor immediately showed that the government was involved in some of the secondary contracts. Indeed, the Report baldly stated that 'Armscor was not precluded from contracting subcontractors directly if this proved to be more cost effective. Armscor did, in fact, nominate and select subcontractors for the supply of the engines for the Light Utility Helicopters and the gearboxes for the Corvettes.'[67]

Regardless of these inconsistencies, the Report ended damply, and exonerated the government of any wrongdoing. Even though the final chapter detailing the conclusions of the investigation reported that 'fair and competitive procurement procedures for the selection of subcontractors were not followed in all cases', the Report stated that 'no evidence was found of any improper or unlawful conduct by the Government. The irregularities and improprieties referred to in the findings as contained in this report, point to the conduct of certain officials of the government departments involved and cannot, in our view, be ascribed to the President or Ministers involved in their capacity as members of the Ministers' Committee or Cabinet. There are therefore no grounds to suggest that the Government's contracting position is flawed.'[68]

The government had been cleared.

BUT WAS THERE A COVER-UP?

The presentation of the Joint Investigation Team Report was met with incredulity by the country's opposition parties. Almost every single one claimed that the Report was a whitewash, and that it had been extensively sanitised. Far from clearing the government, the Report had only served to heighten fears that the government had been covering its tracks.

Thabo Mbeki, using his weekly online column, responded furiously to the claims that the Report was a cover-up. At the root of these claims, Mbeki argued, lay 'the racist conviction that Africans, who now govern the country, are mutually prone to corruption, venality and mismanagement. As soon as the report of investigators was issued yesterday, so soon did the campaign begin to discredit this report. The Truth will not be allowed to stand in the way of what has been proved – that Africans and black people in general are corrupt. We have the facts about the defence acquisition. The question that remains to be answered is whether we have the courage and morality to demand an end to the insulting lie communicated everyday, that, as Africans, we are less than human.'[69]

Mbeki's argument carried little weight with most commentators, especially as revelations about Executive interference in the Arms Deal probe soon came to light. Almost immediately after the Joint Investigation Report was published, for example, the *Mail & Guardian* broke the story that the government, including Mbeki, Chippy Shaik and relevant ministers, had been provided with a draft of the original Auditor-General's report presented to Parliament in September 2000.[70] Allegedly Chippy Shaik had used the space provided to substantially edit the Auditor-General's report to clear his name of any wrongdoing. In the original draft drawn up by the Auditor-General, Shauket Fakie, it was acknowledged that Richard Young's C^2I^2 was the preferred bidder to supply the information management system for the combat suite for the purchased corvettes. Chippy Shaik, upon reading this, allegedly wrote a letter to Fakie suggesting a change of wording: 'The South African Navy did not express "its preference to the C2I2" rather "although the South African Navy appreciated the technical potential offered by the C2I2 this was outweighed by the risk-driven cost".'[71] The Report was duly edited, which, in its final form, read: 'Although the South African Navy preferred the technical potential offered by the local company, this was outweighed by prohibitive risk-driven implications.'[72]

In 2003, Richard Young lodged a legal application with the Auditor-General to receive documents pertaining to the Arms Deal under the Promotion of Access to Information Act. Young won the bid, and Fakie was ordered to hand over the requested documents. He released only a fraction of what was actually requested, however, and in 2005 was forced to hand over the rest or face arrest for contempt of court.

The documents handed to Richard Young showed that the Auditor-General had, in fact, provided the draft of the Joint Investigation Report to the government (including Mbeki) for feedback. Fakie admitted as much in 2003 during a presentation to the now-neutered Scopa, but promised that any changes that emerged from these feedback sessions

were small and insignificant.[73] In fact, when Young was provided with all the documents in 2005, it showed that the
Joint Investigation Report had been extensively edited. The
drafts of the Joint Investigation Report provided to Young
bore testimony to this: they were covered in notation suggesting necessary edits; sections were crossed out, and, in
some cases, blanked-out with Tippex.[74]

As yet, there is no clear indication as to who made the
edits, although Andrew Feinstein notes that 'it was widely
alleged that the instructions were written by the AG himself
in meetings with the executive'.[75]

The sections that were eventually edited out of the report
make for breathtaking reading. One of the most shocking
revelations was that the first section of the final chapter of
the Joint Investigation Report had been included at the insistence of the editor. This section, as noted above, stated
that 'no evidence was found of any improper or unlawful
conduct by the Government.' In the original draft submitted to the Executive, however, this did not appear at all.[76]
Similarly, the original draft had included damning conclusions about the decision to purchase the Hawks favoured
by Joe Modise: 'According to documentation the Minister
could have influenced decisions made by certain role-players
during the process to select BAe/SAAB as the preferred bidder for the Gripen and Hawk Aircraft ... The [Aeromacchi]
MB339FD could have been acquired much cheaper whilst
also meeting the SAAF LIFT requirements adequately...
There were fundamental flaws in the selection of BAe/SAAB
as the preferred bidder for the LIFT and ALFA programme.'[77]
Such concerns were excluded from the final report, which
instead stated that 'the decision to recommend the Hawk/
Gripen combination to Cabinet ... was taken by the Minister's Committee for strategic reasons.'[78]

The draft reports also provided additional damning evidence for the case against Chippy Shaik. The final report noted that Chippy Shaik had failed to recuse himself from meetings that involved discussion of his brother's company, but it held back on the idea that Chippy had directly prejudiced the outcome of ADS's rival bid. In the final report, it was stated that the imposition of the 'risk premium' on the C^2I^2 bid was not 'unreasonable'. This, however, could only have been possible with the excision of two key lines from the draft report. In the first, the draft report noted that Cabinet was informed that Young's product was 'high risk'; in the second line, the draft report noted that 'this statement is contrary to the evidence of all naval and Armscor personnel who testified and to all documents made available to us'.[79]

The draft reports included a further indictment against Chippy Shaik that was excised from the final reports. A three-page section of the draft report was entitled 'Inaccuracies in the presentation to Scopa'. This section provided a full list of inaccuracies in the report of the Defence Department, headed by Chippy Shaik and Jayendra Naidoo, during their disastrous hearings before Scopa. One of these was the claim on the part of Chippy Shaik that his brother's company, ADS, had no connection to the French arms company, Thomson, when the contract was awarded to ADS. In reality, Thomson had bought a 50 per cent share in ADS prior to the awarding of the contract.[80] Another inaccuracy was the claim on the part of the Department of Defence and the South African Navy that Richard Young's C^2I^2 was never the preferred bidder for the supply of the corvette's information management system. In fact, as the draft report made clear, the investigating team was of the view 'that C^2I^2 IMS was the preferred databus of the SA Navy, at least up to a point.'[81] Needless to say, this section was entirely excised from the final Joint Investigation Report.

Taken together, these revelations illustrated that there was still much to learn about the Arms Deal. As Gavin Woods wrote in 2005: 'Was our highly publicised multi-billion rand Arms Deal corrupt? Well, notwithstanding many allegations and reasons for suspicion, we do not really know the answer to this uncomfortable question ... While we remain in the dark about the level of dishonesty (or otherwise) in the deal, there seems to be much to learn about its investigation, and why this failed to produce the answers sought by the public.'[82]

So, was there a cover-up?

It is hard to come to any other conclusion.

CHAPTER 4

THE FIRST CASUALTY: TONY YENGENI

- The *Sunday Times* article that broke the story of Yengeni acquiring a 4x4 through corrupt channels.
- Yengeni's newspaper ad rejecting the claims.
- How the ANC used its majority in the Joint Committee on Ethics and Members' Interests to ensure that Yengeni did not have to answer allegations of corruption before Parliament.
- How Yengeni was arrested in 2001 and what he was charged with.
- What Yengeni admitted to in his guilty plea in 2003.
- Yengeni's four-month prison sentence and how he rose through the ranks of the ANC after his release.

- MARCH 1998 Tony Yengeni travels to Chile and Brazil to view the DaimlerBenz Assembly Plant. Here, he sees a prototype 4x4 Mercedes-Benz which piques his interest. On returning to South Africa, he approaches an executive of DaimlerChrysler Aerospace, Michael Woerfel, to get the car at a discount. DaimlerChrysler Aerospace owns a part stake in a company that is tendering to supply radars for the Navy's corvettes.
- OCTOBER 1998 Tony Yengeni registers his Mercedes-Benz ML320 in his name. He had received the car at a 47 per cent discount from Woerfel.
- DECEMBER 1999 The final Arms Deal contracts are signed. The company in which DaimlerChrysler Aerospace owns a part stake is selected to supply radars to the Navy.

- MARCH 2001 *Sunday Times* breaks the story that Yengeni had received his 4x4 through corrupt channels. Yengeni appears before Parliament after the article is published and tells the Assembly that the 4x4 was not a gift and did not need to be declared in his statement of Members' Interests.

- 29 MAY 2001 The ANC uses its majority on Parliament's Joint Committee on Ethics and Members' Interests to force through the finding that Yengeni did not need to appear before Parliament to explain his 4x4. Opposition parties furiously oppose the motion.

- JULY 2001 Yengeni takes out a full page ad in the national media proclaiming his innocence and calling the allegations against him part of a 'witch-hunt' to ruin his reputation.

- OCTOBER 2001 Yengeni is arrested and charged with fraud, perjury, forgery and corruption. Woerfel is also charged.

- 2003 Yengeni submits a guilty plea admitting to committing fraud with regard to his purchase of the 4x4 from Michael Woerfel. He is sentenced to four years in prison but appeals the sentence. The charge against Michael Woerfel is dropped as a result of Yengeni's plea bargain.

- AUGUST 2006 The Bloemfontein Supreme Court of Appeal rejects Yengeni's appeal for a reduction in sentence and he is ordered to report to Pollsmoor Prison within 72 hours.

- JANUARY 2007 As a result of a presidential pardon that halves the sentences for 'this category' of criminal, Yengeni is released on parole after serving four months of his sentence. He is received at the gates of Pollsmoor by a cavalcade of ANC leaders from the Western Cape.

- DECEMBER 2007 Yengeni is elected to the 21st position on the ANC's National Executive Committee at the National Conference in Polokwane. He is later selected to be part of the 20-member National Working Committee, one of the most powerful organs in the ANC.

Tony Yengeni's Mercedes-Benz 4x4, which he acquired in October 1998,[1] was, by all accounts, a pleasure to drive, marked by its 'plush body-hugging beige seats, tinted windows and metallic green bodywork.'[2] Yengeni loved his car. It was, as he recalled in a 2000 interview, 'like flying a jet … I'm a Mercedes-Benz man. I bought a 4x4 not because I want to drive around in the bundus, but because it's the in-thing and I'm part of the trend.'[3] One problem with the car, however, was the attention it attracted at petrol stations, where people would get out of their cars and 'have a look'. Yengeni wished he could get a break from the attention the car received, lamenting that 'being a public figure I sometimes desire a bit of privacy'.[4]

Yengeni's 4x4 didn't just turn the heads of petrol pump attendants. In 1999, Patricia de Lille announced in Parliament that she had received a document, signed by 'concerned ANC MPs', alleging widespread corruption in the Arms Deal. One of the individuals fingered in the allegations was Tony Yengeni: 'Just before the government confrimed [sic] British Aerospace as a preferred bidder Tony Yengeni bought a Mercedes 4x4 ML 320 Auto. It is alleged that the money came from the British Aerospace.'[5]

THE CASE AGAINST TONY YENGENI

Although such allegations persisted, it was not until 2001 that the story came to full public notice. In March 2001, the *Sunday Times* broke a story that alleged Yengeni had received his 4x4 through inappropriate channels.[6] According to the story, Yengeni's 4x4 was ordered in September 1998 by DaimlerChrysler Aerospace (DASA) from its parent company DaimlerChrysler. DaimlerChrysler owned Mercedes-Benz, and, as a result, was able to order it as a 'staff car', which was subject to a substantial discount. The 4x4 was then delivered to Yengeni, who received it in October 1998. It was registered in his name on 22 October. However, in order for a car to be licensed, details needed to be provided about who had provided the vehicle finance. According to the *Sunday Times* story, Yengeni had registered the title holder as Stannic, even though Stannic had never given him the finance and he had not yet insured the car (a prerequisite for a company such as Stannic to provide financing).[7]

Yengeni did eventually insure the car with Millionsure in March 1999 – 140 days after the 4x4 had been registered in his name. According to the *Sunday Times*, roughly six months before Patricia de Lille presented her 'De Lille dossier' to the press and public, 'rumours began circulating in the corridors of Parliament that Yengeni had received the car as a "gift"'.[8] It was then that Yengeni had finally entered into a finance arrangement directly with DaimlerChrysler Financial Services in May 1999. This was a full seven months after he had received the car, suggesting that he had not paid a cent on the 4x4 up until the signing of the financial agreement.[9] It was also alleged that Yengeni's wife, Lumka, had received a car through the same channels.[10]

What made the dealings around Yengeni's 4x4 suspect was that DaimlerChrysler Aerospace had direct links to the Arms Deal. DaimlerChrysler Aerospace was incorporated into a new company, European Aeronautic Defence and Space (EADS) in July 1999. EADS, in turn, owned a 33 per cent stake in Reutech Radar Systems, which had received a R220m contract to supply tracking radars for the corvettes.[11] Tony Yengeni, during the period of the arms acquisition, held two powerful positions in which he could have influenced the outcome of Arms Deal decisions and, later, any investigation into alleged impropriety: as the Chairman of the Joint Standing Committee on Defence and as the Chief Whip of the ANC. The Joint Standing Committee on Defence acted as a parliamentary oversight body that, amongst other functions, helped to 'assist the Department of Defence in its acquisition of armaments'.[12] As Chief Whip, Yengeni's job was to police ANC politicians working in Parliament.

It was in his position on the Joint Standing Committee on Defence that Yengeni had become friendly with one Michael Woerfel. Woerfel was a representative of DASA, the company that had ordered Yengeni's staff car. Woerfel's main job, according to Yengeni's later admission of guilt, 'was to market the products of Daimler-Benz-Aerospace AG in South Africa. The National Defence Force was a potential purchaser of the products of Daimler-Benz-Aerospace AG.'[13]

The inferences drawn were simple: Tony Yengeni had received a 'gift' from Woerfel, who was a marketing representative of a company with a large stake in the Arms Deal. Yengeni tried to cover his tracks by signing a finance deal with DaimlerChrysler to show that he was actually paying for the car, but only after questions around the car emerged, and even then it was bought at a discount of 47 per cent of the purchase price. If these questions had not emerged, would Yengeni have received the car *gratis*? And did Yengeni receive the car in order to swing matters in favour of EADS in their quest for a slice of the Arms Deal pie?

DENIALS AND DIVERSIONS

Yengeni responded to the allegations immediately, describing them as 'hogwash'. He would not – as Jacob Zuma would also complain – submit himself 'to an investigation by a newspaper when they themselves asked for an official investigation'.[14] Yengeni, however, seems to have felt that consistent quoted denials in disparate newspaper reports weren't enough: he paid for a full-page advertisement in the weekly *Sunday Independent* newspaper, in which he outlined his full defence.

First, Yengeni questioned the motivations behind the investigation into him. Regardless of the fact that one of the main investigative reporters from the *Sunday Times*, Mzilikazi wa Afrika, was black, he argued that 'the issue of racism reared its ugly head once more. It clearly motivated some of the worst forms of McCarthyism during this whole frenzy and witchhunt. How else do you explain the fact that old order politicians who were corrupt to the hilt and embezzled billions of tax payers' money which went straight to their pockets and many of them, including those who are still active in politics today continue to own vast sums of assets including businesses, vast plots of land, farms, wine farms, huge mansions, holiday houses here and in many parts of the world. And this is seen as being normal and acceptable! And that during their time in government and up to this point they drive very big Mercedes Benz cars, and they have never and not once been called 'wabenzi', the question is why?'[15]

Second, he argued that he had, in fact, received no discount and intended to pay for the car. With documents in hand to prove it, Yengeni claimed that the car had been sold as a damaged used car, and that he had put down a R50 000 deposit before he received the car. Stannic had been listed as the holder of the car, Yengeni argued, because the car had actually been registered by the seller, DASA, in Pretoria, and he might have told them that he was approaching Stannic. Stannic belatedly confirmed that they had, indeed, received an application for vehicle finance from Yengeni, albeit nearly three months after Yengeni had received the car.[16] When his Stannic application was refused, he signed a finance deal directly with DASA. This all showed, Yengeni argued, 'that it was never envisaged by the Seller nor myself that the vehicle would not be paid for'.[17] The fact that he had only entered into the finance arrangement as a cover-up after rumours started spreading was also 'devoid of truth'.[18]

Lastly, he argued that he could not have received the 4x4 as a kick-back to help DASA in its pursuit of Arms Deal contracts as he did not hold any position of power that would allow him to do so: 'the Defence Committee [Joint Standing Committee on Defence] and myself were never part of the procurement process at all'.[19] The decision, Yengeni argued in April 2001, was entirely Cabinet's to make as 'Members of the Defence Committee didn't have anything to do with the Arms Deal ... We weren't even asked for submissions.'[20] He had received the car from Woerfel, instead, because Woerfel had claimed that a man of Yengeni's 'caliber driving the Mercedes ML Model will do much to market their product. Convincing me was not a difficult task as I am a Mercedes Benz fan.'[21] Yengeni reiterated this point in an interview with *City Press*, in which he promised that he had 'never discussed the procurement of arms with Michael Woerfel, the managing director of DaimlerChrysler Aerospace'.[22]

Many in the media questioned where Yengeni had got the money to pay for the ad, reported to have cost R250 000 to run. Of greater concern was the fact that Yengeni had chosen this forum, rather than a more appropriate one, to answer these questions. The *Sowetan*, for example, argued that Yengeni's ad 'was a very considered attempt at answering many difficult questions. And he certainly has added some clarity to the circumstances in which he acquired the luxury Mercedes-Benz vehicles in question.' But, the *Sowetan* continued, Yengeni 'would have done himself a great deal more good if he had chosen to offer the explanation in Parliament instead. His decision not to do so has understandably prompted suggestions that he harbours a measure of contempt for his peers.'[23]

This was a vital point. According to parliamentary regulations, any MP who had received a gift or benefit of over R350 was supposed to acknowledge the gift in the Declaration of Members' Interests. Yengeni, however, had not registered his 4x4 as a benefit with Parliament. His argument, addressed to the National Assembly in March 2001, was that the 'acquisition does not in any way amount to a gift or a donation and therefore there was no interest to be declared'.[24] This did not fly with Fezela Mohamed, Parliament's Registrar of Members' Interests, whose job it was to ensure that MPs provided accurate information in their submissions according to the Declaration of Members' Interests. Mohamed recommended that, in order to ensure that Yengeni was not lying to Parliament about his

4x4, he be investigated by Parliament's Joint Committee on Ethics and Members' Interests (JCEMI).[25] JCEMI was similar to Scopa (dealt with in detail in the previous chapter): it was a parliamentary watchdog committee whose main job was to ensure that MPs acted ethically and in accordance with the law in accepting gifts and benefits and declaring them accurately. But there was also another similarity between JCEMI and Scopa: the ANC had the majority vote.

Mohamed, on 28 March 2001, was given the go-ahead by the JCEMI to request that Yengeni submit his explanations contesting the allegations raised in the story broken by the *Sunday Times*. Yengeni twice failed to respond adequately, questioning the JCEMI's procedures in the first reply and then informing the Committee in the second that he would be unable to answer questions until his return to Parliament in May 2001.[26] Finally, on 18 April, Yengeni gave a full response to the enquiry, stating that he had acquired the car legitimately and, as a result, it did not constitute a gift that needed to be declared. This line of reasoning failed to win over Mohamed, who noted in a report to JCEMI that 'Mr. Yengeni's response does not refute the detail contained in the [*Sunday Times*] article nor does he explain the circumstances related to the acquisition or funding of the motor vehicle.' As a result of Yengeni's failure to refute the *Sunday Times*'s allegations accurately, Mohamed argued that 'consideration must be given to the information in the *Sunday Times* report. These allegations cannot be dismissed as unfounded, as on the face of it, it appears that there may be some substance to the report. I recommend that the Committee authorize an investigation to determine the facts.'[27]

The ANC majority did not want Yengeni to appear before the Committee to discuss the 4x4 at all. The 'minority view', however, which was held by seven Members from six different opposition parties, was that 'Mr. Yengeni is refusing to cooperate with the Committee, and this constitutes a contempt of the committee' and that 'the Joint Committee on Ethics and Members' Interests should proceed directly with its own investigation of these matters'. The 'majority view', held by the ANC, was that 'the subject matter of the complaint falls within the scope and ambit of the [Three Agency Investigation] and that a separate investigation by the Committee would traverse the same issues. Therefore a parallel investigation, at this point, into these matters is not desirable.'[28] The motion was carried, with 7 voting for the 'minority view' and the remaining 25 voting for the 'majority view'.

This was the first time that any decision before the JCEMI had been forced to a general vote, suggesting that the Arms Deal had again turned a previously harmonious committee into a partisan playground.[29] And, just as had happened on Scopa, the ANC refused to allow any allegedly corrupt ANC member to appear before the appropriate parliamentary hearing or be investigated by Parliament.

TONY GOES DOWN

The fears that Yengeni would not face sanction eased later that year. In October, he was charged with fraud, perjury, forgery and corruption over the 4x4 matter.[30] Michael Woerfel, too, was later brought to book under similar charges.

Yengeni immediately resigned his position as Chief

Whip of the ANC, but not before taking a broad swipe at the team that had arrested him, the Scorpions (the anti-corruption investigative unit), arguing that 'there is something wrong with that unit. When I went for the interview in their reception I was amazed at the number of white people there. The guys who persecuted us are in control … so it's not surprising that the attention of the unit has changed from cracking serious syndicates and criminals.' Much as Jacob Zuma would later claim, Yengeni inferred the he was the victim of a conspiracy: 'If they thought they would make me the fall guy, they must think again. I'm not going to allow it. If they think I'm going to sit back in a corner and collapse and die, I'm not. I'm going to clear my name.'[31]

He might not have collapsed and died, but after two years of appeals, Yengeni finally admitted his guilt in a plea bargain agreement entered into with the State.[32] Changing the count from corruption to fraud meant that no case could be built to prosecute Michael Woerfel, who had arranged the discounted 4x4 for Yengeni. The case against him was dropped.

Yengeni's confession of guilt was striking. According to his statement, Yengeni admitted that he had 'unlawfully and with intend [sic] to defraud falsely and to the prejudice of the Parliament of the Republic of South Africa failed to disclose to the aforesaid Parliament that Accused No. 2 [Woerfel] gave me a benefit in the form of a discount, and furthermore made the false representations set out [below].'[33] The 'false representations' that were set out effectively destroyed every defence produced by Yengeni at the time the claims of corruption were levelled against him, as is shown in the following pages.

Yengeni's original defence in 2001

'The Defence Committee [Joint Standing Committee on Defence] and myself were never part of the procurement process at all.

'Members of the Defence Committee didn't have anything to do with the Arms Deal ... We weren't even asked for submissions.'

What he admitted in 2003

'4.2 The Joint Standing Committee on Defence was competent to investigate and to make recommendations on the defence budget, functioning, organization, policy and morale and state of preparedness of the National Defence Force and to perform other functions related to parliamentary supervision of the National Defence Force.

'4.3 Further Parliamentary supervision of the Joint Standing Committee on Defence included an oversight function to assist the Department of Defence in its acquisition of armaments. The final decision, however, remained with the Department of Defence.

'4.4 In my capacity as chairperson of the Joint Standing Committee on Defence, I, collectively with other Members, had the power and/or duty to exercise the aforesaid parliamentary oversight.'

Yengeni's original defence in 2001

'Recently media have reported that I purchased a vehicle at a discounted price of R160 000,00 which effectively gave me a discount of approximately 47% on a reported dealer's price of R314 000. It is amazing how the papers have omitted the true state of affairs.'

What he admitted in 2003

'4.7 In March 1998 I was invited by Accused No. 2 to attend an air show in Chile and undertake a tour of the Daimler Benz Assembly Plant in Brazil. Whilst I was in Brazil I learnt that Daimler Benz was due to release a prototype 4x4 Mercedes Benz motor vehicle. I immediately developed an interest in the aforesaid motor vehicle.

'4.8 On returning to South Africa I enquired from Accused No. 2 if I could get a discount if I were to buy the aforesaid motor vehicle. Accused No. 2 agreed to make enquiries and if possible arrange for the discount. I convinced Accused No. 2 to arrange a discount of approximately 50%. After some negotiations Accused No. 2 arranged that discount.

'4.8 During October 1998 Accused No. 2 ordered a motor vehicle, a Mercedes Benz ML320 from Mercedes Benz of South Africa (Pty) Ltd, a sister company of Daimler Benz Aerospace (Pty) Ltd, in terms of a purchase discount scheme available to companies and employees of the companies in the group.

'4.9 Accused No. 2 ordered the said vehicle with the intention to sell it to me at a 50% discount.

'4.10 The retail price of the said vehicle was R349 950,00 and the vehicle was wholesaled to Mercedes-Benz dealers at 10% less ...

'4.13 The new vehicle was sold to me for an amount of R182 563,63 at a discount of 47%.'

Yengeni's original defence in 2001

'I paid a deposit [on the 4x4] of R50 000 ...'

What he admitted in 2003

'4.24 Accused No. 2 and myself made the following misrepresentations in an attempt to account for my improper conduct;

'4.24.3. ... falsely gave out that I paid a deposit of R50 000.'

Yengeni's original defence in 2001

'The dealer's price of R314 000,00 would not apply to a damaged used vehicle ...

'Secondly, the amount paid for the vehicle was not R160 000,00 but R230 052,00.'

What he admitted in 2003

'4.24 Accused No. 2 and myself made the following misrepresentations in an attempt to account for my improper conduct;

'4.24.1 during or about the period May to September 1998 I signed a document dated to October 1998, an agreement of sale in respect of the said vehicle for the falsely inflated amount of R230 052,00;

'4.24.2 ... falsely gave out that the vehicle was damaged during transport and that the vehicle was sold as a used vehicle without a warranty.'

Yengeni's original defence in 2001

'The acquisition does not in any way amount to a gift or a donation and therefore there was no interest to be declared.

What he admitted in 2003

'4.15 The discount that I received was not available to the public, or to dealers. I realized that it was highly unlikely that I would have received the benefit had I not been a high profile person and Chairperson of the Standing Committee on Defence ...

'4.19 The discount that I received from Accused No.2, who represented a supplier of military equipment, was an improper benefit and therefore constituted an infringement of my duties ...

'4.21 I failed to disclose the said benefit, and failed to disclose the receipt of the benefit to Parliament in any other way.

'4.22 My failure to disclose the benefit constituted a

breach of my above duties and was potentially prejudicial to the integrity and reputation of, and trust in Parliament.'

Yengeni's original defence in 2001

'A vigilant and free press is an absolute necessity in our newly found democracy, so that it is able to criticize government and any other institution or citizen for any form of wrong doing, but all this comes with responsibility, in that it is expected that this same press will do its work in a fair and neutral manner and not to be unfair and take sides in the political battles that are raging in the country.'

What he admitted in 2003

'4.24 Accused No. 2 and myself made the following misrepresentations in an attempt to account for my improper conduct;

'4.24.5 ... caused an advertisement to be published in the national press wherein I falsely attempted to give out that there was nothing improper about the benefit.'

THE REHABILITATION OF TONY YENGENI

Yengeni's admission of guilt brought a stern sentence, at least initially. As a result of pressure within the ANC, Yengeni resigned from his position as an ANC MP and had his Membership of the ANC suspended for engaging in 'conduct unbecoming that of a member or a public representative of the ANC'.[36] The magistrate presiding over Yengeni's case, Bill Moyses, lambasted Yengeni in sentencing him to four years: 'What makes the crime even more serious is the planning and ongoing deceit after the benefit became public knowledge. Not only did you not disclose the benefit, but thereafter covered your tracks ... I regret to say the example you set as Chief Whip of the ANC is shocking.'[37]

Yengeni's lawyers found the sentencing 'extremely harsh', and appealed for a reduction for nearly three years.[38] Finally, in August 2006, the Bloemfontein Supreme Court of Appeal rejected the appeal, and he was ordered to report to Pollsmoor Prison within 72 hours.[39] It was to be a remarkably short stay. In January 2007, after spending four months in prison, he was released.[40] Yengeni was allowed to walk early because Mbeki had issued a presidential pardon for 'this category' of criminal in May 2005, which shaved 20 months off his sentence. After serving a sixth of the remaining 20 months, he was freed on parole as a result of good behaviour.[41] Thus, six years after the *Sunday Times* broke the first story of Yengeni's perfidy; four years after he had admitted guilt; and four months after he began serving his four-year prison sentence, Tony Yengeni was a free man.

After Jacob Zuma was fired as deputy president by Thabo Mbeki, the ANC began to split and fray at the seams. On the one side stood Mbeki and his coterie of supporters; on the other side, populated by SACP and Cosatu supporters, stood

Jacob Zuma and his own backers. Yengeni was firmly in the Zuma camp, and by the time he was finally sent to prison he had become somewhat of a *cause célèbre* for those in support of Zuma and critical of Mbeki. Indeed, when Yengeni left prison, he was greeted by a cavalcade of ANC leaders from the Western Cape.

According to the ANC, Yengeni had served his time and would be welcomed back into the fold. The ANC's Western Cape Provincial Secretary, Mcebisi Skwatsha, speaking in his personal capacity, said that Yengeni had 'served his due, no problem ... [the fact that he had been convicted of fraud] does not make him less of an ANC comrade.'[42] Similarly, James Ngculu, the ANC Western Cape Chairperson, attacked those who refused to accept that Yengeni needed to be forgiven: 'some of them expect us to forgive them for having stood in defence of apartheid, but they don't want us to be forgiven. This is the hypocrisy we in the ANC must reject with the contempt it deserves.'[43] Admittedly, it was difficult to forgive a politician who, on his release, seemed to eschew any sense of remorse by defiantly claiming that 'I'm now walking out of the gate of this prison, a place I was not supposed to be in the first place.'[44]

Yengeni's position in the ANC was cemented during the ANC's hugely publicised Polokwane Conference held in December 2007. At the conference, Jacob Zuma was elected by a large majority to be the new head of the organisation. Yengeni, seen as extremely close to Zuma, was elected to twenty-first position on the ANC's 80-member National Executive Council. A month later, he was elected by the ANC to serve on the party's most powerful organ, the 20-member National Working Committee.

In the space of eight years Yengeni had gone, in the words of *The Star*, 'from hero to zero ... to hero.'

CHAPTER 5

'DEATH OF A SALESMAN': JOE MODISE

WHAT'S IN THIS CHAPTER?

- Introduction to the allegations of corruption levelled against Joe Modise.
- What the Air Force initially wanted.
- The role of the British government in lobbying politicians.
- How the procurement process was wrangled to allow BAe's Hawk and Gripen to be considered.
- How the Hawk deal was wrangled to allow the more expensive Hawk to beat other competitors.
- The SANDF's attempt to block the Hawk and Gripen purchases.
- A description of the allegations of corruption that suggest that BAe bribed South African figures to land the Hawk and Gripen deals.

KEY DATES FOR THIS CHAPTER

- 1994 The Air Force reviews what it needs and argues that it only needs to replace one 'tier' of jets: the Impala trainers.
- OCTOBER 1995 The review is formalised, requesting that only the Impala trainers are bought.
- MARCH 1997 After receiving further information from arms companies, the four preferred suppliers to replace the Impala are selected. Neither of BAe's submissions (the Hawk or the Gripen) makes the shortlist as they are too expensive and not suited to the needs of the Air Force.

- OCTOBER 1997 On allegedly 'strict instructions' from Joe Modise, the Air Force changes its purchasing requirements, allowing for BAe to resubmit tenders for the Hawk and Gripen.

- LATE OCTOBER 1997 Further requests are sent out for information from arms companies to supply Advanced Light Fighter Aircrafts. BAe makes the shortlist with the Gripen but the Air Force still favours other jets due to cost and operational ability. BAe eventually wins the Gripen contract after submitting an offset proposal that was later argued to be 'radically inflated'.

- MARCH 1998 BAe allegedly donates R4.5m to the MK Military Veterans Association – Joe Modise is the Life President of the Association.

- APRIL 1998 Arms companies are approached to submit tenders to supply 24 Lead-In Fighter Trainers (LIFTs). BAe submits a tender offering the Hawk, but the Air Force prefers other planes, notably the Aeromacchi MB339FD.

- 30 APRIL 1998 Joe Modise argues that the acquisition team needs to take a 'visionary' approach and not consider the cost of the jets on offer. This favours the Hawk, which is almost double the price of the Aeromacchi MB339FD. He orders a new evaluation be completed in which price is excluded – the 'non-costed option' to be submitted along with the existing evaluation.

- JULY 1998 General Pierre Steyn, amongst others, tries to block the Cabinet from receiving the 'non-costed option' as a basis on which to make its decisions, since choosing weapons without considering costs is considered unethical.

- 31 AUGUST 1998 At a Cabinet briefing session, the 'costed' and 'non-costed' options are presented. Steyn later recalls that no decision was made and the meeting was not minuted. But, after the meeting, he was presented with minutes drawn up by Chippy Shaik that said that the meeting had selected the BAe's Hawk.

- LATE 1998 General Pierre Steyn resigns in protest against the selection of BAe's Hawk.

- JUNE 1999 Joe Modise resigns from Cabinet and his position as Minister of Defence. He immediately takes up a position as an executive with Conlog, a company that was slated to receive massive contracts arising from BAe's offset commitments. He is also alleged to have been bought shares in the company by BAe.

- NOVEMBER 2001 The Joint Investigation Report notes serious problems with the selection of the Hawk and Gripen but clears the government and Joe Modise of any wrongdoing. Joe Modise dies only days later on 26 November.

- JUNE 2003 Britain's Minister for Trade, Patricia Hewitt, admits in UK's House of Commons that BAe paid huge commissions to agents in South Africa.

- MID-2006 The British Serious Fraud Office begins investigating BAe's alleged corruption in the SA Arms Deal. According to their request for assistance, key players in the Arms Deal (including Joe Modise's former advisor) allegedly received huge commissions from BAe during the Arms Deal.

When Joe Modise retired from his post as Minister of Defence in 1999, he went straight into business. As a retirement plan, it was supposed to be an easy way to spend the last years of his life. 'You can't compare the hardship of liberation struggle to this,' he explained. 'It doesn't compare to not knowing whether your food and weapons will be arriving, or seeing comrades being killed.' For many, though, it was an improper and irresponsible move, as it raised the question as to whether he had smoothed the way for future business ventures while in government. Modise's response was simple: 'This is silly. No one can prescribe to you what to do. I would encourage anyone to enter business because it is exciting and challenging. It is your right.'[1]

One of the businesses in question was Conlog, a company that was slated to receive a substantial portion of the offset contracts as part of the purchases of Hawk and Gripen planes from British Aerospace (BAe). Modise, after his retirement, became both a director and (allegedly) a major shareholder.[2] This might, perhaps, have been seen as explicable: it would make sense for a military man to get involved in a company that dealt with military deals. But, since the signing of the BAe Hawk and Gripen contracts, allegations of major impropriety have come to light that shed new light on Modise's Conlog connections and on the selection process as a whole.

WHAT WE INITIALLY WANTED

The selection of the Hawk and the Gripen was an incredibly complex process, and had a long history. The story began in 1994, when the SANDF started investigating a plan to re-equip the SAAF. The SAAF had long employed a three-

tier operational structure. Pilots were trained on two different planes, the Astra Trainer and the Impala MKI and MKII
Trainers, and then graduated to the supersonic fighter, the
Cheetah, which was the plane that would actually be used
in a war situation.[3]

In 1994, only one tier had to be replaced: the Impala
Trainers, which were rapidly becoming technically obsolete. The Cheetahs, the actual war-time fighters, would also
have to be replaced, but only at a later stage as, at the time,
the SAAF had 50 Cheetahs that would be operational until
2012. In October 1995, these needs were formalised by the
agreement of a 'staff target' (which stated what was needed
by the SAAF in terms of equipment to be purchased). According to the 'staff target', a key requirement for the new
trainers to be bought was that they could be used both as
trainer aircraft and as fighters that could be used in military
operations: a smart system that would see the SAAF acquiring two functions (training and fighting) out of buying one
set of planes.[4]

After confirming these SAAF needs, the SANDF invited a
series of international companies to tender for the provision
of the aircraft. A total of 23 responded, and were quickly
whittled down to four preferred suppliers by March 1997.
The four suppliers were: a joint Brazilian and Italian consortium offering the AMX-T aircraft; Daimler-Benz Aerospace
offering the AT2000; Aero Vodochody offering the L159;
and Aeromacchi/Yakovlev offering the YAK/AEM-130.[5]

Although BAe had submitted information about the Hawk
100 and the Gripen, neither made this original shortlist. The
Hawk, it was argued by the SAAF, didn't meet its basic operational requirements, and was more expensive than other
options. The Gripen was simply 'unaffordable'.[6] BAe, at this
stage, was completely out of the running.

ENTER THE BRITISH

In early 1997, the British attempted to muscle their way
back into the acquisitions process. The Defence Export Services Organisation (DESO), an investment arm of the British government, put together an acquisitions package to
be presented to the South African government, which saw
BAe supplying Hawks and Gripens (including other military
matériel) in return for substantial investment in South Africa. The SANDF was worried about the role DESO was playing
at the time: they were concerned that it was lobbying South
African politicians to get its proposal through, even though
the SAAF and SANDF did not want either the Gripen or the
Hawk. HD Esterhuyse, the general manager for acquisition
of aeronautic and maritime supplies for Armscor, recalled
later that, as early as March 1997, DESO was 'clearly in discussions with other government officials and the minister
[Modise] ... At this stage we were already concerned about
the actions of DESO and British companies regarding South
African politicians and parliamentarians'.[7]

So worried was the SANDF about the inclusion of the Hawk
and the Gripen that George Meiring (head of the SANDF)
and Pierre Steyn (Secretary of Defence), even went so far as
to write to Nelson Mandela. Their memo explained that 'the
British proposal does not correspond with the SAAF preference option ... The Hawk option is not optimal because
cheaper options exist for the niche requirement satisfied by
the Hawk.'[8] Similarly, General WH Hechter, the chief of the
SAAF, wrote that 'neither the Hawk nor the Gripen systems
as offered by BAe during its formal response ... satisfied the
full requirement specifications ... In terms of quoted acquisition of life-cycle support costs both aircraft systems were
by far the most expensive options in their respective classes.'

Hechter noted in closing that the BAe option 'would only be considered under extreme duress'.[9]

SHIFTING THE GOALPOSTS

In 1997, after receiving all the information from various bidders, it was decided that the cost of purchasing all this equipment was simply too high. As a result, the SANDF decided to switch from a three-tier system to a two-tier system, which would see trainee pilots moving straight from the Astras already in the SAAF's possession to a new mid-range fighter (also referred to as an ALFA, or Advanced Light Fighter Aircraft) that would now be bought. As a result of this change, the Gripen aircraft from BAe became a far more desirable plane, as the criteria for multi-purpose planes had been shifted. But the Hawk would be excluded, as there was no longer a middle-tier into which it could fit.[10]

In October 1997, the SAAF Command Council (which was overseeing the selection of preferred bidders for the SAAF) met to discuss this change. It was decided, once again, to change the requirements for the purchases. Apparently on the strict instructions of Joe Modise, the SAAF decided to revert back to a three-tier system.[11] But it would not be the three-tier system of old. Instead of filling the middle-tier (between the Astra and the Cheetah) with a plane that could be used to train and fight, the middle-tier would now be filled by a Lead-in Fighter Trainer (LIFT). The LIFT, of which the Hawk was one, could not engage in military operations, and could be used only to train pilots to graduate up to the war-time fighter. No reason was given for this shift in goalposts, but the result was simple: in both cases, the Hawk and

TABLE 3 **Sorry, can you explain the three-tier system again?**			
	TIER ONE	**TIER TWO**	**TIER THREE**
1995 three-tier system	**Astra trainers.** Pilots would train on the Astra fighters before moving on to the Impala trainers. The SAAF did not want to replace the Astras.	**Impala MKI and MKII trainers.** Pilots would train on these planes before moving on to the actual war-time fighter. The SAAF originally wanted this tier to be replaced with an aircraft that could be used for training and combat.	**Cheetah fighters.** After training on the previous two tiers, pilots would graduate to the Cheetah, which was the war-time combat fighter. The SAAF wanted to replace these fighters, but only at a later stage as the Cheetahs would still be operational for over a decade.
Early-1997 two-tier system	N/A	**Astra trainers.** Pilots would train on the Astra and move directly on to the supersonic war-time fighter.	**An ALFA (Advanced Light Fighter Aircraft).** The SAAF recommended purchasing a new fighter to replace the aging Cheetahs that would be used to fight in combat.
Late-1997 three-tier system	**Astra trainers.** Pilots would learn to fly combat planes in the Astra and graduate to the second tier.	**The Lead-In Fighter Trainer (LIFT).** Pilots would train for supersonic flight in the LIFT before graduating to the ALFA. Importantly, the LIFT would have no combat role functions, unlike what was proposed in 1995. BAe's Hawk was the LIFT chosen in 1999.	**The Advanced Light Fighter Aircraft (ALFA).** After completing training on the LIFT, pilots would graduate to flying the war-time combat fighter. BAe's Gripen was the ALFA chosen in 1999.

Gripen could now be resubmitted as realistic options for the SAAF to purchase. They had, in James Myburgh's words, been elevated from 'also-rans to contenders'.[12]

This change in preferred systems was almost certainly unnecessary. First, pilots could actually move straight from the Astra to the war-time fighter, without the need for a middle-tier trainer. Getting a LIFT for the SAAF would be a luxury, rather than a necessity. Second, according to the previous three-tier system, the SAAF would have filled the middle-tier with a 2-in-1 plane that could have been used to train pilots and fight in combat situations. Now, the SAAF would be spending money on a plane that could be used only for training.

Flying a LIFT such as the Hawk in a combat situation could have disastrous consequences. Indeed, Helmoed-Römer Heitman, the South African correspondent for *Jane's Defence Weekly* (the pre-eminent journal on all things military), has joked that it would be 'kinder to take a pilot behind the hangar and shoot him', rather than let pilots fly military operations in the Hawk. 'You can use the Hawk for photo-reconnaissance, for patrolling borders but it hasn't got the speed or the power – or the tracking radar – necessary to fly against enemy interceptors.'[13]

GETTING THE GRIPEN

As a result of the change in SAAF systems, BAe could now re-submit the Hawk and Gripen for consideration by the South African government. The selection of the Gripen happened remarkably fast. In October 1997, three suppliers were shortlisted to provide the ALFA component of the acquisition. These were Germany's Daimler-Benz Aerospace (with the AT2000 fighter), France's Dassault (with the Mirage 2000 fighter) and UK's BAe (with the Gripen).[14] At the time, the Gripen was the SAAF's lowest-rated of the three in terms of technical capability and cost. The AT2000 received the highest score, followed by the Mirage. The AT2000, it was noted, had the 'best cost-effectiveness. Also best operational capability.' The Gripen was a 'capable modern fighter with low development risk but high cost.'[15]

With these three shortlisted, they went through a further evaluation process. According to this process, the technical suitability of the different bidders would be combined with cost, financing options (which showed how the repayments on the loans taken out to buy the equipment would be structured) and the amount offered from offsets, in order to determine the best overall value to the military. During this process, the SANDF was unimpressed by BAe's initial offset offers. Indeed, after meeting BAe, S de Lancey, part of Denel's aviation team, wrote to General PO du Preez, head of staff logistics at the SANDF, arguing that 'industry was united behind the fact that the BAe/SAAB industrial participation offer was very poor, and was aimed at the absolute minimum that they could get away with. The IP offered by BAe/SAAB has been assessed by all industry parties present as being very disappointing … It appeared that BAe/SAAB might have thought they had already won the SA competition and did not feel compelled to make sacrifices for SA trade and industrial imperatives.'[16]

BAe quickly got their ducks in a row, and put together a more impressive offset package that comprehensively beat the French and German proposals. But what really tipped the scales was the financing proposal (which set out how the loans used to pay for the purchases would be structured). In terms of the final evaluation criteria, the financing proposals made up 33.3 per cent of the total evaluation score. When the SANDF requested that the three shortlisted companies submit financing proposals, only BAe provided their proposal. As a result, the French and Germans scored 0 on a portion of the evaluation criteria that counted for 33.3 per cent. With this counting against the French and Germans, the Gripen now emerged as the favoured plane, and was presented to Cabinet as such.

However, it later emerged that the French and Germans had not been given time to submit their financing proposals. During the meeting at which the Gripen was chosen, it was argued that the Germans and French had 'failed to offer financing, notwithstanding repeated requests'. James Myburgh has alleged that the Auditor-General's office, during its investigation of the Arms Deal, could find no record of any such requests and that officials from the Department of Finance and Dassault later denied that requests for financing proposals from the French and Germans were ever drawn up, sent out or received. Whether this was done intentionally is not certain; what is clear is that the Gripen was chosen without a proper comparison between the financing proposals for the Gripen, Mirage and AT2000, even though this comparison made up 33.3 per cent of the final evaluating criteria. Indeed, even the sanitised Joint Investigation Report noted that 'there was no competitive financial evaluation. The aforementioned lack of a competitive financial evaluation played an important role during the overall evaluation process, as the financial evaluation score comprised 33.3% of the total evaluation.'[17]

The Gripen, in other words, had been chosen on a technicality. We would get the Gripen regardless of the fact that it was neither the cheapest nor the technically preferred option.

HAGGLING FOR THE HAWK

At the same time as the Gripens were being chosen, the military was considering proposals for the purchase of the trainer aircraft (the LIFts). After reconfiguring the three-tier system, it was decided in April 1998 to purchase 24 LIFts, and a request for information was issued by the South African government. In total, 20 proposals were received, which, again, were whittled down to four preferred suppliers. These were: BAe with the Hawk 100; Aeromacchi offering the MB339FD; Aero Vodochody with the L159; and the joint Russian and Italian YAK/AEM-130 provided by Yakoklev/Aeromacchi.[18]

After information had been received from the four suppliers, the LIFts were put through an evaluation procedure to determine the best option. At the start, the Hawk fared particularly badly. It came in third, after the L159 in second and Aeromacchi's MB339FD in first place. According to the initial evaluation, the MB339FD scored 100 compared to Hawk's 44.2: in terms of cost-effectiveness and technical suitability the MB339FD was twice as good as the Hawk.[19] This was based on the fact that the MB339FD was the successor to the Impala trainers already used by the SAAF, and that the Hawk was nearly double the cost of the MB339FD.[20] Indeed, buying the Hawk, at the time, by far exceeded the budget set aside for the LIFT project (R2.2bn), whereas the MB339FD just squeezed in.[21]

And yet, Joe Modise, during a meeting of the Armaments Acquisition Council on 30 April 1998, argued that the Council needed to take a 'visionary approach' in deciding the matter, as the deal potentially offered South Africa's own armaments companies the chance to engage in international trade. Based on this visionary approach, Modise instructed the evaluation committee to draw up two evaluation reports: one that evaluated all the aircraft with the cost included, and another that evaluated all the aircraft without the cost included.[22] Even without cost included, Hawk was not the favoured option. At the top was Aeromacchi's MB339FD, followed, now in second place, by the Hawk. [23] In other words, the SAAF still recommended the MB339FD because the plane was, in the end, better suited to its needs than the Hawk. But, as James Myburgh has noted, 'by setting aside the issue of the unaffordability of the Hawk its proponents were able to keep it in play'.[24]

But BAe had a card up its sleeve: an offset package that dwarfed the proposals of the other contenders. Without cost included, the offset package offered by BAe just took it beyond the rest of the contenders, and the Hawk was able to be presented as the preferred LIFT to purchase. However, these offset deals weren't the dream investments that were suggested. In June 1999 (only months before the final deals were signed), the Department of Trade and Industry (DTI) received a report that suggested that the Hawk's offset offer had been radically inflated. According to the report, a 'breakdown' in communication had meant that the DTI had provided the ministers who made the final choice of the Hawk with an 'incorrect impression of the quality of the offer'.[25]

In fact, when the DTI completed a review of the offset proposals in 1999, it found that most of the Hawk's offset offers were unfeasible. Two of the biggest offers were to build a titanium plant and to invest in the manufacture of equipment to be used in the installation of power plants throughout Africa. The latter offer, to invest in power plant manufacture, had actually already been rejected under a different name (the National Power project) as 'neither the investments nor the local manufacturers [had] been defined and the African projects [were] not yet firm.'[26] On closer inspection, the titanium plant was unsustainable, as the company that BAe wanted to establish the plant, Ti-Met, had pulled out.[27] As the Joint Investigating Report pointed out, 'without these two projects, BAe had virtually no NIP package.'[28]

Even with them, the offset figures provided to Cabinet were, by the Report's own admission, overinflated. When the Hawk's offsets proposals were provided to Cabinet, they were estimated to provide just under R10bn in counter-trade. However, after investigating the offers, the DTI estimated that, even with the two unfeasible projects included, offsets would generate just over R1.5bn in counter-trade, or 15 per cent of what Cabinet had been told the Hawks would earn in offsets.[29]

At the very least, the selection of the Hawk raises serious concerns about mismanagement and incompetence. First, the Hawks were not the favoured military option of the SAAF, the very organisation they were being bought for. Second, the Hawks were considerably more expensive than their closest competitors and were only kept in the running after cost had been excluded as a criterion. Lastly, the Hawks were chosen even though the SAAF still favoured the Aeromacchi after cost had been excluded, largely on the basis of the BAe's offset proposals – proposals which the DTI later pointed out were largely hot air.

WHY DIDN'T THE AIR FORCE JUST SAY 'NO?'

When the final deal was signed with BAe at the end of 1999, the SAAF was lumbered with two planes it did not want, to be used in a training-and-fighting system that it had rejected. Looking back on the deal, what is interesting is the fact that the key players had continuously tried to prevent the deals going through. But they were blocked at every turn.

The testimony of General Pierre Steyn provides the best indication of this. Steyn, who was the Secretary of Defence during the arms acquisition process, resigned in 1998 over the purchase of the Hawk. He explained in a 2007 interview that he resigned 'because, as secretary of defence, I was going to have to account for the costs to Parliament, which I couldn't do'.[30] In fact, Steyn has argued that, from the beginning, he attempted to warn government against the deal, but that his protestations weren't heard. This, he argues, was because the government had decided to sign the deal with BAe come hell or high water, as he made clear in an interview he gave to the Auditor-General in 2001: 'Their choice for Hawk was patently clear from the start ... It was clear to most of us that [it was] the preferred choice of the minister and those who supported him ... The decision makers, and those who supported the decision makers, tried various avenues to get to their presumably predetermined choice ... They tried non-costed options, it did not work. They tried, let us consider risk. How they got to the Hawk, has never really convinced me.'[31] Steyn had even warned Joe Modise that the offset proposals included in the Hawk deal were unlikely to come to fruition: 'Minister Modise was clearly under the impression that [the Hawk deal] was a good idea and that costs shouldn't matter, because we were going to get lucrative offset deals that would give us 65 000 jobs. I warned that the offers that were coming in merely contained vague promises of the kind that were not enforceable, but they wouldn't listen.'[32]

Steyn's attempted interventions in the purchase of the Hawk were material and direct. The most startling example can be found in mid-1998. After Modise had argued for a 'visionary' non-costed approach to purchasing the Hawk, Steyn attempted to make sure that the non-costed option never reached Cabinet. During an Armaments Acquisition Steering Board meeting in July 1998 that he chaired, it was resolved that only the costed option (which favoured the Aeromacchi MB339FD plane) should be sent to the Cabinet for consideration.[33] However, in a meeting of the same board the following month, Steyn's intervention was shot down by Modise, even though Steyn pointed out that the 'Hawk doubled the cost of the LIFT aircraft for an increase in performance of approximately 15%.'[34] Modise argued that a choice about cost would have to be made by the politicians, not the generals: 'the political decision needed must not revolve around the operational aspects of the aircraft … we must not prejudge – let the politicians decide.'[35] As a result, Cabinet would be provided with both the non-costed and costed evaluations, even though the former evaluation flew in the face of the need for the government to spend money efficiently and wisely.

On 31 August, the two options were presented to a briefing meeting that included Thabo Mbeki, Alec Erwin, Joe Modise, Stella Sigcau, Ronnie Kasrils, Chippy Shaik, Pierre Steyn and HD Esterhuyse (the general manager for acquisition of aeronautic and maritime supplies for Armscor). Steyn and Esterhuyse (who also opposed the Hawk deal) later recalled that the meeting did not have official decision-making powers and was not properly minuted by a secretary.[36] The government was briefed by Shaik, who told the government of the two options available in terms of the LIFT contracts (the costed and non-costed evaluations). At the time, Steyn and Esterhuyse recalled, no decision was made about the two options.

After the meeting, Chippy Shaik drew up a set of minutes of the meeting. According to the minutes, those attending the meeting had discussed the two proposals in depth (which Esterhuyse and Steyn contested) and had, after lengthy deliberations, chosen the Hawk 'as the best option to meet all Military and National Economic Strategic Requirements for South Africa.'[37] Steyn and Esterhuyse were furious that the Hawk would now be presented to Cabinet as the preferred option. Steyn, in a memorandum to Shaik written a week after the meeting, stated: 'I cannot recall that a decision was made. The merits of neither the Hawk nor the MB 339 were discussed. The fact that the MB 339 meets the SAAF LIFT requirements adequately (with reference to the pre-determined criteria) is not reflected. The Hawk is not the "best option" from a military point of view – the fact that its acquisition cost would solicit substantially more [offsets] apparently carries the day. The SAAF, however, will have to absorb considerably higher operating costs during its life cycle.'[38]

Esterhuyse, in conjunction with Llew Swan, drew up an alternative set of minutes that he believed accurately reflected the meeting. The minutes argued that the whole deal had to be investigated further before any decision was made. According to Esterhuyse, Swan allegedly took the new minutes to Modise, but they were never acted upon. Scarcely two months later, on 18 November 1998, the Hawk was presented to Cabinet as the preferred option. Steyn, as noted above, resigned soon after the decision was made. Esterhuyse took a more proactive approach, and urged Armscor's internal auditors to investigate and block the deal. However, he left Armscor soon after and the audit never took place. Cabinet was now free to choose the Hawk, always operating under the arguably false assumption that it was, indeed, the preferred choice of the SAAF and the arms acquisition team.

BAE'S 'WEB OF INFLUENCE'

As discussed in Chapter 3, the various 'unusual'[39] machinations that eventually led to the signing of the Hawk deal were explained away in the Joint Investigation Report as being taken for 'strategical [*sic*] reasons, including the total benefit to the country in terms of counter trade investment and the operational capabilities of the SANDF.'[40] It went on to explain that making this sort of decision was the prerogative of the government: 'Although unusual in terms of normal procurement procedures, this decision was neither unlawful, nor irregular in terms of the procurement process as it evolved during the SDP acquisition. As the ultimate decision-maker, Cabinet was entitled to select the preferred bidder, taking into account the recommendations of the evaluating bodies as well as other factors, such as strategic considerations.'[41] What these strategic considerations consisted of is not made clear, but what is made clear upon reviewing the Hawk deal is that the government, at almost every turn, was at pains to ensure that BAe received the contract. This may have been because of a long-term view of strategic partnerships with the UK, but more sinister explanations have also come to light: explanations that point directly to allegedly massive corruption in the selection of BAe as the preferred supplier.

The person around whom allegations of corruption have lingered the longest is Joe Modise, who continuously intervened in the BAe deals to ensure a favourable outcome for the UK company, including arguing for the need to purchase the Hawk without considering cost. At the time of these interventions, however, Modise is alleged to have had serious conflicts of interest. The first of these centred on his role in Conlog. Conlog, a company specialising in

'prepayment' services, such as pay-as-you-go electricity me-
tering and vending devices,[42] was slated to receive a considerable contract arising from the offset proposals submitted
by BAe. It is alleged that Modise was a major shareholder
in the company, and that BAe had undertaken to purchase
the shares for him.[43] What is certain is that, by the time of
Modise's retirement in late 1999, he had been openly installed as a director of the company in charge of marketing.[44] It was a startling conflict of interest, as Colm Allen of
the Public Service Accountability Monitor has argued: 'For
Modise to benefit financially as a businessman from decisions that he made whilst he was a Cabinet minister is an
astounding conflict of interests. You don't need a degree in
ethics to recognize that.'[45]

Whether or not Conlog received any benefits related to
possible offset contracts is uncertain. In 2003, BAe spokesperson Phil Soucy claimed that Conlog had actually been removed from the list of possible sub-contractors once Modise's
involvement was known: 'Conlog was on the very first list
of projects that could have been candidates for our off-set
programmes. When we found out Mr. Modise was a shareholder in Conlog it came off the list.'[46] Later the same year,
BAe's South African representative, Linden Birns, claimed
that 'we [BAe] have never done any business with Conlog,
a fact that could have been checked with us or the Department of Trade and Industry, who monitor all offset deals'.[47]
However, in September 1999, the government posted a list
of all projected National Industrial Participation projects (a
list still available from the government's website). According
to the list, it was projected that as late as September 1999, a
good year after Modise had intervened to smooth the way
for purchases from BAe, BAe and SAAB had planned a joint
venture between 'ABB SA [a company that had become "a

SAAB-BAE SYSTEMS NIP Partner in 1998"[48]] and Conlog to produce pre-payment electrical meters and solar power manufacturing for the domestic and export markets ... Feasibility studies and implementation plans completed.'[49] Thus, while it is plausible that Conlog may not have received any benefits from the BAe deal, it is equally notable that, while the Hawk and Gripen deals were being discussed by South Africa's negotiators, and for a good while thereafter, it was fully anticipated that Conlog would, indeed, be the recipient of a joint-venture partnership flowing from BAe/Saab's offset commitments.

The second allegation of conflict of interest arises from Modise's role as 'Honorary Life President' of the MK Military Veterans Association. The Veterans Association was established as a charitable organisation that was supposed to help returning MK soldiers adapt to life in the new South Africa. In March 1998, while the negotiations around the Hawk deal were ongoing (and only a month before Modise urged a 'visionary approach' to selection), BAe pledged to make a donation of R4.5m to the Association. According to the Memorandum of Understanding, still available from the ANC's website, BAe pledged to donate R4.5m to the Veterans Association through a company called the Airborne Trust (of which more later).[50] This was to be used, according to a press statement released by the Airborne Trust and BAe, to fund the development of an 'industrial/agri-business park and training centre near Orange Farm'[51] that was anticipated to train nearly 20 000 former MK soldiers for their reintegration into civil society. Where these funds have eventually landed up is far from clear. In November 2002, five years after the agreement was signed, SABC's *Special Assignment* team visited the area and reported that no activity in this regard could be found, except for some limited farming.[52] As late as September 2007, the *Mail & Guardian* reported that 'unanswered questions remain about the whereabouts of the donation as nothing became of the agri-business park'.[53]

Perhaps the difficulty in tracking the funds derives from the fact that, as BAe has frequently argued, the funds were never in the hands of the Veterans Association. According to BAe spokesperson Phil Soucy, who responded to the breaking of the story in 2003, 'the money was transferred into First National Bank in Pretoria and is administered by a group of trustees called the Airborne Trust'.[54] Whether or not the park materialised, and even if such a donation does not constitute prosecutable corruption, what is clear, as DA MP Raenette Taljaard argued, is that the payment had a 'very clear political flavour ... I certainly have not come across anything this strange before'.[55]

According to ex-ANC parliamentarian Andrew Feinstein, these wranglings were only the tip of the Modise iceberg. While investigating alleged corruption in the Arms Deal in the aftermath of the tabling of Scopa's 14th Report, Feinstein travelled with Gavin Woods to Pretoria to discuss matters with investigators already probing Arms Deal scandals. When they arrived, one of the investigators allegedly took Feinstein and Woods to see 'a sheaf of different sized pages'. The sheaf contained a 'series of bank statements, signed letters, deposit and withdrawal slips'. The investigator explained the documents by dropping a bombshell: '"This," said the investigator, "is a substantial part of the paper trail linking money from a number of the successful bidders to Joe Modise." "How much of the trail is outstanding?" Gavin asked. "Not much. With the resources and legal powers of the investigating team upstairs, we will complete it in a couple of weeks."'[56]

Joe Modise died at home on 26 November 2001. He was

not investigated further by any investigative agency in South Africa, and the matter was quietly left to die with him.

Other, potentially shady, participants in the BAe deal might still face investigation. In mid-2006, the British Serious Fraud Office (a UK organisation similar to the Scorpions) submitted a request for assistance to South African authorities to pursue an investigation into the BAe deals. Attached to the request, which was granted by South African investigators in January 2007, were a series of damning allegations. According to the application, there existed a complex web of agents and intermediaries who had batted for BAe in South Africa. In particular, the allegations fingered one Fana Hlongwane. Hlongwane was an adviser to Modise during the Arms Deal process, and it is alleged by the SFO that they had received documents from BAe that showed that Hlongwane had 'entered into a general consultancy agreement with BAe in 2002 on a retainer of £1-million per annum. In 2005 there was an agreement to pay $8-million as a settlement figure to Hlongwane in relation to work done on the Gripen project.'[57]

Other personalities included in the SFO allegations were Basil Hersov and Richard Charter. Hersov, it is alleged in the papers, received a massive R77m commission for his role in assisting BAe in South Africa (Hersov has admitted to receiving a commission, but claims that the amount he received was tiny compared to the alleged R77m).[58] Hersov was the founder of the Airborne Trust, chaired by Richard Charter. The Airborne Trust was the company through which BAe's donation of R4.5m to the MK Veterans Association was facilitated.[59] Richard Charter, the former chair of BAe Systems South Africa as well as the Airborne Trust (who died during a canoeing accident on the Orange River in 2004), is alleged to have received even more money from BAe. According to the SFO, Charter received a R27m commission as the country's registered agent in South Africa, but this was just one payment in a series of 'covert' payments that allegedly amount to R350m. These payments were allegedly made to a company of which Charter, according to the SFO allegations, was the sole beneficiary.[60]

Whether these allegations prove to have any substance is still to be discovered in the wake of the full SFO investigation. But what is certain is that BAe did pay huge commissions to agents in South Africa for help in securing the Hawk and Gripen contracts. In June 2003, Patricia Hewitt, the British trade minister, confirmed in front of the UK's House of Commons that BAe had definitely paid a commission to agents in South Africa around the deal.[61] The SFO, taking up allegations, has alleged that, in total, these payments come to at least £112m in 'covert commissions': roughly R1.5bn at 2008 exchange rates.[62]

Both BAe and the British government, while admitting the commissions were paid, have argued that these were paid in the normal conduct of business and did not constitute corruption in any way. According to Patricia Hewitt, the British government had been supplied with 'details of agents' commissions ... in order that it can follow its due diligence procedures. In this case such due diligence procedures were followed and no irregularities were detected.'[63] Similarly, BAe, in 2003, released a statement that acknowledged the use of agents in South Africa, but went on to claim that the South African authorities were 'continuously informed of the advisors employed by BAe Systems, as required by South African regulations. The use of such advisers is strictly controlled, both under South African and UK regulations. Like all defence contractors, BAE systems is bound by these regulations. BAE Systems always complies with all relevant regulations. BAE Systems rejects any suggestion that any such payments are corrupt in intent or fact.'[64]

It is thus clear that considerable payments were made to agents in South Africa to assist BAe to win its contracts from the South African government. However, whether such payments constitute prosecutable corruption is still not clear, and will probably remain so until the SFO has concluded its investigation and presented its findings.

CHAPTER 6

AGENT RS452 AND THE RESIGNATION OF BULELANI NGCUKA

WHAT'S IN THIS CHAPTER?

- How the screws tightened around Schabir Shaik, Mac Maharaj and Jacob Zuma from 2001 to 2003, leading to Ngcuka's claim that there was '*prima facie*' evidence of corruption on the part of Jacob Zuma.
- How Bulelani Ngcuka was accused of being an apartheid spy soon after the '*prima facie*' statement and what this allegation was based on.
- What happened at the Hefer Commission of Enquiry to prove that Ngcuka was not an apartheid spy.
- Judge Hefer's findings after the Commission of Enquiry.
- The Public Protector's investigation into whether Ngcuka had abused his position by making the '*prima facie*' statement.
- What the Public Protector found and how Ngcuka responded.
- How and why Bulelani Ngcuka resigned from the NPA.

KEY DATES FOR THIS CHAPTER

- 16 NOVEMBER 2001 Schabir Shaik is arrested the day after the Joint Investigation Report is presented to Parliament.
- 31 JULY 2003 Newspaper reports emerge that allege that Mac Maharaj was guilty of corruption involving payments from Schabir Shaik. Mac Maharaj resigned from Discovery Holdings pending an investigation, but has never been charged with any wrongdoing.
- 23 AUGUST 2003 Bulelani Ngcuka announces that the NPA is to prosecute Schabir Shaik but not Jacob Zuma. Ngcuka notes that while there is a '*prima facie*' case of corruption against Zuma, the NPA felt that it was not 'winnable'.

- 6 SEPTEMBER 2003 The *City Press* runs an article questioning whether Bulelani Ngcuka was an apartheid spy with the codename Agent RS452. It later emerged that the report was based on an intelligence document authored by Mo Shaik, the brother of Schabir Shaik, in 1989. Both Mo Shaik and Mac Maharaj back up the report when asked for comment.
- 16 OCTOBER 2003 The Hefer Commission of Enquiry tasked with investigating whether or not Ngcuka was an apartheid spy begins. Over the next few months, the case against Ngcuka is blown to smithereens as both Mac Maharaj and Mo Shaik admit that they have no hard evidence against him.
- 6 NOVEMBER 2003 Jacob Zuma lays a formal complaint with the Public Prosecutor (Lawrence Mushwana) alleging that Ngcuka abused his position as the National Director of Public Prosecutions by making the '*prima facie*' statement.
- 20 JANUARY 2004 Judge Hefer delivers his findings. He finds that Ngcuka was probably not an apartheid spy, but slams Ngcuka's office for persistent media leaks.
- MAY 2004 The Public Protector finds that Ngcuka has abused his office and infringed on the constitutional rights of Zuma. His findings are attacked by Ngcuka and former Justice Minister Penuell Maduna.
- JULY 2004 Ngcuka resigns from his position.
- AUGUST 2006 According to an affidavit by Leonard McCarthy, the NPA found that Mushwana's findings were incorrect and outside of his legal jurisdiction.

When Schabir Shaik was first arrested in November 2001, many hoped that the trial would be conducted swiftly, thus minimising any potential fallout from the Arms Deal and returning South Africa to a period of post-apartheid stability and unity. However, over the next four years, South Africa was submitted to a gruelling examination of its democratic credentials and was forced to live through some of the most distressing claims and counter-claims made since the founding of the new South Africa.

Over the course of four years, it was claimed that Schabir Shaik was guilty of two counts of corruption and one of fraud, and that the Deputy President, Jacob Zuma, had a corrupt relationship with Shaik (which resulted in his prosecution, yet to be concluded). But perhaps the most controversial of all the claims was that the man who led the investigations into Shaik and Zuma, National Director of Public Prosecutions Bulelani Ngcuka, had been suspected of being an apartheid spy, and that he was attempting to smear Shaik and Zuma because he held a grudge as a result of the suspicions against him. Many, at the time, claimed that Ngcuka was being fingered purely as a means of defending Zuma and Shaik from further investigation. But this could not be established without resorting to a typical feature of post-apartheid's political landscape: a full-blown commission of enquiry. What followed was tantamount to a farce, but one that kept South Africa's increasingly impatient public on the edge of their seats.

SHAIK, ZUMA AND MAHARAJ:
THE SCREWS TIGHTEN

When the Joint Investigation Team presented their report to Parliament in November 2001, they promised that action would soon be taken against those implicated in improper activities: 'The area of conflict of interests of government officials is cause for concern and viewed as extremely serious. We will be taking action in the next 24 hours.'[1] True to their word, the very next day action was taken, but not against Chippy Shaik, whom most expected would face the music after being slammed in the Report.[2] Instead, it was his brother, Schabir, who faced the long arm of the law. Perhaps people should have seen it coming: a month before the Report was presented, the Scorpions had raided a series of properties in France, Mauritius and South Africa, including the offices of Schabir Shaik's company, Nkobi.[3] Amongst the documents found, it later emerged, were confidential Cabinet minutes relating to the Arms Deal.[4]

Shaik was arrested on 16 November 2001 and charged with theft of documents and an offence under the Protection of Information Act.[5] He was released on R1 000 bail and ordered to present himself to the court when the charges would be fully prosecuted.[6] In May 2002, Shaik was brought before the court to answer these charges. The proceedings of the court showed that the minutes in Shaik's possession related to a meeting of the submarine committee in May 1999, at which Chippy Shaik, Jayendra Naidoo, Thabo Mbeki and Alec Erwin were present. Shaik was also allegedly in possession of confidential Cabinet documents and correspondence between the Department of Defence and the Department of Trade and Industry. Shaik's defence team argued, however, that the minutes and documents were inadmissible as the search warrant used to seize the documents was too vague.[7] The State, soon after this court appearance, requested that the trial be postponed until it could add to the charges laid against Shaik.[8]

Over the course of the next two years, the screws began to tighten. First, in November 2002, the *Mail & Guardian* broke a story alleging that Jacob Zuma had solicited a R500 000-a-year bribe from France's Thomson-CSF, the company that had won the contract to supply the combat suites for the newly purchased corvettes and which had included Schabir Shaik's company, Nkobi, as its black empowerment partner in the deal.[9]

Second, in July 2003, Shaik was forced to submit to a seven-hour interview with the Scorpions, strongly suggesting that he was likely to be charged with corruption.[10] A day later, on 31 July, newspaper reports emerged that the former Transport Minister, Mac Maharaj, was being investigated for corruption. At the heart of the investigation was a series of payments totalling R500 000 that had allegedly been paid into Maharaj's account by one of Shaik's firms. The inference was that Maharaj had been paid the money to assist Shaik's Nkobi Holdings in securing a lucrative slice of a R265m contract to supply bar-coded driver's licences.[11] A month later, Maharaj resigned from First Rand in anticipation of an investigation into the claims being completed.[12] On 14 August 2003, First Rand published a report on the matter, which substantially cleared Maharaj.[13] However, the NPA refused to issue any statement that cleared Maharaj; as a result, Maharaj agreed to resign from First Rand and received a settlement of R1m.[14]

On 23 August Bulelani Ngcuka, the National Director of Public Prosecutions, dropped a bombshell of a statement.[15] The statement detailed the investigation that had taken place into Jacob Zuma and his financial advisor. For the first time, it was announced that the NPA was 'charging Mr Schabir Shaik for various counts of corruption, fraud, theft of company assets, tax evasion and reckless trading. We have decided to prosecute the Nkobi group of companies and Thomson CSF on contraventions.'[16] Jacob Zuma, however, was slightly more fortunate. After the conclusion of the investigation into Zuma, it was decided not to charge him. But, in perhaps the most controversial statement of the entire Arms Deal, Ngcuka went on to claim that 'whilst there is a *prima facie* case of corruption against the Deputy President, our prospects of success are not strong enough. That means that we are not sure if we have a winnable case.'[17]

THE STORY OF AGENT RS452

On 6 September 2003, the weekly newspaper *City Press* ran a combustible article. In it, the author wondered whether the head of the National Directorate of Public Prosecutions, Bulelani Ngcuka, was an apartheid spy with the codename RS452. This was based on a set of 'documents leaked to City Press ... by a senior investigative journalist, which are said to have been sourced from the National Intelligence Agency database.'[18] The documents in question were said to have been written and compiled as part of the ANC-in-exile's operation 'Bible Project', which was an ANC intelligence initiative to establish who in the organisation might have been operating as an apartheid spy. 'Bible Project', importantly, had fallen under the direct supervision of Jacob Zuma (who headed the ANC intelligence structures in Lusaka), and the report that fingered Ngcuka had been drawn up by Mo Shaik (who headed ANC intelligence structures in South Africa) in conjunction with operatives from Operation Vula, including Mac Maharaj.[19] Mo Shaik, who it was later confirmed had written the report fingering Ngcuka, was adamant about the claims: 'By late 1989, the unit in South Africa had come to the conclusion that there was a basis for suspecting Bulelani Ngcuka as being RS452.'[20]

The response to the allegations was one of shock and disbelief. Ngcuka's spokesperson, Sipho Ngwena, claimed no comment, but still pointed out the remarkable coincidence of the allegations emerging at the same time as the Scorpions were investigating Zuma.[21] The national media made much the same point. Xolela Mangcu, writing in *Business Day*, wondered 'why the rumours about Bulelani Ngcuka are only surfacing now that Maharaj, Deputy President Jacob Zuma and the Shaik brothers are in the midst of corruption allegations. Also, if the ANC had this information on Ngcuka, why would they then elevate him to the strategic post of literally being the attorney-general of our land? And so what if Ngcuka was a spy? Does that make Maharaj, Zuma and the Shaiks any less corrupt if the allegations are indeed true?'[22] The political commentator Jovial Rantao made the point even more stridently:

> There can only be one reason for unleashing allegations as damaging as these. It is the desire by people – desperate people – to turn the focus away from themselves. It's a smokescreen … Why is this information peddled at a time when Ngcuka is probing serious allegations against his own comrades? What is it that those who supply this information want to achieve? Is the message that Ngcuka committed a cardinal sin by investigating Deputy President Jacob Zuma? If he had not launched an investiga-

tion into Zuma and others, would the spy claims have been revealed? Quite clearly, these are tough times and there are desperate people out there. They are not only desperate but it would seem they are afraid. The innocent are never afraid. They never get desperate.[23]

Mac Maharaj's biographer, Padraig O'Malley, makes the point that Maharaj's involvement in the whole affair was often misread by the media. Indeed, what was clear from the First Rand investigation into his affairs was that there was little case to be made against him. However, Maharaj had become increasingly upset at what he saw as the Scorpions' proclivity for abusing its powers and authority. He was not, as Mo Shaik later admitted he was trying to do, attempting to 'defend the honour'[24] of Jacob Zuma. Instead, as O'Malley notes, Maharaj was 'deeply angry at Ngcuka for his refusal to clear him, which cost him his job and encouraged the media to imply wrongdoing on his part...'[25] Maharaj, increasingly, became 'obsessed with abuse of power in the office of [the Scorpions]'.[26] Whatever the reason, Maharaj threw his cap into the ring to defend the spy claims, using the forum to criticise the Scorpions for what he perceived to be their abuse of power.

THE HEFER COMMISSION OF ENQUIRY

In order to clear the air over the matter, President Thabo Mbeki decided to do what always seemed to be done in these circumstances: he authorised a commission of enquiry into the allegations. It was to be headed by Judge Joos Hefer, who was authorised to investigate a very specific set of questions:

'Whether at any stage prior to 1994 Ngcuka was registered with the security branch or any other security service of any pre-1994 government as an agent under the code name RS452 or under any other code name; and acting as an agent for the security police and/or National Intelligence Service of any pre-1994 government.'[27]

On 16 October 2003, the Hefer Commission of Enquiry started proceedings with a series of public hearings. But only seven minutes of business was conducted. The advocates of the two main accusers, Mo Shaik and Mac Maharaj, requested a postponement so that they could gather more evidence.[28] When the request was granted, Maharaj and Shaik might have felt a degree of relief at being able to marshal their thoughts and evidence more clearly. However, five days later, their case was severely undermined. Vanessa Brereton, a former Eastern Cape human rights lawyer, admitted that she, in fact, was Agent RS452.[29] She confessed that she had begun working for the apartheid security forces in 1985 as an informer after being convinced of the bona fides of the security policemen who acted as her handlers. She was tasked with aiding the security forces undertake 'Operation Crocus', which attempted to infiltrate and gather information on the 'white left'. Her testimony, she claimed, had been made as she struggled to deal with the self-loathing that had come with the actions she now wanted to leave behind her, and in order to clear the air over the Ngcuka debacle. As she so succinctly summarised: 'I was RS452 and I have had enough of the lies and deceit.'[30]

Brereton's confession gave the clearest indication of all that the Hefer Commission was likely to be a farce. And so it proved. On 12 November, the Commission met to hear the testimony of two key witnesses, Mo Shaik and Mac Maharaj. With Agent RS452 now confirmed to be a white woman from the Eastern Cape, Ngcuka's main accusers tried to prove his spying credentials by wheeling out a different story, which they articulated before they eventually took the stand.[31] According to this new account, Ngcuka had sold out his fellow comrades operating in Durban in the early 1980s, Ntobeko Maqhubela, Mboniso Maqutyana and Mpumelelo Gaba, who were all arrested and sentenced to 20 years on Robben Island. The back-story to this was simple: in the early 1980s, the ANC had infiltrated a comrade named Litha Jolobe into the country to work with Maqhubela's unit in Durban. Jolobe was instructed by his ANC handler (who was in exile), to pick up documents from a dead-letter box at the University of Natal. When he did so, he was arrested, suggesting that he had been set up by his handler in exile. Under severe torture, Jolobe spilt the beans on the Durban unit, which led to the arrest of the comrades listed above. Ngcuka's accusers claimed that it was Ngcuka who had sold them out.[32]

These claims were flawed from the start. Maqhubela, when asked about the matter, dismissed the idea that Ngcuka could have sold them out. Speaking before the Hefer Commission at the end of October, Maqhubela referred to the claims as 'puzzling' and claimed that it was 'impossible' that Ngcuka was the spy who sold them out.[33] In fact, Maqhubela noted, Ngcuka was not even aware of the operations of the Durban unit as Ngcuka had been tasked with a different mission: trying to locate the famous lawyer, Griffiths Mxenge, and his wife, Victoria, who had had recently disappeared (and who were subsequently found dead).[34] Indeed, Ngcuka had only found out about the operations of Maqhubela's unit when he was subsequently arrested and spent time in jail with Maqhubela.[35] This was an important point. When Maqhubela was arrested, Ngcuka, amongst others, was brought in by the apartheid state, which attempted to get Ngcuka to testify against his comrades. Ngcuka, who endured severe torture, refused to testify against his comrades and, as a result, was sentenced to three years in prison.[36] Far from ratting on his comrades, it seems, Ngcuka's only action was to suffer immensely at the hands of the apartheid police in order to protect his fellow revolutionaries.[37]

But that was not all. Maqhubela noted that he actually knew who sold them out, whom he referred to as Mr X. Maqhubela refused to divulge who Mr X was as he had subsequently died, and Maqhubela did not want to embarrass the surviving family. To rub further salt into the wounds, Maqhubela claimed that both Mac Maharaj and Mo Shaik were aware of Mr X's identity, suggesting that they both knew that these specific claims against Ngcuka were a load of hot air.[38]

With these refutations ringing in the ears of the Commissioners, Mac Maharaj took the stand in mid-November. He began by arguing that Ngcuka had been abusing his office, and had attempted to sully Maharaj's name. This was based on the claim made by Maharaj that the *Sunday Times* had been informed of a Scorpions investigation into Maharaj's alleged corruption before Maharaj himself had been told. Maharaj believed that the only man who could have done this was Bulelani Ngcuka: Ngcuka had, according to this account, purposefully smeared Maharaj.[39] As he stated: 'The *Sunday Times* story was a fundamental attack on my integrity, which is the only thing I have in my life … I had no way to clear my name. I offered to resign.'[40] Moreover, Maharaj argued, this formed a 'pattern of abuse' on the part of Ngcuka, which proved that Ngcuka had been abusing his office for political ends.[41]

While the evidence against Ngcuka's unit on this score was

not particularly flattering (Hefer later criticised the unit for the number of leaks emanating from it, which he referred to as 'disturbing'[42]), it was not considered germane to the Hefer Commission. After all, the Commission's mandate was very clear: to investigate claims that Ngcuka was an apartheid spy. On this score, Maharaj was less than convincing. Under cross-examination, he admitted that the major source of the document that implicated Ngcuka was Mo Shaik.[43] Indeed, Maharaj had based his claims of spying against Ngcuka solely on Shaik's report, which showed Maharaj had no evidence of his own to present against Ngcuka.[44] Maharaj also admitted that to the best of his knowledge, Ranjeni Munusamy, the journalist who had provided the story to *City Press*, had likewise based her information solely on Shaik's report. After Ngcuka's counsel had systematically rubbished Shaik's report (of which more below), Maharaj was essentially left with no evidence to prove his claims. Finally, after a lengthy cross-examination, he was forced to admit, 'I do not know that Ngcuka was a spy.'[45]

Maharaj's testimony had established that, in reality, all the claims of Nguka's apartheid-era malfeasance emanated directly from Mo Shaik's intelligence. If this intelligence was proven to be faulty, the entire case against Ngcuka would collapse. Shaik's testimony was far from convincing. He began by telling the court why he had gone public with the Ngcuka claims. Confirming many of the media's suspicions about the reason for the claims, he admitted: 'I went public with the allegations about Ngcuka in order to defend the honour of the deputy president of this country [Jacob Zuma]. I believe that a part of this ongoing personal investigation into the deputy president by the national director of public prosecutions is because he is aware that Zuma conducted an investigation into him in the late 1980s.'[46]

But the intelligence on which Shaik had based his original report, Ngcuka's counsel argued, was no more than 'mere gossip'.[47] In addition, many of the factual claims made in the report were shown to be unfounded in reality. All that was left, in the end, was a series of intelligence reports, based on flawed information, which amounted to nothing more than hearsay. The fact that Shaik refused to reveal his sources only confirmed that the evidence was hearsay, as the Commission could not interrogate Shaik's sources.[48] Again, after intense probing, Shaik finally admitted that he only had evidence that suggested that 'it was possible' that Ngcuka was a spy: 'I am prepared to accept that if you have credible information put to you that nullifies any one of the assumptions I have made, I'm prepared to concede that the analysis that I made in 1989 may have been faulty.'[49]

NGCUKA CLEARED (SORT OF)

With the Hefer Commission hearings complete, Judge Joos Hefer retired to consider his judgment. Finally, on 20 January 2004, Hefer presented his findings, which cleared Ngcuka of the charge of spying: 'Mr Ngcuka probably never acted as an agent for the pre-1994 government security service … the allegations of spying have not been established. The suspicion which a small number of distrustful individuals harboured against him 14 years ago was the unfortunate result of ill-founded references and groundless assumptions.'[50]

But this did not mean that Ngcuka or the Scorpions emerged squeaky clean from the Hefer Commission. In particular, Hefer slammed Ngcuka's office for its persistent and irregular leaks of information to the press. Mac Maharaj's testimony, Hefer found, showed that Maharaj had been the subject of unfair media leaks and the attendant vilification of his family, which Hefer found 'most disturbing'. Although Hefer stressed that he could find no evidence that Ngcuka had leaked the information (or, indeed, condoned the leak), he still argued that 'it must be accepted that someone in Ngcuka's office had disclosed the information, relating to a pending investigation, to the press contrary to the provisions of Section 41 [of the National Prosecution Act].'[51] He also severely criticised the undue stress that had been placed on Maharaj as a result: 'Months have elapsed since Mr Maharaj had been questioned by members of the directorate [but] no charges have yet been preferred against Mr Maharaj or against his wife. In the meantime, press reports about allegations against them kept appearing ... one cannot be assured that the Prosecuting Authority is being used for purposes for which it was intended.'[52]

On 6 November 2003, as the Hefer Commission of Enquiry was unfolding, Jacob Zuma lodged a complaint against Ngcuka with the Public Protector's Office, headed by Lawrence Mushwana. In his complaint, Zuma criticised Ngcuka for his '*prima facie*' statement, which, Zuma argued, showed that the 'National Director of Public Prosecutions conducted the investigation in bad faith, motivated not by the need to earnestly search for the truth, but to cast aspersions on my character.'[53] After conducting a five-month investigation, Mushwana delivered his findings to Parliament in May 2004. They were deeply critical of Ngcuka. According to Mushwana, Ngcuka's '*prima facie*' statement had 'unjustifiably infringed upon Mr. Zuma's constitutional right to human dignity and caused him to be improperly prejudiced'.[54] Mushwana also claimed that Ngcuka and the NPA had failed to co-operate during his enquiry, and, as a result, they should both be 'held accountable for failing to co-operate with the public protector in the investigation of the complaint of the deputy president'.[55]

In order to hold Ngcuka and the NPA to account, Parliament agreed to form an ad hoc 17-member committee to discuss Mushwana's report and what should be done about it. If the Committee 'accepted' Mushawana's report Ngcuka might have been dismissed.[56] But not before both Penuell Maduna (the Justice Minister to whom Ngcuka reported) and Ngcuka furiously attacked Mushwana's findings. Ngcuka responded to Mushwana's report by exclaiming: 'I feel really sorry for him because he has no backbone.' Maduna, too, lashed out, stating: 'Mushwana is the saddest case I've ever had to look at intellectually ... No one who has read [the report] would take it seriously. Parliament has been lied to by the public protector [Mushwana], it's as simple as that.'[57] Both Ngcuka and Maduna later apologised for their outbursts, but Ngcuka still vowed to fight Mushwana's findings.[58]

Ngcuka and the NPA dismissed the majority of Mushwana's findings. First, Ngcuka and Maduna rejected the idea that they had not co-operated with Mushwana's investigations. In fact they had explained to him, they claimed, that they could not do so as the Shaik trial was ongoing and that discussing the matters at hand could possibly prejudice the outcome of the trial. This, they claimed, had been explained to Thabo Mbeki, who, on their behalf, sent a letter to Mushwana with this explanation.[59] Second, they rejected out of hand that it was incorrect to make the *prima facie* statement, when, indeed, there *was* a *prima facie* case of corruption against Zuma (which Ngcuka claimed that Mushwana had admitted to him during Mushwana's initial investigation[60]). In fact, the NPA had drafted a response to the Mushwana report in 2004 that only saw the light of day in 2006, in which they claimed that Mushwana 'struggles with the meaning of *prima facie*', suggesting that Mushwana could not realistically gauge whether or not it was appropriate for Ngcuka to make the statement he did.[61] Indeed, according to an affidavit later submitted by Leonard McCarthy, the new head of the NPA, Mushwana had even gone as far as to mislead the presidency:

> It appeared that when the public protector was unable to deal with the fundamental principles of the law raised in the McCarthy letter, he sought the intervention of the president's office on the basis that the national director and the minister were refusing to co-operate. With respect, the view is held that in this regard the public protector did not just mislead the minister and the national director, he went further and misrepresented the office of the president.[62]

With these claims and counter-claims hanging in the air, the Parliamentary Committee met to discuss the report. Almost immediately, as with all the other aspects of the Ngcuka affair, it was plunged into controversy when it emerged that Jacob Zuma had chaired the meeting of the ANC in which it was decided which ANC politicians would be included in the ANC component of the committee.[63] A number of ANC MPs responded to the revelation by arguing that 'there should have been a wall between himself and the decision … It is a move that could raise eyebrows.'[64] The ANC, however, responded to the report by noting that this was an internal ANC matter, and not one of governance, and the ANC could decide exactly how it chose its own members to partake in a parliamentary committee.[65]

Unfortunately, the Committee itself suffered from serious disagreements. As with all the other parliamentary committees that had been tasked to examine any part of the Arms Deal, it was deeply split along party lines. The ANC, along with the NNP, argued that the scope of the Committee was only to engage with Mushwana's report. Opposition parties, however, argued that the Committee should request the documents that had led Ngcuka to make his statement, as well as call Ngcuka before the Committee to explain himself. Ngcuka himself had declared that he wanted to respond to the Committee as he claimed to have proof that would 'smash' Mushwana's report 'to smithereens'. As Sheila Camerer, the DA representative, noted: 'We can't divorce the [*prima facie*] statement from the surrounding context. If he did not make the statement, he would have had to explain why he did not charge the deputy president.'[66] The IFP's chief whip, Koos van der Merwe, was even more blunt: 'Unless [Ngcuka] is given the opportunity to explain why he made such a statement, we don't support [Mushwana's] finding.'[67] It was an intractable debate, which was never fully resolved. In order to prevent any further conflict, the Committee decided on what was essentially a compromise decision in June 2004. According to the Committee, Mushwana's report was 'noted', but not 'accepted'. This meant that, in effect, the Committee did not give any firm opinion on the matter, and, as such, could not recommend that Ngcuka be dismissed.[68]

In the end, it was an academic point. A month later, in July 2004, Ngcuka tendered his resignation. For many, it was a sign that he had been forced from his position due to political considerations stemming from the Zuma debacle. For Ngcuka, however, it was a decision made more in need to protect the Scorpions and the NPA from the pressure that had been put on him. As he stated in an August interview:

'I'm relieved this has come to an end. I feel a heavy burden has been lifted from my shoulders ... it is important that I protect this organisation from further attacks, attacks from a whole range of people and institutions. The focus has been on the person, but it has been about the institution. If I remove myself, I'll give the institution some space.'[69]

As a statement, it was relatively benign. But, seen in the perspective of the entire Arms Deal, Ngcuka's decision to resign could not but reflect badly on the government. One of their own men, appointed by President and Parliament, had felt the need to jump in order to ensure that an organisation that Parliament itself had created was not destroyed in the fallout from the Arms Deal.

CHAPTER 7

THE
CASE
AGAINST
SCHABIR
SHAIK

WHAT'S IN THIS CHAPTER?

- What Schabir Shaik was charged with and what the State presented as evidence.
- What emerged during the trial of Schabir Shaik.
- The judgment of Judge Hilary Squires finding Schabir Shaik guilty on two counts of corruption and one count of fraud.
- A summary of Schabir Shaik's failed appeals against Judge Squires' findings.

KEY DATES FOR THIS CHAPTER

- 1995 – 2002 Shaik 'loans' Zuma R1.2m.
- 9 SEPTEMBER 1999 Patricia de Lille announces in Parliament that she has evidence of widespread corruption in the Arms Deal.
- 30 SEPTEMBER 1999 Schabir Shaik allegedly meets Alain Thetard and requests a bribe for Jacob Zuma.
- 10/11 MARCH 2000 Schabir Shaik, Alain Thetard and Jacob Zuma meet in Durban. Judge Hilary Squires later found that, at the meeting, it was agreed to pay a R500 000-a-year bribe to Jacob Zuma in return for his protection against any investigation into Thomson-CSF. Squires also found that all parties in the meeting knew what they were agreeing to.
- 14 OCTOBER 2004 Schabir Shaik's trial on charges of corruption and fraud begins in earnest.
- END MAY–BEGINNING JUNE 2005 Judge Hilary Squires presents his judgment on the Shaik case. He finds Shaik guilty on two counts of corruption (of having a corrupt relationship with Zuma and of soliciting a bribe for

Zuma) and one count of fraud. Squires sentences Shaik to 15 years in prison.
- 6 NOVEMBER 2006 The Supreme Court of Appeal finds against Schabir Shaik after he had appealed his conviction and sentence as decided by Judge Hilary Squires.
- 2 OCTOBER 2007 The Constitutional Court finds against a further appeal.

In May 2005, Judge Hilary Squires presented his judgment in the corruption case against Schabir Shaik. The judgment was so long that it took a full two days to read it to the court – and the country. But while the judgment may have been somewhat long-winded, it kept the nation on the edge of its seat. That precarious position was threatened when it became clear exactly what Judge Hilary Squires had found: Schabir Shaik was guilty on two counts of corruption, and one count of fraud. And Shaik wasn't guilty of corruption involving just anybody: he was found guilty of corruptly attempting to influence the decisions made by then Deputy President Jacob Zuma. In finding Shaik guilty, Squires set in motion a series of events that are still playing their way out in the full glare of the media: events that have raised serious questions about the resilience of South Africa's young democracy.

THE CHARGES AGAINST SCHABIR SHAIK:
COUNT ONE OF CORRUPTION
(Shaik and Zuma's 'mutually beneficial symbiosis'[1])

Shaik was first arrested in 2001 and charged with the theft of state documents. This trial was postponed as the State went about putting together a more substantial charge sheet. Finally, on 23 August 2003, the head of National Prosecutions, Bulelani Ngcuka, announced that Shaik was to be prosecuted on more serious charges of corruption and fraud. On 25 August, during a hearing at the Durban Regional Court, Shaik was handed a 45-page charge sheet outlining the State's case against him.

Shaik was charged on three separate counts, along with 10 of the companies he represented. The first charge he had to face was of one of corruption in relation to a generalised pattern of corrupt behaviour between himself and Jacob Zuma. This charge held that Shaik had made a number of payments to Zuma, to which Zuma was not legally entitled, with the intention of influencing Zuma to act in such a way as would benefit Shaik and his companies. As the full charge sheet noted:

> IN THAT during the period 1 October 1995 to 30 September 2002 and at or near Durban in the district of Durban, the accused unlawfully and corruptly gave the abovementioned schedule benefits, which were not legally due, to Zuma, upon whom the powers had been conferred and/or who had the duties as set out in the preamble, with the intention to influence Zuma to commit and/or omit any act in relation to his powers and/or duties to further the interest of the accused and/or the entities associated with the accused as set out in the preamble and/or with the

intention to reward Zuma because he so acted in excess
of such powers or any neglect of such duties, as set out in
the preamble.[2]

What this meant, in layman's terms, was that Shaik was to
be tried for paying money to Zuma in return for Zuma inappropriately assisting Shaik's business activities. To substan-
tiate this charge, the State needed to provide three things.
First, an indication of what actions Zuma would have to
have undertaken in order to have 'acted in excess of such
powers or any neglect of such duties'. Second, that Shaik
had indeed made payments to Jacob Zuma, and that these
were not legally due to Zuma. Lastly, the State had to present
evidence to show that Jacob Zuma's influence had, indeed,
been used to unfairly and inappropriately assist Shaik and
his companies.

On the first point (that Zuma had acted inappropriately
according to the terms of his office), the State noted that
Zuma was bound to abide by the laws that governed his
holding of four different positions: as a member of the Kwa-
Zulu-Natal legislature (from May 1994); as Deputy President
of the country (from 17 June 1999); as the Leader of Government in Parliament (from 17 June 1999); and as a member
of Cabinet. According to Section 136 of the Constitution,
Zuma may not have undertaken the following activities
while holding all of these positions:

(a) undertaken any other paid work;
(b) acted in any way that is inconsistent with his office,
or exposed himself to any situation involving the risk of
a conflict between his official responsibilities and private
interests; or
(c) used his position or any information entrusted to

him, to enrich himself or improperly benefit any other person.[3]

As a member of Parliament, Zuma was supposed to abide by the following rules:

> Zuma was duty bound to maintain the highest standards of propriety to ensure that his integrity and that of the political institutions in which he serves are beyond question. ... Zuma was duty bound not to have placed himself in a position which conflicts with his responsibilities as a public representative in Parliament, nor may he have taken any improper benefit, profit or advantage from the office of Member.[4]

If the State could prove that Zuma had broken any of these rules in his relationship with Shaik, it could therefore argue that their relationship had resulted in Zuma acting 'in excess of [his] powers or any neglect of [his] duties.'

By arguing that Zuma had acted 'in excess' of his powers and in 'neglect' of his duties, the State was making sure that any inappropriate behaviour on the part of Zuma, either by commission or omission, would be considered as breaching the rules governing his political position. To give a simple example: Zuma would have acted in 'excess' of his duties if he had used his political clout to shut down an investigation into any act of impropriety committed by Shaik. But Zuma would also have acted in 'neglect' of his duties if he had been aware that Shaik had committed an offence of corruption and done nothing about it, as the positions he held gave him a constitutional and legal obligation to do something.

On the second burden of evidence (that Shaik had made

payments to Zuma that were not legally due to him), the State presented evidence purporting to show such payments. The State argued that Shaik had paid Zuma R1 340 078.01 from 1 October 1995 to 30 September 2005.[5] In addition, the State argued that these payments were highly irregular for a host of reasons. These were:

1. That the payments made 'no legitimate business sense'[6] because neither Shaik nor his companies could actually afford to make them. In reality, the State argued, in order to pay the money to Zuma, Shaik and his companies had to borrow money from banks and exceed their overdraft in order to make the payments.

2. It was strange that Shaik would borrow this money from banks 'at prevailing interest rates', only to make payments to Zuma that were interest free.[7]

3. None of these payments had been reflected 'as a liability in any financial document relating to Zuma' and had not been 'reflected as an asset in any financial documentation relating to' Shaik.[8]

4. That, while loan agreements between Zuma and Shaik had been signed, these were 'patently incomplete and irregular, being undated, seemingly hurriedly signed in the wrong place, and indicating interest-free loans with no date of repayment.'[9]

5. And, lastly, because Zuma could 'at no stage afford to repay the "loans"', a reality that Shaik would have been all too aware of as Zuma's financial advisor with an 'intimate knowledge of Zuma's financial affairs'.[10] As proof of this, the State noted that Zuma's 'expendi-

ture constantly exceeds his income' and that 'Zuma's
financial record reflects an unfortunate history of dis-
honoured cheques and unmet debit orders.'[11]

In other words, the State argued that Shaik had made payments to Zuma that Shaik's companies could not afford, and
that Zuma had no real way of paying these amounts back.
The only inference that could be drawn from acting in such
a way, the State argued, was that 'the group's survival depended on obtaining profitable new business, *inter alia*, with
the assistance of Zuma'.[12] In more straightforward language:
Shaik and his companies would only have made these payments if they expected that they would help them land fat
contracts.

The third thing that the State needed to prove to make
this charge of corruption stick was that Shaik had used his
connection to Jacob Zuma to help Shaik and his companies.
The State advanced a number of examples of this, one of
which was directly related to the Arms Deal. This related to
the working relationship between Shaik's Nkobi Holdings
and the French company Thomson-CSF.

Both Thomson and Nkobi owned and ran a series of subsidiary companies in South Africa, which are highly confusing to try and follow (see Appendix C for a full low-down
list of all these, as well as Appendix A). But the essential
point of all these holding companies was this: Thomson
and Nkobi were joint venture partners, and Thomson was
the company that won the contract to supply the combat
suites for the corvettes.

The State, however, argued that Shaik was uncertain as to
whether Thomson planned to include Nkobi in any potential bid. According to the State, Thomson had always wanted
to get a slice of the Arms Deal action.[13] To get this, Thomson-

CSF acquired a stake in a company called Altech Defence Systems, which was later renamed African Defence Systems (yes, *the* African Defence Systems that was fingered in the Joint Investigation Report). Typically, Thomson, which already had a joint venture partnership with Shaik's Nkobi group of companies, would have given Shaik a slice of the company so that Shaik could be submitted as Thomson's black empowerment partner. But, according to the State, Thomson were 'wracked by uncertainties over the "suitability" of their political contacts in South Africa',[14] largely because Thomson believed, for some reason, that Thabo Mbeki disapproved of Schabir Shaik and his Nkobi Group (it was later alleged that Mbeki was far more impressed by Futuristic Business Solutions, which later received a small shareholding in ADS and was owned, in part, by Tsepo Molai, the son-in-law of Joe Modise[15]).

As a result, Thomson tried to make sure that Shaik and Nkobi would get no slice of ADS. This would be achieved by a sleight of hand: Thomson-CSF would buy directly into ADS, and not through its SA subsidiary, Thomson Holdings or Thomson Pty, of which Nkobi was a shareholder. Needless to say, the State argued, Shaik, Nkobi and Zuma were none too pleased with this turn of events. To resolve the situation, on 17 March 1998 Shaik conveyed to Jean-Paul Perrier, the head of Thomson-CSF International, that Zuma wanted to meet with Perrier to resolve the issue.[16] On 2 July 1998, Schabir Shaik, Jacob Zuma and Perrier met in London, although it is unclear what transpired at the meeting.[17] Enter Chippy Shaik. Seven days after Zuma met Perrier in London, Chippy Shaik met with Bernard de Bollardiere (a representative of Thomson) and Alain Thetard (the director of Thomson Holdings, the SA subsidiary of Thomson) on 9 July 1998.[18] According to the State, Chippy told both of them that 'he would facilitate matters for Thomson if Thomson's position with partners and friends was convenient to Chippy Shaik. He would otherwise make things difficult.'[19]

With this threat ringing in the ears of Thomson, Schabir Shaik met with the company on 9 June 1998. The State claimed that, according to minutes of the meeting, Shaik expressed his intense displeasure at being bypassed, and threatened to take out a court interdict to ensure that Thomson acted in good faith in terms of its joint venture agreement.[20] Zuma, too, weighed in with his view. On 18 November 1998, the same day the government selected the German Frigate Consortium and Thomson as the preferred suppliers for the corvette bid, 'Minister JZ', Pierre Moynot, Perrier and Schabir Shaik met at the Nkobi offices to resolve the matter. Thomson, who had been told by Chippy that Zuma was likely to be the next deputy president, agreed to submit to mediation over the matter, with Zuma acting as the mediator on the day. After this meeting, Thomson transferred a 10 per cent share of Thomson's holdings in ADS to Nkobi Investments (owned, in turn, by Shaik's Nkobi Holdings), which meant that, after months of struggle, Schabir Shaik would be sure to get his own little slice of the Arms Deal pie.[21] The State was clear on the matter: Zuma was 'there as a mediator to resolve the dispute' and the result of the meeting was that 'Nkobi Investments, with Zuma's assistance, became a joint venture partner with Thomson in the German Frigate Consortium and so joined the successful bidder in the corvette bid.'[22]

So, to summarise this first charge of corruption: it was claimed by the State that Shaik had paid Zuma a considerable amount of money (over R1m), which Shaik's companies could not really afford, and which Zuma had no realistic means of paying back. In return for these payments, Shaik turned to Zuma for help in securing business contracts, and, in one specific Arms Deal-related case, to smooth the way for Shaik to become the joint-venture partner of Thomson in its bid for a slice of the Arms Deal.

THE CHARGES AGAINST SCHABIR SHAIK: COUNT TWO OF CORRUPTION (The Bribe)

The second count of corruption that Shaik faced was related to the solicitation of a bribe for Zuma. This is the matter that has attracted most of the media attention around the Shaik and Zuma trials, and is also the charge in which the famous 'encrypted fax' was material.

According to the strict legalese of the indictment, Shaik was to face the following charge:

> IN THAT during the period 30 September 1999 to 2001 and at or near Durban in the district of Durban, the accused unlawfully and corruptly agreed and/or offered to give and/or gave the abovementioned amounts of R500 000 annually, as described in the preamble, which were not legally due, to Zuma, upon whom the powers had been conferred and/or who had the duties as set out in the preamble, with the intention to influence Zuma to commit and/or omit any act in relation to his powers and/or duties to further the interest of the accused and/ or the entities associated with the accused, as set out in the preamble.'[23]

The State's case on this count was relatively straightforward.

According to the State, the story of this count began in November 1998, when, as discussed in Chapter 3, the investigations into the Arms Deal began. In September 1999, De Lille presented her dossier in Parliament, which raised serious questions about the rectitude of the Arms Deal. This was followed, in February 2000, by allegations raised in the media about the corvette deal, which started appearing in the same month as the Heath Unit expressed interest in investigating the Arms Deal.[24] On 30 October, Scopa issued its now-famous 14th Report, in which it was recommended that a super-investigating team be established to investigate allegations of corruption in the Arms Deal; the Heath Unit was to be part of this recommended team.

According to the State, Schabir Shaik met with Alain Thetard in Durban on 30 September 1999, as it was becoming apparent that the Arms Deal was likely to be the subject of an intense investigation.[25] During (or sometime after) this meeting, the State alleged, Schaik requested that Thetard arrange a bribe of R500 000 per year to be paid to Jacob Zuma until dividends were paid by ADS in 2001, which meant that the requested bribe amount would be R1m.[26] The objectives of the bribe were straightforward: in return for the money, Zuma would provide protection during the current investigations as well as support any future Thomson projects in South Africa.[27] Thetard responded by asking that Zuma confirm, by way of an encrypted code, that he was amenable to the bribe agreement. This was provided by Zuma, according to the State, on 11 March (later changed to 10 March) 2000 during a meeting between Zuma, Shaik and Thetard in Durban. Thetard then told Thomson-CSF head offices in France and Mauritius that Zuma had agreed to that arrangement.[28]

According to the State, Shaik had considerable difficulty in actually getting any money out of Thomson. In the end,

Shaik and Zuma only received R250 000 of the R1m bribe, which was paid into the Absa account of one of Shaik's subsidiary companies, Kobitech, on 16 February 2001. The bribe was hidden from public scrutiny through a complicated arrangement. At the end of 2000, Nkobi and Thomson-CSF International (France) entered into a service-provider agreement, which, not so coincidentally, was to see Nkobi earn R500 000 a year, the same amount as the bribe. The State was damning about this service provider agreement: 'Nkobi did little by way of any service to justify this fee of R1 million (or the amount of R250 000 that was paid during February 2001), beyond providing a letter dated 15 April 2001 referring to a submission regarding guidelines and procedures for counter trade offset obligations that would follow and a letter dated 16 July 2001 dealing with potential offset projects, all of which in any case would have benefited Nkobi.'[29]

By this date, however, Zuma had started incurring some serious costs. On 20 July, Zuma authorised that construction should begin on his traditional homestead at Nkandla in KwaZulu-Natal. According to the tender submitted before the construction began, it was to cost R1.34m to build.[30] It was such a big expense that Schabir Shaik even attempted to stop the development going ahead in October 2000, but was overruled by Zuma. Zuma was to pay for the property in two ways: through taking out a bond, and by receiving payments from third parties (in fact, when Zuma did get a bond in 2002, one Vathasallum Reddy, a businessman, signed surety on the bond and accepted responsibility for meeting the monthly repayments).[31]

This is where it starts getting complicated. On 4 December 2000, Zuma withdrew a cheque to the amount of R1m from the account of Development Africa (which the State noted was registered entirely in Reddy's name). Zuma presented the cheque to his Nkandla contractor, but, only three days later, Shaik stopped payment on the cheque. Instead, Shaik waited until he had received the first R250 000 from Thomson on 16 February 2001. This amount was then transferred, seven days later, from Shaik's Kobitech company into which the R250 000 had been paid by Thomson into the account of Reddy's Development Africa. A further three post-dated cheques of R250 000 each were drawn up by Shaik to be paid from the Kobitech account to Development Africa, seemingly in anticipation of Shaik receiving the remaining R750 000 from Thomson. In April 2001, following a February meeting with Jean-Daniel Chabas (a member of Thomson's senior management) in which Thomson raised the possibility that the remaining R750 000 be paid from dividends owing to ADS (only due in September 2001), Shaik cancelled the post-dated cheques drawn in favour of Development Africa. This suggested that, without payments coming from Thomson, Shaik would be unable to pay Development Africa, which was slated to pay for the costs of Nkandla.[32] Two further payments totalling R125 000 were eventually made by Shaik to Development Africa in September 2001.

What was left to explain, on this count, was that Zuma acted on this bribe agreement. According to the State's charges, the smoking gun in this matter was the letter written by Jacob Zuma to Gavin Woods of Scopa in January 2001. In it Zuma informed Woods that the government did not think it was necessary to include the Heath Unit in the investigation into the Arms Deal, and subtly accused Scopa of trying to 'find the Executive guilty at all costs, based on the assumption we have already mentioned, that the Executive is prone to corruption and dishonesty.'[33]

So, to summarise this charge: Shaik had, according to the State, solicited a R500 000-a-year bribe from Thomson to be paid to Zuma. This was done in order to influence Zuma to protect Thomson against any problems arising from the investigations into the Arms Deal. This bribe, the State claimed, was to be disguised by means of a service provider agreement between Nkobi and Thomson that exactly matched the amount of the bribe to be received by Zuma. Further, the State alleged that the payments did end up as part of Zuma's assets as the payments were channelled to Development Africa, which, at the time, was one of the companies belonging to the businessman, Reddy, who was paying for Zuma's Nkandla rural village. And, lastly, Zuma had acted on the bribe agreement by writing a stinging letter to Gavin Woods of Scopa attempting to prevent Scopa from leading a full-fledged investigation into Arms Deal corruption.

THE CHARGES AGAINST SCHABIR SHAIK: COUNT THREE OF FRAUD (The Accounting Fudge)

The third and final charge laid against Shaik was of fraud. As the indictment stated:

> 'IN THAT during or about the period February 1999 to early 2000 accused 1 unlawfully falsified and/or made false entries in any book, register, document, financial record or financial statement of any company, to wit accused 2 to 10
>
> IN THAT the aforementioned amounts as set out in the preamble, were irregularly written off under the description development costs of Prodiba; and/or
>
> IN THAT the accounting records failed to reveal, in

circumstances where it should have been revealed, that the abovementioned write-off had the net effect of extinguishing certain of accused 1's and/or accused 9's and/or accused 10's and/or Zuma's supposed debts in the books of the Nkobi group, as described in the preamble.'[34]

This charge was very straightforward. According to the State, on 28 February 1999, an amount of R1 282 027,63 was written off in the accounting records of the Nkobi company, Kobifin. This amount, the State claimed, was the amount that Schabir Shaik, Floryn Investments (a Shaik company) and Clegton Pty (another Shaik company) owed to the Nkobi group. Part of this debt of R1.2m was made up of a payment to Zuma. However, the amount was written off irregularly, as it was entered into the accounts under the description of development costs for Prodiba (a contract earned by Shaik and others to provide bar-coded driver's licences). This was not true, the State alleged, and further led to a misrepresentation of the actual financial status of Kobifin. As the State summarised: 'The write-off to Prodiba development costs is false, irregular and does not comply with GAAP (Generally Accepted Accounting Practice).'[35]

THE TRIAL

Schabir Shaik's trial began in earnest on 14 October 2004. The trial was to be presided over by Judge Hilary Squires, who was brought out of retirement to hear the case in the Durban High Court.

On this day, the battle lines in the Shaik trial were drawn. The State spent a good three hours outlining its case against

Shaik, as detailed above. This was made easier for everyone to understand as the State's lead prosecutor, Billy Downer SC, delivered a three-hour Powerpoint presentation to the court, in which he explained all the various links between the role players in the Shaik trial.[36] Shaik, in turn, opened his defence with a deceptively brief statement: 'I am accused Number One in this matter and I also represent the corporate accused. I plead not guilty.'[37]

Shaik then proceeded to outline what his defence on these charges would be. He admitted, upfront, through his lead advocate Francois van Zyl, that he had made payments to Zuma, which were used to pay school fees for Zuma's children, clothing bills, the repair of cars, air fares, a number of attorneys, and settling debt obligations that Zuma had with Standard Bank where Zuma had a home loan and chequing account.[38] But, Shaik argued, these payments were not inappropriate or corrupt at all: they were made purely out of friendship, as Zuma and Shaik shared a deep and close bond. In particular, Shaik noted how his relationship with Zuma stretched back into the mists of exile: 'My association with Zuma began in the 1980s during the struggle against apartheid. I went to London where I met Zuma and Aziz Pahad. Zuma recruited me for the ANC and sent me for training … I was often in charge of carrying information from my brother, Mo, to Zuma.'[39] Shaik began paying Zuma money when he realised that 'between 1996 and 1997, Zuma had dire financial problems and he wanted to leave politics'.[40] Shaik, deeply concerned by the possible loss to politics of Zuma and solicitous of his friend's wellbeing, took it upon himself to support Zuma, which was an attempt, Shaik noted, to 'help in an effort to keep him in politics'.[41]

These payments, Shaik argued, were never conceived of as donations, but, rather, as forming part of a loan agreement. According to Shaik, Zuma insisted that he would re-pay Shaik, and they entered into a loan agreement to this effect. Importantly, this loan agreement did not include any interest charges, Shaik claimed, 'because of my religious be-liefs'[42] as a Muslim, which provided clear condemnation of the institutions of interest and usury.

As to the other charges Shaik faced, he issued flat denials. On the charge of fraud, he acknowledged that he had writ-ten off the R1.2m from the books of Kobifin, but that this was a mistake of which he was not at first aware. When he learnt of the mistake, he argued, he instructed the matter to be rectified in the books.[43] On the charge of soliciting a bribe, he argued that he had never done so, and that he had never entered into the complex set of payments described above to hide the bribe.[44] He admitted that he had indeed met Zuma and Thetard in Durban on that day in March 2000, but claimed that the meeting was to discuss the pos-sibilities of Thomson making charitable donations to the Jacob Zuma Education Trust.[45]

Over the course of the next six months, the State argued its case against Shaik by admitting reams of evidence and calling on the testimony of nearly 40 witnesses. And, from the start, it did not look very good for Schabir. The first wit-ness called by the State was one Professor Themba Sono, who had joined Shaik's business empire in 1996 after Shaik had promised that he would 'make [Sono] a millionaire.'[46] Shaik's business empire was to be founded on very little as Nkobi was started with almost no money and very little ex-pertise, as Sono admitted: 'It had nothing really.'[47] The one thing the company did have was 'political connectivity', which Shaik had argued should be judged in real monetary terms by the companies that entered joint venture agree-ments with Nkobi. During a meeting between Nkobi and

Thomson over the signing of the Prodiba deal, Sono recalled Shaik arguing that 'we are bringing a lot of goodwill here, we are an empowerment company. This is the new South Africa. If we are going to open doors you must regard our goodwill in monetary value.'[48]

According to Sono, Shaik's 'political connectivity' was assured by his relationship with two political heavyweights: 'There are names that always cropped up. Two of the names that always cropped up were Jacob Zuma and Mac Maharaj.'[49] Indeed, Sono claimed that Zuma's name was frequently dropped right from the time Sono had joined the company in 1996. As he recalled: 'He asked me, "You know president Mandela is to retire soon, and deputy president Mbeki would become the president, and minister Zuma would be the deputy president?" And he says, "What do you think if I become a director general in deputy president Zuma's place?".'[50] Sono's testimony also cast some doubt as to the 'sunniness' of Shaik's character. Sono noted that he resigned from the company because of his run-ins with Shaik, which he referred to as stemming from the 'non-sunny side' of Shaik's personality.[51] In particular, he was upset at the 'boorish and autocratic' way in which Shaik treated his staff, and at a harangue delivered by Shaik in which he attacked Sono's political connections and blackness: 'Listen here my friend, your blackness means nothing to me ... Your connection to Mandela and Mbeki means nothing in the company,' Sono recalled Shaik saying.[52]

Another academic, Professor John Lennon, gave testimony that painted much the same picture as Sono's. Lennon flew in from Glasgow for a single day to give his straightforward testimony. In 1998, he had flown to South Africa as part of a trade delegation.[53] His intent: to set up an ecotourism school in KwaZulu-Natal that would create jobs and develop the tourism industry. At the time, Lennon had been told by people in Britain that he would need the support of political figures, such as Zuma, in order to get the project off the ground. As a result, Lennon met with Zuma at Zuma's Durban office, where he outlined the potential project. At the time, Lennon recalled, Zuma was 'very keen, very enthusiastic' about the project, and promised to provide a letter of support. After waiting a number of months, Lennon received the letter from Zuma, which was sent, not from Zuma's office, but from the Nkobi fax machine. The letter expressed support for the project, but suggested that Zuma had spoken to Nkobi about the project and that Lennon should possibly speak to Nkobi about including them as a joint venture partner in the project.[54]

Lennon found it 'peculiar' that the letter had been sent from the Nkobi office.[55] But things were about to get even more peculiar. Lennon felt that the suggestion to include Nkobi was irregular, as Lennon already had two local firms slated as joint partners. On 4 February 1999, Nkobi wrote to Lennon expressing interest in the deal, while, on the same day, a letter from Zuma was sent to the Development Bank of Southern Africa expressing his support of the deal. Lennon was perturbed by this series of events, and wrote back to Nkobi suggesting that they meet with Lennon's South African partners, Ash and EDP.[56] This did not meet the liking of Nkobi, whose Martyn Surman (the business development manager of Nkobi) sent a response to Lennon on 16 February. The response stated that Shaik felt 'insulted' by Lennon's suggestion, and unfairly 'marginalised' after Lennon had received the letter of support from Zuma. It was demanded, in the same letter, that Lennon and Nkobi develop a business plan and a workshare agreement. If this was not delivered, there would be comeback: 'Mr Shaik has asked me to advise you that he is prepared to give you three days … failing which he would go back to Minister Zuma.'[57]

The threat was clear: include Nkobi in the deal, or Shaik would tell Zuma to withdraw his support for the project. As Lennon noted, the letter implied that Shaik was the 'only person' who could wrangle Zuma's support for the project, which Lennon felt was 'unusual and irregular'. In addition, Surman's letter suggested to Lennon that Shaik had a 'degree of influence over Minister Zuma and that if I didn't do as I was told … Zuma might potentially withdraw his support'.[58] But it was all academic in the end: Lennon's project never took off after this exchange of letters, which he decried as 'unusual, unfortunate and tragically unforgivable'.[59]

The next damning witness called by the State was Bianca Singh, Shaik's former secretary, whose testimony provided some of the quotes that lived long in the media's memory. Singh's testimony painted a relationship between Zuma and Shaik that was, somewhat understatedly, 'quite close'.[60] According to Singh, Shaik kept two red files in his office, which contained details of Zuma's financial affairs. Both Zuma and Shaik were in constant contact about Zuma's financial affairs, which Shaik managed by accessing Zuma's accounts via the internet. As Singh recalled: 'Mr Zuma would often speak to Mr Shaik to check on the balance of his account and deposits into his account.'[61] Singh also recalled how frequent payments were made to Zuma: 'Transfers of money would be made to Mr. Zuma's account, Kobifin [one of the accused corporate entities] and Mr. Shaik's account to Mr. Zuma and Mr. Zuma would phone in and check.'[62]

The payments made to Zuma were, in some instances, quite absurdly ad hoc. One on occasion, Singh recalled, she answered Shaik's cellphone to find that Zuma was calling, so she called Shaik out of a meeting to speak to him. Shaik then asked her how much money there was in petty cash. 'I had R500. I gave Mr Shaik the R500 and he took out another R200 from his pocket. He asked me for an envelope, placed the money into the envelope, then asked me to call Mr Isaacs [the Nkobi group accountant]. He then told me I need to go with Mr Isaacs to the airport and then ... to take the envelope to the deputy president [Zuma].'[63]

Arguably, all this testimony proved was the Shaik was admirably fulfilling his obligations as Zuma's financial advisor. However, Singh's testimony went further in noting how close Zuma and Shaik were in their business dealings. One instance that Singh recalled related directly to the Arms Deal. According to Singh, in late 1998 she was in Shaik's office when his cellphone rang. Shaik answered the call, which was from his brother, Chippy. After a brief conversation, Schabir told his brother not to worry. Immediately after, according to Singh, Shaik dialled a new number and said: 'Hello, my brother JZ ... Chippy's under pressure and we really need your help to land this deal.' Singh recalled that Shaik often referred to Zuma as 'JZ', and that she was convinced that they were talking about the Arms Deal, as this was the only affair that Shaik referred to as a 'deal'.[64] That Shaik was interested in the Arms Deal by this point was certain in Singh's mind, as she recalled that, when she first arrived to work at the company in 1996 (after being spotted by Shaik at a Durban pizzeria), she noticed, in Shaik's office, a laminated, black and white copy of the diagrams of the corvettes later bought in the Arms Deal.[65]

This ability to call up important friends in time of need didn't mean that Shaik was always happy with how his 'political connectivity' acted out in his relationship with the ministers and black empowerment partners at his disposal. Singh recalled that, although Nkobi argued that it had black empowerment credentials, Shaik would often admit to Singh that 'oh, he's just tired of black people'.[66] On another occasion, Singh recalled (in words that were to resonate with media reportage of the trial for long after its conclusion) that Shaik had ridiculed the type of relationship he had with 'various ministers': 'He said he has to carry a jar of Vaseline because he gets fucked all the time but that's okay because he gets what he wants and they get what they want.'[67]

The result of this testimony was simple: if the court accepted Singh's version of events, the State would have a part of the evidence that proved that the relationship between Zuma and Shaik was one in which Shaik paid Zuma sums of money and that, as a consequence, Shaik could call on Zuma for assistance in any business transaction. In other words, Singh's testimony went some way to proving that Zuma had received benefits that were not 'legally due' to him, and that Shaik had given them 'with the intention to influence Zuma to commit and/or omit any act in relation to his powers'.[68]

But Singh's testimony went further than this and provided some proof towards the verification of the second corruption charge that Shaik was facing (of soliciting the bribe). Singh recalled that in November 2000, she travelled with Shaik to Mauritius for a meeting with Alain Thetard, the director of a South African subsidiary of the French arms giant Thomson-CSF. Prior to the meeting, Singh recalled, Shaik emphasised the need for Singh to bring along with her a file of newspaper clippings about the investigations into the Arms Deal that were just beginning. During the meeting, from which she was eventually ejected after Shaik had pointedly said to her, 'I hope you're not minuting all this,' Shaik raised the matter of the investigation into the Arms Deal. As Singh recalled: 'Mr. Shaik said they needed to discuss damage control with regard to newspaper articles on the Arms Deal. Shaik said that if the Heath Investigating Unit continues we are going to be under an amount of pressure and if a certain ANC member – I can't remember his name – were to open his mouth we would be in real trouble.'[69]

Singh's relationship with Shaik ended soon after this meeting. On the same night that the meeting took place, Singh recalled, she was summoned to Shaik's room. What happened next is unclear, except that they had an 'incident of a personal nature' that deeply upset Singh. The next day, she flew back home, resigned from Nkobi, and never spoke to Shaik again.[70] Nkobi insisted that Singh sign a confidentiality clause, as she knew too much about Shaik's relationship with Zuma.[71] But, this diversion aside, what was clear from Singh's testimony (if the Court accepted her version) was this: Shaik was, by November 2000, worried about the investigations into the Arms Deal, and felt that they needed to do damage control to prevent any embarrassment potentially suffered by Thomson and Nkobi. That he told this to Thomson meant that they were, in turn, aware of the potential problems that an investigation could cause. This, remember, was roughly eight months after Shaik had allegedly solicited a bribe for Zuma from Thomson; only two months before Zuma had written his stinging letter of rebuke to Gavin Woods of Scopa (which was later shown to have been written by Thabo Mbeki, although signed by Zuma himself); and only three months before Zuma was alleged to have received his first bribe payment from Thomson.

It was the bribe and its solicitation that was one of the hardest things for the State to prove. The 'smoking gun' piece of evidence was the 'encrypted fax' sent by Thomson director Alain Thetard to Yann de Jomaron, Thomson's sales director for Africa. When the State tried to get the fax admitted into evidence, Shaik's defence counsel argued that it was inadmissible. This was because, they claimed, it was hearsay. Squires responded to the submission by allowing it to be submitted into evidence temporarily until he had reached a judgment on the matter. This judgment was delivered by Squires during the course of the trial. It was not good news for Shaik. Squires, to baldly summarise a lengthy legal argument, ruled that it was fair for the fax to be admitted because Shaik had been given the right to lead his defence evidence on this question, and, as a result, the State should also be given the right to present its evidence. This did not mean, however, that the Court necessarily had to agree that the contents of the fax supported the State's case. As Squires stated in some fine legalese:

> ... it seems to me that as the accused's explanation of the common purpose for the solicitation of money from Thomsons is an entirely innocent one, then the interests of justice require that the State's version of this common purpose in the form of this encrypted fax, also at least be placed in the scales. Once there of course, for the State to succeed, the scale would have to come down to the necessary level of proof beyond a reasonable doubt for its version to be accepted. But at least the interests of justice require that it be placed in the scale to start with.[72]

But what did the fax actually say? The typed version was headed FAX CRYPTE, and was given the subject line: 'Subject: JZ/S.Shaik.' The body of the fax read:

> Dear Yann: following our interview held on 30/9/1999 with S. Shaik in Durban and my conversation held on 10/11/1999 with Mr J.P. Perrier in Paris I have been able

(at last) to meet JZ in Durban on the 11th of this month, during a private interview in the presence of S.S. I had asked for S.S. to obtain from J.Z. a clear confirmation or, at least, an encoded declaration (in a code defined by me), in order to validate the request by S.S at the End of September 1999. This was done by JZ, (in an encoded form). May I remind you of the two main objectives of the 'effort' requested of Thompson-CSF are:

- Thompson-CSF's protection during the current investigations (SITRON)
- JZ's permanent support for the future projects
- Amount: 500k ZAR per annum (until the first payment of the Dividends by ADS).[73]

The State argued that this fax proved that Shaik had, in September 1999, requested that Thomson pay a bribe to Zuma, and that in March 2000, Zuma and Shaik had met with Thetard. During the March 2000 meeting, the fax suggested, Zuma had given a thumbs-up to the bribe, which, in return, would lead to Zuma providing protection for Thomson against any investigations taking place during the Arms Deal at the time.

Shaik's defence had a somewhat strange argument to offer in defusing the encrypted fax. Taking their cue from an affidavit signed by Thetard (which directly contradicted one he had initially written in return for not being prosecuted), Shaik's defence argued that the fax had never been sent. Thetard claimed in his second affidavit that the note was actually just a rough note of a document 'in which I intended to record my thoughts on separate issues in a manner which was not only disjointed but lacked circumspection. It is for this reason that I did not fax this document or direct that it be faxed. I crumpled it and threw it into the waste paper basket from where it was possibly retrieved and provided to the state.'[74]

This account was directly contradicted by the testimony of Sue Delique, Thetard's former secretary. Delique claimed in her testimony that she had been given the handwritten note by Thetard, after what she assumed had been a meeting with Shaik and Zuma in Durban. Delique then typed the note up and sent it via an encrypted channel as Thetard had requested. The State had got hold of the handwritten note, as well as the computer disk on which Delique had saved the typed-up version, directly from Delique. In April 2000, Delique resigned from her position at Thomson/Thales, which seriously upset Thetard. Under Thetard's watchful eye, Delique was forced to quickly pack up her things and leave the premises. Amongst the items on her desk was the handwritten note, as well as the computer disk. As she explained: 'When I left Thomsons … I had a rather unpleasant experience with Mr. Thetard … I feared for my safety … I grabbed what I had on my desk and I ran out of the office.'[75]

But Delique's testimony in this regard wasn't enough. The State still had to prove that the fax note was, indeed, in Thetard's handwriting, as well as that Delique hadn't just typed up the document when she resigned as an act of malice. Two expert witnesses solved this problem. The first was handwriting expert Superintendent Marius Rehder. Rehder testified that it was his opinion that Thetard had definitely written the note.[76] The second witness was Bennie Labuschagne, a computer forensics expert from the company Computer Security and Forensic Solutions. He testified, with the aid of a projector and a laptop (which led Squires to quip that 'only two thirds of us are computer literate so don't assume anything'[77]) that he had examined the disk on which the fax was saved, as well as a printout from the Thomson fax machine and Thomson's telephone records.[78] Labuschagne noted that the fax was definitely typed up on a Thomson computer, and the fax and telephone records showed that Delique had almost immediately printed out the fax and sent it using Thomson's fax machine.[79] Putting together Delique's testimony, as well as that of the expert witnesses, the State had made what seemed to be a watertight case for proving that the fax had been written by Thetard and faxed as per his instruction.

Perhaps the most important witness for the State, however, was a forensic auditor from KPMG named Johan van der Walt. He had been employed by the State to undertake a full forensic audit of both Zuma and Shaik's financial records (aided by 10 other auditors), which was then presented to the court in a 259-page report, in turn supported by a whopping 20 lever arch files of relevant records.[80] In total, Van der Walt spent 16 days in the witness box, 'armed with throat lozenges, a sense of humour and an unshakeable confidence that he was right',[81] outlining the exceptionally complex web of companies and payments that made up the financial relationship between Schabir Shaik, his companies, and Jacob Zuma.

In essence, Van der Walt walked the court through all the financial ins-and-outs that were included in Shaik's original indictment, as described above, and which were included in the KPMG report. Two key points established by the KPMG report stood out. The first was that, between July 1996 and December 2003, Zuma's salary amounted to R3.86m. Unfortunately, Zuma spent R4.29m, leaving Shaik's businesses to settle the R1.2m shortfall (which included a number of debts).[82] If, as Shaik's defence argued, Zuma had intended to pay back Shaik with his pension money, he would have owed Shaik half of the pension he was due.[83] This reflected the fact that, at almost all times, Zuma's style of living extensively outstripped his income. Only a few examples of these financial difficulties included the following:[84]

1. In 1995, Zuma took out a bond for a home in Killarney worth R400 000. However, by 1997, the bond was R30 000 in arrears. Shaik and one of his companies paid in R40 000, but it was too late. Later in the year, Standard Bank sued Zuma for R443 000 plus interest. This was resolved when the debt was paid by a number of third parties.

2. In June 1997, Standard Bank informed Zuma that his current account was in arrears. In October of the same year, they sued him for R118 842, the amount outstanding on the overdraft account. It seemed that the amount was never really settled as, by the time of the Shaik trial, Zuma still owed Standard Bank R128 301.

3. In 1997, Zuma bought a Mercedes-Benz, but wasn't able to pay even the first instalment on the car.

4. In 1998, Zuma bought yet another Mercedes-Benz for roughly R250 000. Almost from the start, debit orders to settle the car financing failed. Mercedes-Benz threatened action, but the amounts were settled by Shaik's Kobitech company.

5. In May 2001, Zuma financed a Mitsubishi Pajero for R275 000. By December 2003, he still owed a huge R350 000 on the car, of which about R129 000 was in arrears. This even though Shaik had made a payment of R47 000 towards the financing of the car in 2002.

The second was that Shaik's Nkobi companies were almost always in financial difficulty. Although it secured some key contracts, Nkobi was always in a 'cash-starved' position. This meant that, in order for Shaik and his companies to pay R1.2m to Zuma, Nkobi had to finance the transfers by using its bank overdrafts.

Some of the other notable testimonies included:

Ahmed Paruk: Paruk was an auditor from David Strachan & Taylor, the auditing firm hired by Shaik. Paruk testified that he had written off R1.2m from Nkobi's books on Shaik's instructions. This contradicted the claim that he was not aware of the writing-off of the loans and ordered his accountants to rectify the matter when he found out. This testimony was central in proving that Shaik had committed fraud in rigging Nkobi's books.[85]

Marion Marais: Marais was, like Sue Delique, one of Thetard's secretaries. She testified that Thetard was extremely volatile and temperamental and was prone to throw things around when upset. She confirmed that Thetard was extremely excited to meet Zuma.[86]

Celia Bester: Bester was a former bookkeeper for Shaik. She testified that she was horrified to find that a huge amount of money had been written off Nkobi's books: money, she claimed, that had been used to pay 'a lot of ministers' in cash.[87] She saw these amounts 'purely as bribe money'. Bester was also furious at the writing off of the R1.2m from Nkobi's books, listed as development costs for Prodiba, as the only costs to Nkobi incurred by Prodiba were for paying staff salaries: Nkobi was not liable for any development costs. Bester also testified that she had constantly written to Shaik to warn him that Nkobi could not afford to consistently make payments to Zuma when the company was always in overdraft.[88] Lastly, Bester presented the resignation letter that she gave to Shaik in December 1999. It was a stinging letter: 'The funds being paid to the ministers should be taxed in their hands as well as your (referring to Shaik's) income. If we are not transparent at this level there is no hope for South Africa. ... If you as the financial adviser to [Deputy President Jacob Zuma] are not transparent, heaven help South Africa when you formally return to politics.'[89]

Gavin Woods: Woods, of Scopa fame, walked the court through the operations of Scopa and how Judge Willem Heath was sidelined from the investigating team. Woods's testimony also focused on the letter written by Jacob Zuma and sent to Woods (later proven to have been written by Mbeki), which Woods found 'strongly worded and hostile' and 'intimidating'. He also noted that it was most unusual for government ministers to send letters such as these to arms dealers – Zuma had copied the letter to Thomson.[90]

Schabir Shaik: Shaik took the stand to argue in his defence. In essence, he denied all of the claims made by the State, and reiterated that any payments to Zuma from him were made out of friendship. Judge Hilary Squires later found that his testimony was less than impressive.

Finally, after nearly six months of gruelling testimony and the submission of mounds of evidence, the Shaik trial finally came to its conclusion on 4 May 2005. All eyes now turned to the man whose decision on the Shaik trial would affect not only the accused, but the future of South African politics.

5. THE VERDICT

Squires' judgment was a lengthy and detailed exercise. After summarising the case against Shaik, and what the burden of evidence would need to be in order to prove the State's case, he went on to analyse the State's case, as well as the defence put forward by Shaik.

He started this, some 20 pages into his judgment, by noting that much of the supporting evidence produced by the State was in the form of oral testimony from a host of witnesses (nearly 40 in total). These were, in many instances, directly contradicted by Shaik in his defence. So, a good place to start would be to judge whether or not Shaik was a credible witness. Squires ran through a host of reasons that suggested Shaik was not a credible witness. First, he noted how Shaik had consistently overblown his academic qualifications and his business victories.[91] This was not necessarily 'indicative of a fundamental dishonesty'.[92] But the way in which Shaik responded to these matters when they were raised in court could not but make him look dodgy: 'the disturbing aspect of these falsehoods, in our view, was the conspicuous lack of any embarrassment or remorse on the part of the witness when the falsity of these claims was admitted. That lack of any expression or sign of regret at practising such a subterfuge, seems to indicate a mentality that appears quite untroubled by the thought of resort to duplicity or falsehood to gain one's ends.'[93]

Second, Squires noted that this was just one occasion of Shaik using duplicity to achieve his ends. Perhaps the most dramatic case acknowledged by Squires involved Nelson Mandela. When Mandela was still President, he became concerned that personal debt was hindering Zuma in doing his job properly and offered to help him out with a personal loan. Mandela requested that Zuma submit a list of creditors to show just how deep in the mire he was. Shaik put together this list of creditors, which included an entry of R200 000 owed to an entity called the Pitzu Trust. The Pitzu Trust belonged to Shaik and his wife, but Mandela and Mandela's lawyer did not know that. The reality was, as Squires noted, that Shaik had attempted to hide the fact that Zuma owed him money because Mandela was not such a huge fan of Shaik. He had, in effect, deliberately lied to Nelson Mandela. As Squires noted: 'the identity of the real creditor was deliberately concealed from Mr Mandela because Shaik did not want him to know that he, Shaik, was one of Zuma's creditors, for fear of the anticipated reaction. That too was a confessed falsehood purposely done to mislead Mr Mandela and his then attorney. It is likewise a small matter in the overall scheme of things, but it also demonstrates the tendency to avoid an unwanted result by resorting to falsehood.'[94]

Third, Squires found that Shaik's performance as a witness was not exactly brilliant. The problems with Shaik's testimony included irrelevant and long-winded answers; the fact that Shaik contradicted himself during his testimony; the fact that he contradicted his original plea of defence during the testimony (which suggested that he was 'extemporising' responses as he needed to); and the fact that he often made claims about other witnesses that his counsel had not thought to ask them during their cross-examination (one example of this was Bianca Singh, who Shaik claimed had asked to return to work at Nkobi after she had left in November 2000, which she was never questioned about by Shaik's counsel). All this did not necessarily make him guilty – but it did not help his cause very much either. As Squires summarised:

> In the result, we were not impressed by his performance as a witness, either in content of evidence, or the manner in which he gave it. That, of course, does not make him guilty of any offence. It does not even mean he is never to be believed in anything he says. Some of his evidence was plainly truthful. But measured against an otherwise convincing State witness, it may be something of a disadvantage.[95]

After assessing Shaik's credibility, Squires moved on to assess the case against Shaik on the first count of corruption (of having a corrupt relationship with Zuma). Starting at the beginning, he traced the various instances in which Shaik turned to Zuma for help before Zuma became Deputy President. These instances included using Zuma's name in his discussions with Professor John Lennon (described above), and in turning to Zuma to help him 'land' his slice of the Arms Deal. After running through all of these instances in detail, Squires found that Shaik could always turn to Zuma, and Zuma was almost always willing to help:

> These four episodes show in our view that Zuma did in fact intervene to try and assist Shaik's business interests. While it may be accepted that his intervention on behalf of Shaik to relieve the threatened exclusion of Nkobi interest in ADS and the munitions suite contract, was un-

dertaken as Deputy President of the ANC and would not, in the absence of any alleged and known duty vested in that office that was discharged or subverted for Shaik's benefit, constitute a contravention of Act 94 of 1992. But it clearly shows, as do those in the Renong, Eco-Tourism and Venson situations, a readiness in both Shaik to turn to Zuma for his help, and Zuma's readiness to give it.'[96]

The next thing for Squires to assess was whether or not these interventions were motivated by anything other than friendship. Squires described, first, the way in which Shaik had helped Zuma with his finances, noting that Shaik had almost total access to Zuma's finances by means of 'computer contact with and control of Zuma's account with ABSA', and that Shaik was, at almost all times, there to help Zuma out of any financial difficulty. As he noted:

> The evidence showed that notwithstanding the regular ongoing payments to institutions of secondary and tertiary learning and the lengthy period of time over which the post-dated cheques issued by accused No 9 in payment of Mangerah's claim every now and then some sudden and unexpected expenditure incurred by Zuma or occasionally by his wife, would cause a temporary crisis in the management of his finances, until other arrangements could be made by Shaik to accommodate the immediate emergency and stabilise matters once more.[97]

He then moved on to discuss the idea of payments made out of friendship, which he systematically demolished. Squires noted the testimony of Celia Bester, which showed that Nkobi was, at most times, deeply cash-strapped while it was making payments to Zuma. Similarly, he noted that Zuma could never really pay back the money, and that Shaik must have been aware of this. The clear inference to be drawn was that Shaik had paid money to Zuma in order to achieve some business-related end:

> In our view no sane or rational businessman would conduct his business on such a basis without expecting some benefit from it that would make it worthwhile …
>
> It would be flying in the face of commonsense and ordinary human nature to think that he did not realise the advantages to him of continuing to enjoy Zuma's goodwill to an even greater extent than before 1997; and even if nothing was ever said between them to establish the mutually beneficial symbiosis that the evidence shows existed, the circumstances of the commencement and the sustained continuation thereafter of these payments, can only have generated a sense of obligation in the recipient.
>
> If Zuma could not repay money, how else could he do so than by providing the help of his name and political office as and when it was asked, particularly in the field of government contracted work, which is what Shaik was hoping to benefit from. And Shaik must have foreseen and, by inference, did foresee that if he made these payments, Zuma would respond in that way. The conclusion that he realised this, even if only after he started the dependency of Zuma upon his contributions, seems to us to be irresistible.[98]

Squires also noted that Shaik had, on numerous occasions, advertised his political connection to Zuma. These advertisements included letters to various potential business partners inviting them to meet with Zuma, as well as Shaik's 'self-assumed title' of 'financial advisor to the Deputy President', which had been 'blazoned across letterheads, business cards and business brochures'.[99] For Squires, it was the final nail in the coffin against the argument that Shaik had not used Zuma to further his interests:

> Genuine friendship, we think, would not have resorted to such blatant advertising of the association with Zuma if these payments were really given for that reason. They are patently aimed at attracting business partners on the basis of political support for any eventual joint venture would be forthcoming from Jacob Zuma and in our view, that clearly underlies the reason why these payments were made.[100]

He then turned to the claim that Zuma and Shaik had entered into a loan agreement, which showed that Shaik had never just 'given' money to Zuma, which was allegedly proved by documents purporting to be loan agreements between Zuma and Shaik. Squires, however, rejected (after another lengthy discussion) that these loan agreements could be considered valid in any way. They were rushed and incongruous, and were arguably only written up when 'this sort of information had to be disclosed by Members of Provincial Executive Councils and it would have been a suspicious circumstance if these payments had not been recorded as a loan'.[101] As he neatly summarised: 'In our assessment, therefore, this document can also be safely disregarded as acceptable proof that these payments were loans. [They were] merely for public consumption and not reflective of a genuine obligation to repay these amounts.'[102] What's more, if these payments to Zuma *were* loans, they were highly unusual in that they were not levied with any interest, they were given without any security and were made available to Zuma who was a 'borrower with a bad record of default in repayments': all to help Zuma 'live at a level of expenditure that his regular income could not afford'.[103] All of this, Squires found, showed that, even if they were loans, they could still be described as a 'benefit' under the terms of the Corruption Act.[104]

Considering that Squires was deeply impressed by many of the witnesses who gave evidence against Shaik on this count of general corruption, he could have no option but to come to this conclusion:

> Accepting then the evidence of these witnesses as the truth
> of the matters they described, makes the case on Count
> 1 not just convincing in total, it is really overwhelming.[105]

On Count 1 of having a corrupt relationship with Zuma, therefore, Shaik was found guilty.

After considering the matter of fraud, which Squires found Shaik guilty of committing, Squires then turned to a lengthy discussion on the matter of Count 3: that Shaik had solicited a bribe of R500 000 a year from Thomson-CSF for Zuma, in return for protection against any investigation into alleged corruption on the part of Thomson. After discussing the cases presented by the State and Shaik's defence counsel, Squires provided a chronological discussion of all the events surrounding the solicitation of the bribe. This, in effect, formed the court's accepted version of events, and is perhaps one of the most important narratives in explaining Shaik's guilt and Zuma's complicity in accepting the bribe. It essentially agreed with the entire case provided by the State in proving the bribe claim, which Squires further found in favour of after the chronology had been completed. Of course, the arguments, as well as the chronology, are incredibly complex, but this table should help you understand them a little more easily:

TABLE 4 The Zuma bribe timeline (Date, events and finding)[106]

9 September 1999

De Lille makes her presentation in Parliament about alleged corruption in the Arms Deal. Presidency issues a denial that Zuma is involved in 'any shady arms deals'.[107] Squires found that, at least by 30 September, Shaik would have been aware of corruption allegations and Zuma's response, as well as the fact that Thomson and ADS had been implicated in these claims.

28 September 1999

Defence Minister Lekota gives the Auditor-General the right to investigate the Arms Deal further.

29 September 1999

Wesbank writes to Mr Colin Isaacs, Nkobi's in-house accountant, to inform him that Zuma's Mercedes car is in arrears to the tune of R46 618, 89 although Kobitech has already paid R66 000 towards the car's financing.

30 September 1999

Alan Thetard and Shaik meet in Durban. During the meeting, Shaik raises the possibility of paying Zuma an amount of money to get him to help protect Thomson against any investigation into the Arms Deal. The following day, Shaik writes to Thetard, referring to the previous day's discussion, and asks for a meeting with Perrier.

9 February 2000

City Press runs an article detailing claims that a high-profile official had intervened in the selection process to get Thomson and ADS selected as winning bidders in the Arms Deal. Thetard hears of the report, asks his secretary to get him a copy, and reads it.

11 February 2000

Shaik faxes a 'cryptic' memo to Thetard which states: 'I refer to our understanding re Deputy Pres Jacob Zuma and issues raised. I will appreciate it if you can communicate to me your availability to meet.' Thetard replied: 'At this occasion I propose to have a meeting with you regarding issues raised in your fax.'

February – March 2000

Jacob Zuma sets about building his Nkandla residence, which increases his financial burden. As Squires noted: 'the cost would plainly be more than Zuma could afford if he still needed Shaik's help to live on his remuneration as Deputy President. So he would have a need for money, not only to meet his current needs but also to pay for this acquisition.'

169

25 February 2000

Shaik meets Thetard in Durban.

2 March 2000

Zuma meets Shaik in Johannesburg.

8 March 2000

Thetard writes to Shaik confirming a meeting with Zuma on 10 March.

11 March 2000

Perhaps the most important day in the entire story. Shaik, Zuma and Thetard meet. According to the infamous 'encrypted fax' (which Squires accepted meant exactly what it said), Zuma gave Thetard the requested signal that showed that he accepted the agreement to be paid R500 000 a year in return for protection for Thomson against any further investigations and a commitment to support Thomson in any future government project.

In discussing the fax, Squires found that the meeting could not actually have discussed a donation to the Jacob Zuma Educational Trust: 'We have no doubt eventually, for these reasons, that the explanation advanced by the accused that the agreement described in the fax was for a donation is not only not reasonably possible, it is nothing short of ridiculous and we reject it as false.'

Vitally for Zuma, Squires also found the idea that all parties were not aware of what the meeting discussed was also ridiculous: it was clear that everybody at the meeting, Zuma, Thetard and Shaik, were fully apprised of the fact that the meeting was to agree to a bribe being paid to Zuma in return for his political protection. As Squires noted: 'Whatever that code was, Shaik's evidence made it clear that all the parties knew what was discussed and what was concluded.'

17 March 2000

Thetard instructs his secretary to type up and fax the 'encrypted fax'.

July – October 2000

Construction continues on Zuma's Nkandla residence, but the contractor hired for the job, Eric Malengret, only receives limited payments for work done. By 5 October, Malengret had done about R226 000 worth of work, but had only received about R140 000 in payment.

31 August 2000

Shaik writes a letter to Thetard complaining about not receiving payment: 'I have also raised a very important matter with Mr Jean-Paul Perrier which he had sanctioned for implementation by yourself. This was done during our last meeting in Paris several months ago and, despite my several attempts to raise this issue with you in order to resolve the undertaking, you have continually ignored this concern. You leave me no choice but to seek alternative remedy to this matter and therefore I wish to put the above matter on record with you.'

Mid-September 2000 – 30 October

Scopa begins its investigation into the Arms Deal, which includes investigating concerns raised about Chippy Shaik's failure to recuse himself from meetings at which Thomson/ADS is discussed. On 30 October, Scopa presents its 14th Report, which recommends a super-investigation team, including the Heath Unit, to probe the Arms Deal.

5 October 2000

Shaik learns of Zuma's Nkandla development.

16 October 2000

Zuma receives a R2m cheque from Mandela, which he deposits into his personal bank account. R1m is transferred to the Jacob Zuma Education Trust, while the other half is a gift from Mandela to help Zuma over his financial hump so that he can do his job as Deputy President properly. Of the R1m in Zuma's account R900 000 is left after erasing his overdraft.

18 October 2000

Noticing that Zuma has R900 000 in his bank account, Shaik uses his cash-focus internet banking to transfer the money from Zuma's account into the fixed deposit account of one of his companies, Floryn Investments. A good portion of this is transferred out of the Floryn account in November 2000, when over R700 000 was transferred into the cheque accounts of Floryn and Kobitech Transport Systems, while a further R100 000 is used to reduce the overdraft of Kobitech.

19 October 2000

Shaik orders Malengret to stop building. Zuma overrules Shaik and orders Malengret to continue, assuming that he has R900 000 in his bank account with which to pay.

1 November 2000

Shaik fills in a form to apply for a 'service provider agreement' with Thomson, which the State found was cover for the bribe to Zuma. The agreement stipulates that the fee owed to Nkobi is R1m, which is the amount of Zuma's bribe payment.

6 November 2000

NPA starts its investigation into the Arms Deal. On the same day, Shaik leaves for Mauritius, where he meets Thomson officials, including Thetard, the following day. He informs Thomson, according to Bianca Singh, that they need to do 'damage control' with regard to the Arms Deal investigation.

7 November 2000

Businessman Vivian Reddy opens a bank account with Nedbank in the name of Development Africa. Squires found that, despite the defence's claims, Development Africa was not a trust for the benefit of the ANC, but the 'alter ego' of Reddy. Reddy is an advisor to Zuma. Reddy eventually signs surety for the R900 000 mortgage that Zuma takes out to pay for his Nkandla village and, as of November 2004, has paid all the instalments on the mortgage.

6 December 2000

Zuma deposits R1m into the account of Development Africa, which seems to have been intended to be used to pay for the Nkandla homestead nearing completion in March 2001. Shaik, however, stops the deposit as he has already transferred the money from Mandela out of Zuma's account. This means that, in effect, Shaik owes Zuma and Development Africa money.

8 December 2000

Needing to replace the R900 000 owed to Zuma and Development Africa, Shaik faxes Thetard. There is, according to Squires, a 'sense of urgency' in the fax, which reads: 'Herewith application for the service provider agreement, as discussed. Kindly expedite our arrangement as soon as possible as matters are becoming extremely urgent for my client.' Squires noted of this fax: 'If that was to be genuinely a payment in terms of the service provider agreement, then it was being requested before any service had been performed by Shaik and, as though such payment was expected in terms of some arrangement related to the agreement.'

1 January 2001

Nkobi/Shaik and Thomson sign the final version of the 'service provider agreement'. According to Squires, there is no doubt that the service provider agreement formed part of an exercise to disguise the bribe payment intended for Zuma and paid by Thomson: 'The inference which the State asks us to draw from them is that the service provider agreement was intended to be the means by which Thomson was to pay the R500 000 a year to Zuma until the ADS dividends became available. The accused disputes that, and says it was only introduced to help him earn an income to replenish the money for Development Africa that he had appropriated from Zuma's account. But that explanation cannot be true, because it is in conflict with the admitted fact that he first completed an application form for the service provider agreement well before he learned he had to make good the money he had taken from Zuma. In our eventual conclusion then, that inference is certainly consistent with all the proved facts and those facts exclude any other reasonable inference, particularly as there is clear proof that the accused's explanation cannot be true.'

19 January 2001

Zuma writes to Gavin Woods informing him that the Heath Unit will be excluded from the investigation into the Arms Deal. Squires noted of the letter: 'It is almost as if the writer is taking a special delight in rubbing the collective nose of Scopa, and Woods in particular, in the rejection of its recommendation. That is conspicuously not the attitude of someone who was supportive of the investigation being pursued by Scopa. Moreover, this scathing and humiliating rebuke was made widely known to a number of other interested persons, including the contractors, some of whose conduct was perceived to justify the investigation that had been refused.'

9 February 2001

R250 000 was deposited by Thomson (Mauritius) into the bank account of Kobitech. Squires noted that this was 'plainly' the first payment of the anticipated R1m forthcoming.

24 February 2001, April 2001

A R250 000 cheque is drawn from the account of Kobitech and paid into the account of Development Africa. Shaik draws up a further three post-dated cheques, each for R250 000 (making a total of R1m in all payments), for Development Africa. But, in April 2001, he orders his bank to cancel the cheques: the suggestion being that he could not honour these amounts as no further amount was forthcoming from Thomson.

August 2001

Shaik and Collin Isaacs are in Mauritius, and try to make it look as if Nkobi had submitted reports on the offsets that would be required to show that Nkobi had filled its obligation in meeting the service provider agreement. These were falsely back-dated to April and July 2001 in an attempt to justify the payment of the R1m service provider agreement.

December 2002

In the end, only R250 000, already paid by Thomson, was ever received by Shaik according to the service provider agreement, meaning that R750 000 of the original bribe was never paid. The service provider agreement was formally cancelled in December 2002.

With this chronology explained, and Shaik's defence left in tatters, all that was left was for Squires to hammer the final nail in the coffin. Shaik was found guilty on all counts, and sentenced to 15 years in jail (15 years for count 1, 3 for count 2, and 15 for count 3, all to be served concurrently).[108]

Moreover, in a later judgment, Squires ordered to the proceeds of the corruptly acquired business undertaken by Shaik be seized by the State: over R30m in total. Shaik was not only going to go to jail, Squires decided, but he would not reap the benefits of corruption while he was there.

THE APPEALS

After Squires had read out his judgment, Schabir Shaik looked like a broken man. But Squires, in July 2005, offered

Shaik a glimmer of hope. In assessing his own outcome, Squires gave Shaik the leave to appeal two of his charges: the charge of fraud and the charge of corruption relating to the solicitation of Zuma's bribe.[109] Squires, however, denied Shaik the right to appeal the first charge on which he was convicted of having a corrupt relationship (that Squires referred to as a 'mutually beneficial symbiosis') with Zuma.[110] Squires' judgment on this point was damning: he found that it was unlikely that any other court would deliver a different judgment to the one he had made. In other words, the evidence was overwhelming.

Shaik was able to contest the other two charges on specific grounds: on the charge of fraud, he was allowed to contest whether or not he had actually told his accountants to make the R1.2m write-off (suggesting that the veracity of the testimonies on which this conviction was based could be reconsidered); on the charge of corruption, he was allowed to contest whether or not the State was correct in admitting the 'encrypted fax' as evidence.[111] However, he was not allowed to contest the three-year sentence given to him for fraud, as Squires noted that this was a very lenient sentence, the maximum sentence for fraud being 15 years.[112]

Shaik leapt at the opportunity, and lodged his appeal, which was heard by the Supreme Court of Appeal in Bloemfontein in September 2006. The appeal went beyond the mandate that Squires set above: Shaik and his lawyers also contested the fact that they were denied leave to appeal on the first charge of corruption (the 'mutually beneficial symbiosis' charge). So, the Supreme Court of Appeal would, essentially, be reviewing the judgments reached by Squires on all three counts on which Shaik was charged.

Unlike the Squires case, the matter was to be heard by a roster of judges instead of just a single trial judge. The verdict they finally delivered on 6 November 2006 was devastating for Shaik: unanimous confirmation of the rectitude of all of Squires' judgments. On the first count of a 'generally corrupt relationship',[113] the Supreme Court of Appeal rejected all of Shaik's defence pronouncements. As the summary, kindly written by the court for use by the media, noted:

> We find a wealth of evidence to show that the friendship [between Shaik and Zuma], which we accept exists, was persistently and aggressively exploited by Mr Shaik for his own and his group's business advantage. In particular there were four occasions revealed by the prosecution evidence in which interventions by Mr Zuma at Mr Shaik's instance advanced, or were aimed at advancing, Mr Shaik's commercial interests.
>
> The most important one concerned the Defence Force's arms procurement program. Mr Zuma's efforts contributed to Mr Shaik acquiring a material interest in a highly lucrative contract to supply the armaments for the Navy's new corvettes. The evidence also showed that when the payments were made Mr Shaik was in no position to afford them without substantial borrowings and Mr Zuma had no realistic prospects of repayment.[114]

On the count of fraud (for the write-off), the Judges were equally succinct:

> The main evidence for the State was given by one of the auditors. The trial court found him an unsatisfactory witness. We agree. We also agree, however, with the trial court's conclusion that the auditors would not have had reason, unprompted, to contrive the write-off by themselves and that circumstantial evidence and the testimony

THE ARMS DEAL IN YOUR POCKET

of two other prosecution witnesses pointed to Mr Shaik's having been a party to it. The other legal elements of the crime of fraud being present, we think that Mr Shaik was correctly convicted on count 2.[115]

On the third count, the Supreme Court of Appeal also found that Squires had reached the correct judgment: that Shaik had, indeed, solicited a bribe for Zuma with the intent of influencing Zuma to protect Thomson-CSF from any investigations stemming from the claims of irregularity and corruption discussed at length in Chapter 3 of this book. Again, the summary of the judgment was succinct on this matter:

In addition, not only does the fax prove that Thetard wrote the words it contains but there is abundant surrounding evidence to find that there was proof beyond reasonable doubt that what Mr Shaik requested of Thomson was a bribe to Mr Zuma.

Even if Mr Zuma was unaware of the request or had not agreed to accept the bribe there was nevertheless proof of commission by Mr Shaik of all the necessary elements of the offence charged. Mr Shaik's evidence that he, Mr Zuma and Thetard had indeed met shortly before the date of the fax but that the subject matter of their discussions was a request that Thomson make a donation to the Jacob Zuma Educational Trust, was rightly rejected by the trial court. He was therefore correctly convicted on count 3.[116]

The only thing left to be discussed was the sentence that Squires had imposed. On this point, the Appeal Court was as damning, if not more so, that Squires. The sentences were to be upheld: Shaik had to serve his 15 years in prison.

In reaching this judgment, the Supreme Court sided with Squires in rejecting the idea that Shaik's struggle credentials should act in mitigation of his sentence, and submitted one of the most devastating attacks on corruption to be found in any court judgment:

> As a country we have travelled a long and tortuous road to achieve democracy. Corruption threatens our constitutional order. We must make every effort to ensure that corruption with its putrefying effects is halted. Courts must send out an unequivocal message that corruption will not be tolerated and that punishment will be appropriately severe. In our view, the trial judge was correct not only in viewing the offence of corruption as serious, but also in describing it as follows: 'It is plainly a pervasive and insidious evil, and the interests of a democratic people and their government require at least its rigorous suppression, even if total eradication is something of a dream.' It is thus not an exaggeration to say that corruption of the kind in question eats away at the very fabric of our society and is the scourge of modern democracies.[117]

Shaik, the man who had once fought for South Africa's freedom, was, in other words, guilty of lowering 'the moral tone' of South Africa and threatening 'our constitutional order'. In the new South Africa, it is difficult to think of greater crimes against the memory of the struggle and the South African public.

Shaik had one more appeal up his sleeve. In 2007, he took the matter to the Constitutional Court. It, too, rejected Shaik's appeals, finding that 'an appeal against conviction and sentence does not bear any reasonable prospect of success'.[118] The final nail in the coffin came in May 2008, when the Constitutional Court ruled that the seizure of his assets ordered by Squires was correct.[119] Not only would he be sent to jail, finally, for 15 years, but he would do so without the succour of his ill-gotten gains.

In total, Shaik's case had been heard by a veritable coterie of judges in three separate courts (Squires in the High Court, five in the Supreme Court of Appeal and 10 in the Constitutional Court), and all had found him guilty on all three charges.[120] As *The Star* summarised: '16 judges, 3 trials, 1 verdict.'

CHAPTER 8

THE
CASE
AGAINST
JACOB
ZUMA

WHAT'S IN THIS CHAPTER?

- What Jacob Zuma was charged with in 2005.
- What has happened to all the appeals surrounding documents seized by the Scorpions in August 2005.
- How Jacob Zuma's legal team got his case 'struck from the roll' in September 2006.
- What the extended charges were in Jacob Zuma's 2007 indictment.
- What appeals Jacob Zuma lodged during his second trial on charges of corruption and racketeering and what appeals he may make in future.

KEY DATES FOR THIS CHAPTER

- END MAY–BEGINNING JUNE 2005 Judge Hilary Squires presents his judgment on the Shaik case. He finds Shaik guilty on two counts of corruption (of having a corrupt relationship with Zuma and of soliciting a bribe for Zuma) and one count of fraud. Squires sentences Shaik to 15 years in prison.
- 14 JUNE 2005 Jacob Zuma is released from his duties as Deputy President of South Africa.
- 29 JUNE 2005 Zuma appears in court for the first time to answer charges of corruption.
- 18 AUGUST 2005 Scorpions conduct raids on Zuma's homes in Johannesburg and KwaZulu-Natal, as well as the offices of his attorneys and the French arms company Thint (formerly Thomson). In total, the Scorpions seize 93 000 documents from 22 different sites.
- SEPTEMBER 2005 The High Court rules that the Scorpions' raid on Zuma's attorney Juleka Mohamed was illegal.

- FEBRUARY 2006 The High Court rules that the Scorpions' raid on Zuma's attorney Michael Hulley was illegal.
- JULY 2006 The High Court rules that the seizure of documents from Thint was legal and can be admitted in evidence.
- SEPTEMBER 2006 Zuma's case is struck from the roll after he submits a request for a permanent stay of prosecution. Although Judge Herbert Msimang is harsh on the State's delays in prosecution, he leaves the way free for the State to recharge Zuma when ready.
- 8 NOVEMBER 2007 The Supreme Court of Appeal overturns the earlier High Court rulings on the Scorpions search and seizure operations. Three out of five judges declare all the seizures (on Zuma, his attorneys and Thint) legal, allowing the State to include this as evidence if they recharge Zuma.
- DECEMBER 2007 Zuma is charged for a second time by the Scorpions only days after winning the election to become President of ANC at the organisation's National Conference in Polokwane. He is charged with two counts of corruption, one count of money laundering, one count of racketeering and 12 counts of fraud.
- MARCH 2008 The Constitutional Court hears Zuma and Thint's appeals to overturn the Supreme Court of Appeal's findings. At the same time, Zuma travels to Mauritius to block the SA State from acquiring documents from Mauritian authorities. Zuma claims in his affidavit that there is a conspiracy against him and that the Mauritian court should not act to further this conspiracy. His claims are rejected by the State, while the Mauritian Attorney General has also submitted an

affidavit rejecting Zuma's motion.

- MAY 2008 Reports emerge that Zuma will not stand trial on 4 August 2008, but will, instead, submit an application for a permanent stay of prosecution.
- JUNE 2008: Jacob Zuma's legal team submit an application to have the charges against him dismissed. Zuma's team claim that the NPA had violated his constitutional right to be included in a 'review' of the decision to prosecute him reached in 2005.
- 30 JUNE 2008: The Mauritian Court rejects appeals lodged by Jacob Zuma to prevent evidence held in Mauritius being given to South African authorities.
- 31 JULY 2008: The Constitutional Court rejects the appeals launched by Jacob Zuma and Thint to have the search warrants used to raid the properties of Zuma, Thint and others declared illegal. This allows the State to include the 93 000 documents seized during the August 2005 raids in Zuma's upcoming corruption trial.
- AUGUST 2008: After filing a responding affidavit to Zuma's appeal to have his case dismissed, the State, along with Zuma's legal team, lead their heads of argument in the High Court over the application. High Court Judge Chris Nicholson, hearing the arguments, notes that he will deliver his judgment in September 2008. However, it is rumoured that Zuma, if he loses the application, will both appeal this application and submit a further application for a permanent stay of prosecution.

The last two and a half years have made quite a difference in the life of Jacob Zuma. On 14 June 2005, two weeks after Judge Hilary Squires had found the Deputy President's financial advisor guilty of corruption, Thabo Mbeki addressed Parliament with a terse statement relieving Zuma of his position. After a digression distancing the government from the subcontracts and defending the primary contracts signed by the government with arms companies, Mbeki stated that, while Zuma must be presumed innocent until proven otherwise, it would be in the best interests of the country if he was released from his duties:

> As President of the Republic I have come to the conclusion that the circumstances dictate that in the interest of the Honourable Deputy President, the Government, our young democratic system, and our country, it would be best to release the Hon Jacob Zuma from his responsibilities as Deputy President of the Republic and Member of the Cabinet …
>
> Personally, I continue to hold the Hon Jacob Zuma in high regard, and I am convinced that this applies to most Members of Parliament. We have worked together under difficult and challenging conditions for thirty years. In this regard, I wish to thank him for the service that he has rendered as part of the Executive, at national and provincial levels, sparing neither strength nor effort to ensure that with each passing day, we build a better life for all South Africans.'[1]

Two weeks after this, Zuma appeared in court to answer charges of having a 'generally corrupt' relationship with Schabir Shaik.[2] And yet, two and a half years later, he was riding the crest of a wave. The case against him had been struck from the roll by Judge Herbert Msimang (although the NPA could still lay fresh charges)[3] and he was at the centre of the ridiculously named 'Zunami'[4] that saw him swept into power as the President of the ANC in December 2007. The fact that the NPA laid an expanded set of charges against him (including racketeering and multiple charges of fraud and corruption) only days later was like water off a duck's back. He had come this far without having to contest the case against him. As it stands, it seems unlikely that he will do so before the national elections in April 2009,[5] which, if the ANC wins, will mean that Zuma will most likely be the third president of South Africa – and the first to come to power facing criminal charges.

How did this come to pass?

THE JACOB ZUMA TRIAL (TAKE ONE)

When Jacob Zuma was served with his charge sheet and the State's Summary of Substantial Facts, he might have been forgiven for feeling that he had read it before. Indeed, the documents presented against Zuma in June 2005 were almost a mirror image of the charge sheet that had been presented against Schabir Shaik. The major difference was that, this time, the arms companies involved in the alleged corruption would be charged as well. Accused 1, according to the charge sheet, was Jacob Zuma.[6] Accused 2 and 3, however, were Thint Holding (previously known as Thomson-CSF Holding) and Thint Pty (previously known as Thomson Pty), both represented by Jean-Pierre Robert Moynot, who had acted as a director for both companies.

In total, there were four corruption charges laid: two

against Jacob Zuma (accused 1) and two against Thint (accused 2 and 3). These charges were explained in the previous chapter, so they won't be dealt with in as much detail here. But, the essential facts of the charges against Zuma were:

Count 1 ('general corruption')[7]

1. That Zuma had received payments totalling R1 282 027,63 from Schabir Shaik and 'relevant corporate entities within the Nkobi Group'.

2. These payments made 'no legitimate business sense', as Shaik and Nkobi were in a 'cash-starved position' and could not afford to make them.

3. However, the payments did make sense inasmuch as Nkobi's 'survival depended upon obtaining profitable new business, *inter alia*, with the assistance of [Zuma]'.

4. That the payments made by Shaik and a series of 'undetermined benefits' (which, the State alleged, included payments made after 2002 from Shaik to Zuma) 'were intended as bribes, whatever their description'.

5. The schedule of benefits (payments to Zuma) constituted further benefits (over and above just being bribe payments) to Zuma as they consisted of funding which he would not have been 'able to obtain … commercially … This is a benefit.'

6. That Shaik acted as his financial advisor without payment constituted a further benefit to Zuma.

7. That Zuma had violated the terms of the offices he held

as a member of government and Deputy President of the country by accepting these benefits and acting on them.

8. That Zuma, as a result of the benefits paid to him by Schabir Shaik/Nkobi and by Thomson (the bribe claim, to be dealt with next), had improperly intervened to help Shaik secure his business interests by using the formal and informal weight of his political office.

9. One of these interventions included interceding on Nkobi's behalf as a mediator to resolve a dispute involving Thomson and Nkobi. The dispute was about the failure of Thomson to include Nkobi, through a shareholding agreement, in Thomson's tender (which included African Defence Systems) to provide combat suites for the corvettes. Thomson was allegedly reluctant to include Shaik's Nkobi as it had heard that key players in the South African government did not want Shaik's company involved in the Arms Deal. The matter was resolved when ADS shares were transferred to Thomson (Pty), which was partially owned by Nkobi Investments (owned by Nkobi Holdings) and Thomson Holdings (partially owned by Nkobi Holdings). This meant, in effect, that Nkobi came to own a portion of African Defence Systems, which was part of the winning corvette tender, and Zuma had helped this happen by acting as a mediator.

10. That, besides his dealings with Thomson, Zuma had either allowed his name to be used by Shaik, or had directly intervened to Shaik's benefit in numerous business transactions.

Count 2 ('specific corruption': the bribe)[8]

Once again, the charges levelled against Zuma and Thint on this point followed much the same route as in Shaik's trial. The essential allegations levelled by the State's case were:

1. Schabir Shaik, acting on behalf of Jacob Zuma, met with Alain Thetard on 30 September in Durban. During or before the meeting, Shaik requested that Thetard arrange for Thomson-CSF to pay a bribe to Zuma.

2. The bribe was intended to ensure that Zuma provided protection for Thomson-CSF against any investigations taking place into the Arms Deal at the time, and to secure Zuma's support for any future Thomson projects.

3. This meeting was the first documented 'marker in a series of payments that constituted the development of a conspiracy between Thomson-CSF (France) and/or Thomson-CSF (International) and/or Thales International Africa Ltd (Mauritius) and/or accused 2 and and/or accused 3, together also with Shaik and his Nkobi group, to pay [Zuma] the amount of R500 000 per annum … as a bribe …'

4. At some stage, Thetard requested that Shaik get Zuma to confirm the bribe agreement by means of a code determined by Thetard.

5. On either 10 or 11 May, Zuma, Thetard and Shaik met in Durban. In the meeting, Zuma somehow provided the code to Thetard according to which the bribe agreement would come into effect.

6. The above meeting was recorded by Thetard in a handwritten fax and transmitted by encrypted channels to de Jomaron and Perrier of Thomson-CSF in France and Mauritius. This served as confirmation that the meeting

did happen and the bribe was discussed and agreed to by all parties, and further evidence of a conspiracy on the part of Thint Holding/Thint Pty on behalf of Thomson-CSF. It also sought 'further approval and ultimately to secure payment of the bribe as agreed'.

7. The bribe was disguised when Shaik entered into a 'service provider agreement' with Thomson-CSF Africa Ltd in Mauritius. The 'fee' owed to Shaik equalled the exact amount of the bribe requested (R500 000 a year over two years, so R1m).

8. The 'service provider agreement' was spurious as Nkobi did not undertake any work to justify the 'fee'.

9. The money was channelled to Zuma through payments from Shaik's company, Kobitech (which received R250 000 from Thomson-CSF Africa on 16 February 2001) to Development Africa, which, at the time, was in the name of Vivian Reddy and was paying for the development of Zuma's Nkandla residence.

10. One sign that Zuma had been honouring the terms of the bribe was the letter written to Gavin Woods of Scopa on 19 January informing Woods that Judge Willem Heath had been excluded from the Arms Deal investigation. The letter was copied to the media and to Thomson-CSF.

DELAYS, DELAYS, DELAYS

The trial was beset by problems almost from the start. On 18 August 2005, the NPA conducted a series of raids on the Johannesburg and Nkandla homes of Jacob Zuma and the offices of his attorneys (Michael Hulley and Julie Mahomed), among other locations. In total, 93 000 documents were seized from 22 different sites.[9] Since then, they have been subject to a series of appeals: Zuma and his legal team have now argued in three separate courts that the documents were seized using search warrants that were illegal and unconstitutional. What exactly were these appeals about?

The difficulty in following all the appeals is that there were actually two appeal processes flowing from the August seizures: one was a set of a appeals lodged by Zuma's legal team, and the other was a set of appeals lodged by the legal team of the company also charged, Thint. In broad terms, Zuma scored more early successes than Thint. The first success came in appealing the seizure of documents from his lawyer, Julie Mohamed. Zuma's legal team argued that the seizure of documents constituted a violation of attorney-client privilege and was based on a set of search warrants that were incomplete.[10] Judge Ismail Hussain, hearing the matter in the High Court, agreed to declare the searches illegal, but on a very specific point: he found that the search and seizure warrants had been obtained without giving full details to Judge Bernard Ngoepe (who had issued the warrants), as the State had failed to fully explain to Ngoepe that Mohamed was Zuma's attorney[11].

Immediately following this success, Zuma's legal team challenged the validity of other raids on Zuma, including those on his properties and the offices of his other attorney, Michael Hulley.[12] A decision on this matter was reached in February 2006, when Judge Joel Hurt ruled in favour of Zuma's team. Hurt found that the search and seizure warrants were overly broad and vague. Specifically, Hurt found that one paragraph that gave the Scorpions the right to seize 'any records' of 'any nature' was, in his words, so broad as to be of 'breathtaking proportions'.[13] As a result, Hurt urged that the NPA hand back all the documents seized: a major blow to the State, as the State allegedly seized all of Zuma's financial records up until 2005 from Hulley's offices. They were at Hulley's offices, the State claimed, because Schabir Shaik had sent them to Hulley after he resigned as Zuma's financial advisor in 2005. These financial records were apparently to be used in expanding Zuma's charges to ones of fraud and tax evasion (as was later done in the 2007 indictment).

Thint was not so lucky. In July 2006, after bringing an application to have the documents seized from its offices returned, Pretoria High Court Judge Ben du Plessis found that, in this instance at least, the Scorpions had conducted legal raids. Du Plessis argued that, unlike in the case of Zuma, the raids were legal as they did not constitute raids on any attorney's offices (and therefore did not violate attorney-client privilege) and that the search warrants used against Thint were not 'overly broad'.[14]

That three different judges could disagree on the search warrants gave the NPA a glimmer of hope. After securing the right to appeal against the judgments in the Zuma search-and-seizure cases, the NPA did exactly that, setting the scene for a major showdown in 2007. In 2007, the State presented its case to have all the documents seized from Zuma, Mohamed and Hulley declared legal. This time, Zuma's legal team scored no victories. The Supreme Court of Appeal delivered its judgment on 8 November 2007. It was a close call: the ruling split the Court.[15] Three judges found that the raids were legal, allowing the State to use the documents seized as evidence. Two judges sided with Zuma and his team. Thint's evidence, too, was considered during the judgment.[16] In relation to Thint, they upheld Judge Ben du Plessis's ruling that the raids on Thint's offices were legal.[17] The result: all the documents seized by the State were declared legal by the Supreme Court of Appeal. The NPA claimed this was a 'vindication' of the manner in which the State had conducted its investigations.[18] It also cleared the way for the State to submit its 'super-charges' against Zuma and Thint in December 2007 (discussed later in this chapter).

Just as Shaik would do with his appeal process, Zuma and Thint's legal teams refused to take the ruling lying down. They had one more court to which they could appeal: the Constitutional Court. They did this, with hearings taking place in March 2008. Again, the hearings were simple: both Zuma and Thint's legal teams requested that the search and seizure warrants used to search their premises be declared illegal and the documents seized returned.

The Constitutional Court hearings soon took a more worrying turn. On 30 May 2008, roughly eight weeks before it was to deliver its final verdict, the Court referred a complaint against the Judge President of the Cape High Court, Judge John Hlophe, to the Judicial Services Commission. According to the original media statement, the complaint was lodged after Hlophe had allegedly approached two Constitutional Court judges 'in an improper manner to influence this Court's pending judgment' in the Zuma and Thint applications.[19] On 17 June, a more substantial listing of the grievances was provided; in it, it was alleged that Hlophe had approached two separate judges, Judge AJ Jafta and Judge J Nkabinde, at the end of March and on 23 April 2008 respectively, at their offices at the Constitutional Court, and had attempted to 'improperly persuade [the judges] to decide the Zuma/Thint cases in a manner favourable to Mr. J.G. Zuma'.[20] In his discussion with Judge Nkabinde, Hlophe allegedly claimed that 'he had a mandate', and that he was aware that Nkabinde was writing up an important part of the eventual judgment because 'he had connections with the national intelligence'.[21] Even more worrying was the allegation that he had informed Nkabinde that 'some people were going to lose their positions after the elections ... [Hlophe] had outgrown the Cape High Court and ... was going to make himself available for appointment at the Constitutional Court and that [Judge] Jafta should also make himself available for appointment to the Court'.[22]

Hlophe responded furiously to the complaint lodged by the Constitutional Court judges. In an extensive statement to the Judicial Services Commission, he agreed that he had, in fact, met both judges. But the content of their discussions had nothing to do with the Thint and Zuma trials, and neither of the judges had indicated 'any discomfort about anything that we had discussed in their chambers'.[23] While they had discussed general approaches to legal issues to be discussed in the Zuma and Thint applications, neither of the conversations directly led to Hlophe addressing an opinion about either in any way. Hlophe, instead, asserted that they had talked mostly about personal issues, including discussions about the fact that both of the judges allegedly had problems with the 'weak management' of the Constitutional Court provided by Chief Justice Pius Langa.[24]

It was at Chief Justice Pius Langa and Deputy Chief Justice Dikgang Moseneke, however, that the Hlophe's response directed most of its ire. Echoing Zuma's claims that his prosecution was the result of a 'political conspiracy', Hlophe claimed that the decision to lay the complaint, and to release the complaint to the media, evinced an ill-defined 'ulterior motive':

> ... there was an element of impropriety in the conduct of, in particular, the Chief Justice Pius Langa and the Deputy Chief Justice Moseneke, the motive for which remains a

mystery, but more likely being an inexplicable desire to get rid of me, to get me impeached, and to suggest that I am not fit to be a judge anymore, – the kind of bandwagonism that has been in vogue since I published my racism report a few years ago. I make bold to link this to the racism report fully cognisant of the fact that both Langa and Moseneke are Africans and Black, but the point here is that for their own reasons, they have climbed on the bandwagon of those who, since the racism report, have been campaigning for my impeachment on the basis that I am ill-qualified to be a judge.

The way they have seized on my so-called attempt to improperly influence judges of the Constitutional Court, and the way they rushed to the media to cause a public sensation about what I was alleged to have said without even as much as raising this issue with me by phone, email, or letter, just to get my version at least before going public with untested allegations, when those to whom I was alleged to have made the alleged pronouncements had clearly disavowed themselves of any inclination to complain at all – all this conduct clearly shows a motive by Chief Justice Langa and Deputy Chief Justice Moseneke to get rid of me at all costs, whatever it took, even if it meant dealing with me in public without due process, or even bringing the whole judicial edifice crashing down in disgrace – anything at all as long as, in the process, in their view, I would be got rid of. A close examination of the conduct of the Chief Justice and Deputy Chief Justice – their total disrespect for my constitutionally entrenched rights to privacy and dignity shows a single-mindedness that can only be attributed to people who were acting with an ulterior motive.[25]

In his own response, Langa set about explaining his actions. In arguing for why the complaint was laid, and the matter made public, he stated that the decision was made because of the severity of the complaints and their implications for constitutional democracy:

> An attempt to influence the judges of the highest court to determine a case in a particular manner is a threat to the institution of the judiciary, one of the pillars of our constitutional democracy ... The other judges were shocked and distressed by the reports. None of the judges had experienced such an affront to the integrity of the judicial process in their careers as judges and the matter was accordingly viewed in the gravest possible light. In the absence of any possible reason to suggest that our colleagues would manufacture reports of such a serious nature, we accepted the accuracy and veracity of what they had been told and continue to do so ...[26]

Significantly, Langa argued that the decision to go public was based on a need to keep the Zuma and Thint applications free from claims of bias. The reasoning was simple: we could talk about this now, and deal with the consequences, or we could not tell the public, deliver a verdict, and have the matter crop up in the future, only to then raise questions about whether or not the Court had been negatively influenced in an eventual decision reached by the Court. As Langa noted:

> In circumstances where the independence of the Constitutional Court had been threatened and the integrity of the administration of justice in South Africa generally, it was considered imperative and appropriate that

this be publicly disclosed. Should the facts have emerged at a later stage there would have been a serious risk that the litigants involved in the relevant cases and the general public would have entertained misgivings about the outcome and the manner in which the decisions were reached. It was especially important that the litigants and the general public were informed of the attempt and that the Constitutional Court had not succumbed to it.[27]

As it stands, the matter has not yet been heard by the Judicial Services Commission, which is the appropriate constitutional body to deal with the complaint. Arguably, it is only once this has been done and the Commission has delivered its verdict that we will begin to achieve clarity on these issues.

However, what is certain is that the public spat between these eminent judges foregrounded the eventual judgment delivered by the Constitutional Court in a way that, once again, raised the political temperature of the country. In delivering the Constitutional Court judgment on 31 July 2008, which rejected the appeals of Zuma and Thint in their entirety, Langa was pressed to deal with the Hlophe issue upfront:

All the members of the Court who sat in the two applications now before us (as well as in two applications heard simultaneously, which concerned a letter of request to Mauritian authorities for documents relating to Thint and Mr Zuma), have considered their position in the light of the events mentioned above and their responsibilities as Judges of this Court. We are satisfied that the alleged acts that form the basis of the complaint to the JSC by Judges of this Court have had no effect or influence on the consideration by the Court of the issues in these cases and in the judgments given. It is recorded in the statement of complaint that there is no suggestion that any of the parties in these cases have had anything to do with the alleged conduct that forms the basis of the complaint by the Judges of the Court. The issues relating to the complaint have accordingly been kept strictly separate from the adjudication process in these cases. It is however important to emphasise that the cases have been considered and decided in the normal way, in accordance with the dictates of our Oath of Office and in terms of the Constitution and the law, without any fear, favour or prejudice.[28]

But what did the judgment say about the search and seizure warrants? One of the key arguments advanced by Zuma's legal team was that the search warrants that had underpinned the searches were overly broad, illegal and unnecessary: the State, Zuma's legal team argued, should not have sought a search warrant, but, instead have used the right to subpoena to get access to the required documents. In addition, Zuma's team claimed, the warrants were issued without all 'relevant' facts being provided to the Judge who issued the warrant, and the searches were conducted in a way that would infringe on Zuma's legal privilege (because some of the searches were conducted at the offices of his attorney, Michael Hulley).[29]

In short, nine of the Court's judges found in favour of the State, while one found in favour of Zuma and Thint. First, the Court found that the State had fulfilled its obligations in informing the judge issuing the search warrant of all the material facts. In fact, the Court found that the claims by Thint and Zuma that additional material should have been provided would have meant that the test for 'materiality' would be 'set at a level that renders it practically impossible for the state to comply with this duty in the context of complex criminal cases'.[30] Second, the Court found that the State had successfully made a case for the need to search premises, rather than use the power of subpoena. As the Court's handy media summary noted: 'there was, in the circumstances of these cases, a real risk, although no certainty, that a subpoena would not have yielded the desired evidence and may even have resulted in its loss or destruction'.[31] Thirdly, the Court found that the alleged 'catch-all phrase' that allowed the State to seize whatever documents it felt were necessary to the investigation was lawful, except in the case of the raid on Michael Hulley's property. However, seeing as the powers conferred by the 'catch-all phrase' were not actually used during the search, it meant that 'Messrs Hulley and Zuma suffered no prejudice'. The logical action, in this case, was to excise the offending section from the warrant (which was never actually activated during the searches), rather than declare the entire warrant invalid. Fourth, and linked to the above, the Court found that the warrants were not overly vague in that they passed the test of intelligibility. Lastly, the Court found that the claims that the searches were conducted in violation of the legal professional privilege held by Zuma (especially in regard to the searches on Hulley's property), were unfounded: largely, as the Court noted, because there was no evidence presented that any prejudice was actually suffered as no complaint about any specific privilege being violated had been presented.[32]

In the wake of the Hlophe matter, it was perhaps unsurprising that the final judgment elicited a strong response. Blade Nzimande, general secretary of the South African Communist Party, cast his own doubts over the verdict: 'We expected this. The whole Hlophe matter, we have said, was actually preparing us for this. [This case] will go down in history as the first political trial, post-apartheid.'[33] The South African Students Congress (Sasco), was even more forthright, stating that 'Sasco views this ruling as part of an invincible political hand that handles judges in order to achieve political and factional agendas. We remain resolute that the Constitutional Court judges have lost integrity and impartiality when dealing with the JZ [Jacob Zuma] issue, therefore only a permanent stay of prosecution can bring justice to this case.'[34] The ANC, in a somewhat ambiguous statement, said that they respected the judgment, but continued to argue that 'the manner in which this case has been handled by authorities over the last few years has reinforced the perception that the ANC president is being persecuted rather than merely prosecuted. It has also fuelled doubts about his chances of receiving a fair hearing.'[35]

But, as this matter rumbled on, Zuma and his legal team started yet another appeal process. In the same judgment in 2007 that declared the search and seizure warrants valid, the Supreme Court of Appeal gave the State the right to ask Mauritian authorities to hand over documents seized from the Mauritian offices of Thales. The documents in question allegedly include one 'smoking gun': the diary of Alain Thetard. Zuma's legal team, as well as that of Thint, approached Mauritian authorities to get them to refuse to hand over the information. Standing before the Mauritian court, Zuma's legal team argued that the documents should not be sent to South Africa as the trial against Zuma was part of a 'political conspiracy' against him: the inference being that, if Mauritius agreed to the State's request, it would be party to this conspiracy. He was opposed by the South African State, which denied the charges of a conspiracy, and the Mauritian Attorney-General, who submitted an affidavit to block Zuma and Thint's appeals.

Much like the Constitutional Court Appeal, Zuma's appeal to the Mauritian Court was rejected. In a brief final judgment, the presiding Mauritian Judge, R. Mungly-Gulbul, found that Zuma's application to 'intervene' in the process of providing documents seized by Mauritian authorities to the State was unfounded. In particular, he found that the idea that Zuma could ask to intervene because he feared the documents would be used in his prosecution was spurious:

> I am of the view in so far as the investigation is concerned, the Applicant is in the same situation as a person in respect of whom incriminating bank books or cell phones have been secured from a third party's premises. In an *ex parte* application by the prosecution authorities before the Judge in Chambers in order to have access to these bank accounts and telephone records, can this person claim that he has a right to intervene in the proceedings before the Judge in Chambers because he stands the risk of being prosecuted as a result of the evidence uncovered? The logical answer to this question is in the negative.
>
> Any person who stands the risk of being prosecuted as a result of a search carried out in the course of an investigation, does not have any absolute right to intervene in any pre trial application by the prosecuting authorities for obtention of records or documents from public or private institutions that may be used by the prosecution authorities, should they deem it necessary and relevant for the purposes of their investigation. He may, at his trial, raise objections for instance as to the production of the items secured in the course of the search. But at the stage of the investigation, the person cannot claim that he has

an absolute right of intervention. It is to be noted that the documents in issue here, were not secured from the Applicant's premises ... so that Applicant cannot possibly claim, for instance, breach of his right to privacy or invasion of his property.[36]

Moreover, much as the State would argue in opposition to Zuma's attempt to have the second set of charges against him dismissed (of which more below), the Mauritian Judge found that it was not in the purview of the Mauritian Court to get involved in discussions as to whether the documents seized could be used as evidence in Zuma's trial, or whether or not the trial was motivated for political ends. Indeed, the Judge found that, if the State presented these documents as evidence in an eventual Zuma trial, his lawyers could contest their validity during the criminal trial: 'Whatever *bona fide* belief that [Zuma] may hold to the effect that he is being persecuted and his trial politically motivated, may be raised before the proper forum which, in this case, is the trial Court of South Africa.'[37]

Now that both the Mauritian Court and the Constitutional Court have ruled in favour of the State, the case against Zuma seems to have been strengthened by being able to include documents up until 2005: documents that, the State has argued in its most recent charge sheet, show that Zuma continued to receive 'benefits' from Shaik all the way until 2005, pushing the amount he received from Shaik from the R1.2m shown to have been paid in the Shaik trial to a cool R4m. The documents also, allegedly, form part of the State's case that Zuma engaged in acts of fraud and tax evasion.

Perhaps this is why, in May 2008, it became clear that Zuma's trial may be held up by applications by his legal team for a number of years further. While all the search-and-seizure warrants have been declared valid in such a way that Zuma can no longer appeal their validity, he still has the legal right to appeal his current prosecution, and it looks increasingly likely that he will be using all available legal opportunities to do just that: it has been mooted, for example, that he will submit another application for a permanent stay of prosecution in September 2008, meaning that he may only face charges, if he ever does, in 2009 or even 2010.

STRUCK FROM THE ROLL: IT'S A 'CONSPIRACY AGAINST ME'[38]

If Zuma's legal team does file for a permanent stay of prosecution in 2008, it will be the second time that they have done so. In June 2006, a month before the trial was due to start, the NPA sent a letter to Zuma and to KwaZulu-Natal Judge President, Vuka Tshabalala. The letter requested a postponement of the trial until February 2007, largely as a result of the appeals that had been lodged by Zuma's team against the search and seizure operations, which had diverted the State from being able to process the documents in their possession.[39] They also weren't exactly helped by the fact that Schabir Shaik was to hear his appeal before the Supreme Court of Appeal in August 2006, roughly a month after the Zuma trial was slated to start: an appeal that would have to be attended to by the Shaik prosecution team, which also made up part of the Zuma prosecution team.[40]

Responding to the news of a potential delay, Zuma's supporters went on the attack. Ignoring the State's argument that it was appeals lodged by Zuma and Thint that had de-layed the presentation of the State's case, the Congress of South African Students threatened to 'down pens' if the trial was postponed, issuing the grammatically fraught state-ment that 'even a grade 10 learner will be able to be aware that the NPA at some point is being used for political in-fighting'.[41] The Eastern Cape branch of Cosatu mooted the idea of a general strike to register their dissatisfaction at the State's vacillation.[42] Three days before the trial was to start, the KZN deputy general of the Young Communist League tub-thumped that the 'crooks' in the NPA were delaying for a very specific reason: 'If the case is postponed, it means the NPA does not have a case against him.'[43]

With this outpouring of NPA-baiting in the background, Zuma, Thint and the State's legal teams met in court on 31 July 2006. The State presented its request for a postpone-ment; Zuma and Thint's legal teams opposed it. But they went even further: Zuma's legal team submitted an affidavit that requested a permanent stay of prosecution. This would mean that the case would be dismissed altogether, rather than just being removed from the roll. But the series of af-fidavits submitted over the course of the next month were of perhaps even greater significance: this was the first time that the claims that there was a 'political conspiracy' against Zuma were fully expressed and contested.

Zuma's affidavit, nearly 100 pages long, made a series of arguments in support of the demand for a permanent stay of prosecution. The first was that the trial against him was political in nature and that, as a result, it was essentially malicious.[44] As he argued: 'I verily believe that the charges against me have been initiated and certainly fuelled by a po-litical conspiracy to remove me as a role player in the ANC. It has become clear that because of my past record of service to the organisation, the only feasible imperative is an indirect attempt to undermine me to achieve this.'[45] To support this claim, Zuma referred to three incidents:

1. The 4 July 2003 'off-the-record' briefing given by NPA head Bulelani Ngcuka to various newspaper editors. During the briefing, which was ostensibly to brief the media on the smear campaign launched against Ngcuka, he allegedly asked the editors to tell him their sources to aid him in the prosecution attempt against Zuma. Zuma claimed that Ngcuka had attempted to recruit the editors in 'a furtherance of the conspiracy against me'.[46]

2. Ngcuka's August 2003 announcement that there was *prima facie* evidence of corruption on Zuma's part. Zuma described this as 'character assassination of the highest order' and an attempt to 'poison the minds of the public … there was no need for such pronouncements – they were meant to prejudice and they did'. He also noted that Lawrence Mushwana, the Public Protector, had found in Zuma's favour when the matter was referred to him.[47]

3. The 2001 letter signed by Jacob Zuma and sent to Gavin Woods, which Zuma claimed that Mbeki had written and, further, that Zuma had only signed the letter at Mbeki's behest. 'The letter in question was not drafted or composed by myself or my office. It was word for word drafted by the President's office and forwarded to me with an instruction that I should sign it. I did comply. There can be little doubt that even the most superficial investigation must have revealed that to the Prosecution. I can only infer that the Prosecution knew this at the outset and indeed also when it drafted the indictment in this case. It knew full well the indictment would be eagerly published in various formats by the press. It must have known that

the passage in question, together with the exposition in the Shaik judgment would give the very clear impression that the composing and signature of that letter by me were exactly what I got paid for. It knew and knows that that is, in fact, false.'[48]

This wasn't the only time that Zuma brought up Mbeki in his affidavit. In fact, he was mentioned twice more. First, Zuma argued that it was strange that the State had not called Thabo Mbeki as a witness in the trial, because Mbeki could prove that Zuma had played a limited role in the Arms Deal, and could therefore clear the air in explaining that there was no way that Zuma could manipulate the Arms Deal in favour of Shaik. As he stated in the affidavit:

I further point out that there is not a single State witness involved in the Arms Deal process who contends that I ever even remotely requested or suggested that he or she act in an improper manner in the process or that I tried to influence the process or its outcome in any way. If there is, I challenge the Prosecution to give details thereof. I indeed had just about nothing to do with the entire Arms Deal.

Honourable President Mbeki was in his position as the then Deputy President and member of the Cabinet, very much involved in the Arms Deal process. He took an active interest and part in it. He engaged with various of the role-players and other interested parties. He has been scurrilously accused of being party to improprieties in this regard ...

I distance myself from these and condemn the accusations as false. However, he is a person who is ideally and obviously suited to depose to the absence of corruption in the award process.[49]

The second time that Mbeki was embroiled was in Zuma's statement about the decision Mbeki made to fire him. He argued that, shortly after the Shaik trial was concluded, Mbeki, through various intermediaries, had asked him to resign. However, Mbeki, who could not present any legal argument to justify this, still went ahead with sacking him on 14 June – six days before he was formally charged. Zuma believed that the only reason that Mbeki could have made his decision to charge him was that the National Director of Public Prosecutions, Vusi Pikoli, had presented new evidence to Mbeki during a trip to Chile five days before Zuma was fired. Zuma then challenged Pikoli to present this 'new evidence'. But, if Pikoli did not have new evidence, Zuma argued that the only reason why the State would charge him was because Mbeki had instructed Pikoli to do so in order to make the decision to fire Zuma look more legitimate. As he stated in the affidavit:

> The President, I believe, could not have made the decision to dismiss me simply because I was implicated in Shaik's conviction. I was not an accused and the Shaik trial's outcome was expected on the State's version. If there was to be no prosecution, how could my situation then ever be resolved? I can only surmise that the NDPP, Mr. Pikoli, briefed the Honourable President on the upcoming charges, either at an earlier occasion or during the approximately 5 days the National Director was with President Mbeki during their visit to Chile immediately prior to my dismissal. It is after all inconceivable that the President would have instructed Mr. Pikoli to prosecute

me – that is, after all, the only other inference.[50]

The second argument he presented in favour of a permanent stay of prosecution was that the delays in the trial, and any that might occur in the future, would prejudice the case against him and violate his constitutional rights. The latter point was simple: the Constitution provides that a fair trial includes the right to have it prosecuted 'within a reasonable time'.[51] Zuma argued that, if the State were to get its request for a postponement, the resultant delay would have 'devastating consequences' for him.[52] These 'devastating consequences' included prejudicing his quest for a position in the ANC at the 2007 Polokwane Conference: 'if these charges against me are still pending, then it will greatly strengthen the resolve and capabilities of those who seek to exclude me from any meaningful role'.[53] He also complained bitterly about the financial costs entailed in any further postponement,[54] adding, somewhat tendentiously, that the raids on his lawyers 'had the sinister objectives of discovering my defences and my defence strategies after I had been charged'.[55]

The State responded in double-quick time. On 14 August 2006, two weeks after Zuma's first affidavit, the State submitted six affidavits in response. These were from Penuell Maduna (former Minister of Justice), Bulelani Ngcuka (by now resigned from his position as head of the NPA), Leonard McCarthy (an NPA advocate), Vusi Pikoli (then head of the NPA), Advocate Johan du Plooy and Advocate Billy Downer (the lead prosecutor in the Shaik case). The affidavits rejected almost all the claims made by Zuma.

Bulelani Ngcuka's affidavit made for exceptionally interesting reading. It was argued in strong and forceful language that suggested that Ngcuka, by this time, was fed up with being implicated in a 'political conspiracy' against Zuma. Two of the most notable points regarded his behaviour to Zuma during the outbreak of scandal and the 'off-the-record' briefing he allegedly gave to the media. As he stated:

> The purpose of the meeting was to dispel certain defamatory and damaging rumours that were being circulated about me. It had come to my attention that these rumours had also been sent to certain sections of the media. I considered it necessary to meet with relevant role-players to scotch these rumours before they were widely published, with the attendant and obvious damage to me, my family and the NPA.
>
> I explained to them that these rumours were being invented and circulated in order to tarnish my reputation as a result of a number of high profile investigations in which I, as head of the NPA, was involved. I do not intend to go into further details of these rumours and the discussions that I had in regard to them with those present, as this would entail publishing and perpetuating defamatory matter. Suffice to say that they included the allegation, which was later brought into the public domain by a certain ex-journalist who now acts as a media consultant to Accused No 1, that I was an apartheid spy …
>
> I furthermore deny that the purpose of the meeting was to further any sort of political conspiracy against Accused No 1 or anyone else. I should point out that this was not the sort of secretive, shadowy meeting that Accused No 1 and his collaborators seek to portray. It was also attended by two of my most senior colleagues in the NPA, which would hardly be likely if I were intent on the sort of subterfuge that Accused No 1 alleges.

It must be pointed out that the allegations in regard to this meeting contained in Accused No 1's affidavit, as well as his complaint to the public protector, are based **entirely upon hearsay.** The main source of his allegations appears to be Vusi Mona, ex-editor of the City Press. This is a man whose integrity and reliability were thoroughly discredited in the Hefer Commission. In his evidence before the Commission, Mona repeated the allegations contained in the annexure E1 to Accused No 1's affidavit, but in the words of the Chairperson *'he was forced to make one damning concession after the other'* with the result that by the end of cross examination *'his credibility had been reduced to nil'*. The Commission concluded, regarding Mona's version of what transpired at the meeting, that *'[a]s far as I am concerned one simply cannot accept its factual basis'*.[56]

Vusi Pikoli made much the same noises. In his affidavit, he rejected the idea that the decision to fire Zuma had been based on any conversation he might have had with Mbeki in Chile. He also rejected the claim that he was party to a political conspiracy to charge Jacob Zuma and ruin his career:

I reject these allegations in unequivocal terms. I note that Accused No 1 has put up no facts upon which such serious accusations could reasonably have been founded, but has chosen instead to rely on rumours, press reports, speculation and innuendo. I am advised that these accusations are scurrilous and unfounded, and that they appear to be part of a concerted publicity campaign.[57]

Perhaps the most controversial of all the affidavits was presented by Penuell Maduna. In it, he both rejected the claims of a political conspiracy, and argued that it was not the state that had divulged the identity of Zuma during the investigation into the Arms Deal. Instead, it was his friend and advisor, Schabir Shaik:

> If there was any conspiracy at the time, then it was a conspiracy designed to discredit Ngcuka and the NPA simply because they were doing their job without fear, favour or prejudice (as demanded by the Constitution). This resulted in a shameful smear campaign against Ngcuka, culminating in the allegations that he had been an apartheid spy. These allegations were publicly and thoroughly discredited in the Hefer Commission. It is significant to note that, despite the fact that all interested parties (including Accused No 1) were invited to make submissions to the Hefer Commission, there were no allegations at that time that there was any such political conspiracy against Accused No 1 or that Ngcuka was part thereof …
>
> I was made aware by the NPA at an early stage of the investigation into the Arms Deal. The name of Accused No 1 did not feature at all at that stage. I am advised that the events which led to Accused No 1 becoming a suspect in this investigation are set out elsewhere in these papers. Suffice it to say that I am personally aware that, once evidence was uncovered that required an investigation to be conducted in relation to Accused No 1, the NPA made every effort to handle the investigation with the utmost discretion and sensitivity. The steps taken by the NPA to avoid public disclosure of the investigation of Accused No 1 are listed in Ngcuka's press release. These efforts were successful until Mr Shaik deliberately and cynically revealed in court papers the identity of Accused No

1, who had hitherto been referred to in all of the State's papers only as 'Mr. X'. This was discovered by the *Mail and Guardian*, which published this fact in November 2002.'[58]

Adding significantly to Judge Herbert Msimang's required reading, Jacob Zuma submitted his second affidavit on 21 August, responding to the State's affidavits submitted only a week previously. In it, he attacked the State's affidavits, and, after rejecting Pikoli's account of events in Chile, claimed that the State had not fully dealt with the following concerns:

1. The state's delay in coming to trial.
2. The impact on Zuma of the investigation into him since mid-2001, and especially November 2002, when he first read about it 'in the press'.
3. The impact on Zuma of Ngcuka's *prima facie* statement.
4. The impact of the decision of the decision to prosecute him in 2005.
5. The 'purpose' of the investigation and charges (political conspiracy).
6. The impact of further postponements, which Zuma argued that the state was trying to engineer.[59]

He also further attacked the NPA, claiming that it had failed to investigate him fairly. He based this claim on the following events:

1. The 'cynical' extension in October 2002 of an investigation – *de facto* started in mid-2001 – so as to legitimise what had gone before and what would be done thereafter.

2. The 'cynical' abuse of power in extending the investigation in August 2005 to include allegations of Zuma's defrauding Parliament and tax evasion.
3. A 'cynical' use of state power in executing the search warrants for raids in 2005.
4. The apparent total reliance on the Shaik judgment, which, Zuma argued, is, in law, irrelevant to his trial.[60]

The last affidavit to be submitted in this flurry of legalese came from Leonard McCarthy on 29 August. Beyond being fiery stuff, it was also incredibly important in discussing the whole Ngcuka–Mushwana spat covered in Chapter 6. Zuma had referred to Mushwana's decision (that Ngcuka had violated his constitutional rights) in his first affidavit to prove that Ngcuka was hell-bent on making Zuma's life a misery. But, McCarthy argued, Mushwana's decision could not be taken seriously. This was because Mushwana didn't actually have the legal right to question NPA decisions:

> Since the NPA is, in terms of its functions and powers, subject only to the constitution and the law, no other institution can question or review such decisions, except the courts. Any person who is dissatisfied with a decision in this regard can have it reviewed by the courts. The public protector therefore does not have the power to review or question such a decision.[61]

Even more striking, however, was the claim that Mushwana had actually acted in bad faith. This was based on a complicated argument, but the essence was this: according to McCarthy, Mushwana and the NPA, during Mushwana's investigation, had agreed that Mushwana should halt the investigation as Zuma's complaint could materially affect the outcome of the upcoming Shaik trial. McCarthy argued, therefore, that by presenting his report, and undertaking the investigation, Mushwana had broken this agreement. McCarthy also argued that Mushwana had misled the Presidency on the matter. This was because Mushwana had approached the Presidency to intervene after the NPA had clearly stated that the reason they weren't answering his questions was due to the possible impact on the Shaik trial. Mushwana, McCarthy argued, had misled the Presidency inasmuch as he argued that the NPA's response (that the probe could affect the Shaik trial) consisted of non-compliance on the part of the NPA. As McCarthy stated in his affidavit:

> However, the public protector reneged on this agreement and used the position taken by the NPA as evidence supporting his finding that there was a failure or reluctance (by Ngcuka and Maduna) to co-operate ...
>
> It appeared that when the public protector was unable to deal with the fundamental principles of the law raised in the McCarthy letter, he sought the intervention of the president's office on the basis that the national director and the minister were refusing to co-operate ...
>
> With respect, the view is held that in this regard the public protector did not just mislead the minister and the national director, he went further and misrepresented the office of the president.[62]

With this required reading in hand the trial judge overseeing the hearing, Judge Herbert Msimang, retired for just under three weeks to digest all the documents in hand. When the court reconvened on 20 September 2006, Msimang delivered a telling body blow to the State's attempt to prosecute Zuma. He argued that the trial was always going to struggle:

'It has dawned on us that it was inevitable that the State's efforts to prosecute in this matter would flounder. From the very outset, when a decision was taken to prosecute, those efforts were grounded on an unsound foundation.'[63] In fact, Msimang found, the State's case had 'limped from one disaster to another',[64] as evidenced by the decision to include documents seized in the raids in August 2005 when these documents were still under appeal.[65] In fact, Msimang found that the major reason to decline the State's request for a postponement was not that he necessarily believed the 'political conspiracy' theory woven by Zuma and his legal team, but, rather, because he felt that the decision of the State to include documents whose founding search warrants were being contested was an act of poor judgment. As Msimang stated:

> The position regarding the availability of the contested documents on the trial date is therefore presently uncertain ... to make use of those documents when their legal status have not been clarified would not be a sensible move. I shudder to think of the consequences should the Appeal Court thereafter dismiss the appeals thus upholding the decisions of the High Courts.[66]

The result of this was simple: the trial was struck from the roll. Zuma no longer faced charges of corruption.[67]

As the decision was announced in the court, Zuma supporters began loudly celebrating, forcing Judge Herbert Msimang to comment 'please go outside. That is where people can do as they please. Not inside.'[68] And celebrate they did. Outside the court, Zuma fans loudly championed their hero; a small group, responding to the rumour that Mbeki had trumped up the charges against Zuma for his own political ends, carried a coffin with Mbeki's face blazoned on the top.[69] The party moved to Johannesburg, where Zuma addressed a Cosatu rally the following day. To the rapturous applause of 2000 delegates, Zuma made noises eerily similar to Tony Yengeni in dismissing the Scorpions: 'I said [to the Scorpions] "I must tell you, you are doing what the apartheid state did not do." I said, "you [the Scorpions] are worse than them."'[70] At the same conference, Zwelinzima Vavi, the Secretary General of Cosatu, made the argument that came to typify the response of Zuma supporters to Msimang's decision: 'The overwhelming majority of working people, of the working class, the poor, the marginalised should be very happy today ... This was all a political-conspired case to prevent him from advancing his political career.'[71]

The ebullience might have been understandable, but it was sadly misplaced. In fact, far from dismissing Zuma's case altogether, what Msimang had ordered was that it be struck from the roll. While this gave Zuma a major leg-up for the upcoming ANC National Conference in Polokwane, it also gave the State the right to press new charges if it so wished. Zuma's 'victory' here was mixed: his allies could certainly portray Msimang's decision as vindication of their oft-stated conspiracy theories, but the reality was that Msimang had not actually fulfilled Zuma's request. Remember that Zuma's legal counsel had argued for a permanent stay of prosecution. This would have meant that Zuma could not be charged under the same terms again. But Msimang's decision had rejected this: the State could recharge Zuma whenever it wanted, albeit with a more prepared case up its sleeve.

THE ZUMA 'SUPER CHARGES'[72]

Recharge is exactly what they did in December 2007 when they presented Zuma with a new indictment. This time he would have to face more than just two charges of corruption.

In total, Jacob Zuma faced 16 charges, along with Thint, who were charged with three counts of corruption. In reality, the charges were based on much the same narrative of events that was presented in the Shaik trial and the first indictment served on Zuma in 2005. As such, they will not be dealt with in detail here. The major difference, in terms of narrative, was that the State extended the timeline of payments from Zuma to Shaik. Whereas the original June indictment listed just under 300 payments from Shaik to Zuma totalling just over R1m, this indictment (serviced by an exhaustive forensic report) listed 783 payments starting on 25 October 1995 and ending on 1 July 2005 (a full month after Shaik had been found guilty by Judge Hilary Squires, and, tellingly, a month before the raids were undertaken on Zuma and his attorney's property).

These payments, painstakingly set out according to a 17-page 'schedule of payments', had totalled R4,072,499.85 by 1 July 2005.[73] It certainly was an exhaustive document: large payments, such as R400 000 allegedly paid by Kobitech to Development Africa (the company paying for Zuma's Nkandla residence) on 23 June 2005, appeared alongside amounts of R25 allegedly paid for a mini car-valet for Zuma's car in October 2000, R140 allegedly paid in April 2000 for Zuma's petrol and R393.80 allegedly paid in July 2005 for insurance on a Toyota Tazz.[74] If this 'schedule of benefits' is ever presented before the court, and proved to be valid, what is clear is that Shaik was, in many ways, running Zuma's financial life and supporting his lifestyle; a fact amply attested to by the litany of payments listed under the following descriptions: 'Zuma household costs', 'Zuma children education costs', 'Zuma family costs', 'Zuma/Zuma family travel costs', 'cash for Zuma/Family', 'Zuma/Zuma family medical costs', 'Zuma children allowance', 'Zuma legal costs', 'Zuma traffic fine' and the slightly more vague, 'Zuma expense'.[75]

But what were the charges that Zuma faced? The majority were related to fraud: 12 in total. Two of these, in turn, were related to fraud that Zuma had allegedly committed in his relationship with Parliament. The first case of fraud (count 8), was that Zuma had knowingly failed to declare the payments from Shaik to Parliament or Cabinet between 28 September 2000 and 14 June 2005 in his schedule of Members' Interests. The State argued that, in total, he had failed to declare 613 payments that he was legally obliged to do, amounting to R2 813 705.71.[76] The second count of fraud specifically related to Parliament (count 9) was that Zuma had knowingly misled the Assembly in answering questions posed by DA MP Reinette Taljard (actually Raenette Taljaard, but it was misspelt in the original indictment). Taljaard had, in a series of questions issued to Zuma, asked if he had met Shaik and Thetard on 11 March 2000, or with Thetard on any other day. Zuma had responded that he had not met them on 11 March, nor had he met with Thetard to discuss the 'bribe' on any other day. As a result, he 'failed to reveal, when he had a duty so to reveal, that he had met Shaik and Thetard on 10 March, if he had not met them on 11 March 2000.'[77] He did this, even though 'he well knew that he had met Shaik and Thetard on 11 March alternatively on the 10 March 2000, and/or that he had met Shaik and Thetard on either 10 or 11 March to discuss the payment of a bribe.'[78]

The other fraud charges (counts 10 to 18) levied by the

State related to his alleged failure to declare the benefits that he had received from Shaik in his tax returns to the South African Revenue Service.[79] Specifically, in both his September 2003 tax returns and 'during the period after 28 February 2004 to 27 June 2005 on a precise date to the prosecution unknown', he had failed to declare R2 779 514,20 of the benefits paid by Shaik to him, over and above an 'additional tax liability: gross income' of R1 167 971,00 and 'Interest Free Loans' totalling R522 470,00.[80] In other words, Zuma had failed, between September 2003 and June 2005, to declare taxable income or loans totalling R4 460 955,20 that he had received between 1996 and 2004.[81]

The other charges comprise two of corruption, one of money laundering (count 6), and one of racketeering (count 1). The two charges of corruption (counts 2 and count 4) are similar to the corruption charges levelled against Zuma in June 2005 and against Shaik in his trial. Count 2 argued that Zuma had received payments from Shaik (totalling R4m) in return for using the weight of his political office to intervene to help Shaik further his business interests (a mirror image of the 'mutually beneficial symbiosis' charge on which Shaik was found guilty by Judge Squires).[82] Count 6 related specifically to Zuma accepting a bribe from Thomson in return for his protection against any Arms Deal investigation and in return for a promise to support any of Thomson's future projects in South Africa.[83] Count 6, of money laundering, flowed from the bribe charge. This charge alleged that Zuma had knowingly, and with the cooperation of Thomson and Shaik, attempted to 'disguise' the 'nature, source, location, disposition or movement' of the bribe payment of R500 000 a year.[84]

By far the most serious charge that Zuma faced was that of racketeering. Racketeering, in layman's terms, is when a seemingly legitimate company actually bases all of its business activities on corrupt methods. It is, in other words, a legitimate-looking front for illegitimate activity. In its argument alleging that Zuma was guilty of racketeering, the State made the following argument.

First, that Nkobi Investments (owned by Nkobi Holdings) was an 'Enterprise'. An Enterprise was defined as an entity that included 'any individual, partnership, corporation, association, or other juristic person or legal entity, and any union or group of individuals associated in fact, although not in a juristic person or legal entity'. An Enterprise, in other words, was any collection of people, companies or single individuals which worked together in business, even if this was not formalised into a legal company. Nkobi Investments ('the Enterprise'), the State argued, engaged in racketeering activity because it was a company that, while legitimate on the surface, actually was based on corrupt activity. This was, in turn, based on two arguments. First, the State argued that 'the Enterprise', although positioning itself as offering a BEE partner, had little to offer any potential joint venture partner by way of expertise or finance, and could only offer 'political connectivity'. As the indictment noted:

> The Enterprise through its subsidiaries and associated companies, as more specifically set forth in the General Preamble to the Indictment, operated as an ostensibly legitimate group of companies, whose main business was to form joint ventures with foreign and local businesses, more particularly as a 'Black Economic Empowerment' ('BEE') partner, and so to bid for lucrative contracts, primarily in the public sphere.
>
> The Enterprise and its subsidiaries had little to offer in the way of capital or expertise and relied primarily on

Shaik's much heralded 'political connectivity' to attract partners with these resources and to secure an advantage over any competitors in obtaining contracts.

Apart from the legitimate objectives of the Enterprise, it also pursued certain illegitimate objectives, as set out further below, acting both in its own capacity as well as through various subsidiaries and associated companies and persons, including Shaik and the accused.[85]

Second, the 'Enterprise' used methods and attempted to attain objectives that were corrupt. These activities and methods were, according to the indictment:

> To cultivate and maintain corrupt relationships with persons in positions of political power and high government office, including accused no. 1, in order to cultivate 'political connectivity;
>
> To make payments to and on behalf of such persons in return for their services in advancing the interests of the Enterprise as and when required;
>
> It was part of the objectives of the Enterprise that it, its employees, and persons and entities associated with it, would conceal or disguise payments to persons of political power and high government office, including accused 1;
>
> It was nevertheless also part of the objectives of the Enterprise to procure funding or future funding from potential business partners ... through its reliance on political connectivity, with the intention of enabling the Enterprise, its subsidiary and associated companies and Shaik to maintain the payments to persons of political power and high government office, including accused 1, in return for their services in advancing the interests of

the Enterprise and its business partners as and when required;

To advertise political connectivity to or create the perception of political connectivity in the minds of potential business partners and thereby to induce, persuade or intimidate such partners to enter into, and maintain, joint venture agreements with the Enterprise and on terms favourable to the Enterprise and thereby also to enable the Enterprise to maintain its payments to persons of political power and high government office;

To attempt, through corrupt means, to secure lucrative contracts in the public sphere, either alone or through joint venture partnerships with other business partners;

Nevertheless to maintain the appearance that the Enterprise was a legitimate business.[86]

But, you may be asking, where did Zuma fit into all of this? Very centrally, the State argued. After arguing that Nkobi Holdings was, at best, a glorified Ponzi scheme, the State argued that Zuma was actually an employee of Nkobi. This was based on the argument that the benefits that were paid to Zuma over the 10 years from 1995 to 2005 'amounted to a salary in the form of a retainer, in return for which accused 1 would perform services for the Enterprise as and when required. This amount to accused 1's *de facto* employment by the Enterprise.'[87] Even if the court failed to recognise that Zuma was an employee, it could still be swayed by the State's argument that, even if Zuma was not necessarily an employee, he was still closely connected to the Enterprise and helped to further its corrupt activities. He was connected to the Enterprise, the State argued, by the following means:

- 'Through his close and longstanding association with Shaik, the manager of the enterprise;
- Through Shaik's position as his personal financial advisor and/or special economic advisor;
- Through the schedule benefits which he received from the Enterprise;
- Through the service and facility benefits which the enterprise provided to him;
- Through his *de facto* shareholding in the Enterprise;
- Through the 'political connectivity' which he provided to the Enterprise; and/or
- Through the services which he performed on behalf of the enterprise.[88]

Further, he had assisted the Enterprise 'through a pattern of racketeering activity' by:

- Advising, counselling and/or assisting Shaik in the management or conduct of the Enterprise's affairs;
- Corruptly accepting the schedule benefits set out in the Schedule … each payment constituting a separate racketeering act;
- Corruptly agreeing to accept the annual benefits until the first payment of ADS dividends;
- Furthering and/or attempting and/or agreeing to further the business of the Enterprise;
- Protecting and/or attempting and/or agreeing to protect the Enterprise from criminal investigation and/or prosecution;[89]

In more simplistic terms, the gist of the racketeering argument was this: Shaik's Nkobi Investments could offer nothing by way of expertise or finance, and could only offer corruptly gained 'political connectivity' to potential partners; that the Enterprise engaged in various corrupt activities to make money; and that Zuma was either an employee of the Enterprise or, if not seen as an employee, closely linked to the Enterprise for which he undertook a series of illegal services flowing from the powers vested in his political office.

Needless to say, this is serious stuff. One can only wonder, at this stage, how Zuma would respond to these charges if they were ever presented fully in court.

WILL JACOB ZUMA EVER GO ON TRIAL?

Even though the Constitutional Court has now, after years of legal machinations, cleared the use of the documents seized in August 2005, and even after the Mauritian Court has rejected Zuma's appeal to block the repatriation of evidence, there are a handful more possible appeals to be lodged before he ever faces charges. The State may be 'trial-ready',[90] but it will have to fend off a further set of appeals that seek to have the case dismissed.

This was made very clear in June 2008, two months before Zuma's trial was set to begin. Much as they did in 2006, Zuma's legal team submitted an application for his case to be dismissed. The nub of his application was simple. According to Zuma's application, Section 179 (5) of the Constitution required of the National Director of Prosecutions that he/she may 'review a decision to prosecute or not to prosecute, after consulting the relevant Director of Public Prosecutions and after taking representations ... from the following: the accused person, the complainant, any other person or party whom the National Director considers to be relevant'.[91] However, Zuma's team argued, Zuma had constantly been denied the right to make representations to the National Director of Prosecutions when decisions were made to 'review' the decision to prosecute him. According to Zuma's affidavit, the State decided, on two occasions, to 'review' the decision. The first occurred when the State decided to prosecute Zuma in 2005 in the wake of the Shaik trial; this, they argued, was a review of the decision taken by Bulelani Ngcuka not to prosecute Zuma in August 2003 (as evinced in his infamous '*prima facie*' statement). The second decision to review was when the State again decided to prosecute Zuma in December 2007, after the matter had been struck from the roll. In simple terms, Zuma thus argued that the State had 'reviewed' decisions regarding his prosecution, and that the Constitution and the NPA Act required that he be allowed to make representations at each point of review: the fact that he was not allowed to do so, therefore, was a violation of his constitutional rights (at the most) or just purely illegal (at least), and that, as a result, the case against him should be dismissed.[92]

Of course, the argument was not made in such dispassionate terms. In fact, the affidavit submitted was replete with assertions that he was being unfairly pursued by the State. The most obvious example of this, Zuma argued, was the charges of tax evasion he was to face, which 'typif[ied] the improper convict Zuma at all costs "leitmotif" which permeates the NPA's prosecution of myself'.[93] In this case, Zuma argued that, in fact, the appropriate body to lay charges against him over tax issues was the South African Revenue Service, and not the NPA; the fact that the NPA had done so suggested that they were over-eager to prosecute Zuma 'at all costs'. In addition, Zuma had, according to his affidavit, settled all outstanding payments necessary to be made to the Revenue Service, which had stated that it intended to bring no charges against him.[94]

The State responded immediately to the application. After setting out a lengthy chronology of the various decisions to prosecute (or not prosecute) Zuma, the State rejected Zuma's reading of what it meant for a decision to be 'reviewed', and whether the law, in fact, was to be interpreted in the way Zuma had suggested. First, the State argued that the decision taken by Vusi Pikoli to prosecute Zuma in 2005 was not a 'review' of Ngcuka's earlier decision in any real way:

> ... the [Pikoli] decision does not, in fact, amount to a 're-view', properly said, at all. The Pikoli decision did not purport to review or pronounce upon the correctness of Mr. Ngcuka's decision. On the contrary, the decision involved a reconsideration of the question of whether there was a reasonable prospect of a successful prosecution taking into account all the new facts and developments that had transpired since 2003.[95]

Second, the decision to prosecute in 2007 (referred to as the 'current decision') also did not amount to a review:

> The current decision is not a review of a decision to prosecute or not to prosecute but merely re-institutes charges against the applicant subsequent to the striking off by Msimang J. The Pikoli decision expressly indicated that the applicant would be charged with 'at least' the charges framed in the 'provisional' indictment. The current decision accordingly authorized an expanded set of charges in the current indictment.
>
> Inasmuch as this was precisely what the Pikoli decision had envisaged would be the case, the current decision is

not a review of the Pikoli decision. The current decision
therefore does not amount to a reconsideration or review
of a previous decision.[96]

With these affidavits presented, the Zuma trial started in the
Pietermaritzburg High Court on 3 August, only four days
after the Constitutional Court delivered its judgment ruling
the search warrants issued in August 2005 valid. As on other occasions, Zuma's appearance at the Court precipitated
massive outpourings from Zuma fans who questioned the
rectitude of his trial, and responded rapturously to his pronouncements of how he would run the country if he was to
become President: 'I love you all and I will always listen to
what you say. When you ask me to do something, I won't
argue, I'll do exactly that.'[97] As a testament to the rapidly
increasing political temperature, Ramatuku Maphutha, the
Deputy National Secretary of the MK Military Veterans Association (the organisation of which Joe Modise was once
President) issued a chilling warning: 'We want to make this
very clear. We are not going to allow this country – or any
other country – to destroy the ANC or its leader, comrade
Jacob Zuma. We are going to make sure that Zuma becomes
the next president of this country, no matter what. No
Zuma, no country.'[98]

Inside the somewhat more sedate courtroom, the presiding judge, Chris Nicholson, heard the arguments for and
against Zuma's application. He then adjourned the Court
and served notice that he would give a ruling on the application on 12 September. However, even if Nicholson finds
in favour of the State, it looks unlikely that Zuma will have
to face charges any time soon, and certainly not before the
April 2009 elections. Indeed, if Nicholson finds in favour of
the State, this matter will, as Zuma's attorney Michael Hul-

ley has confirmed, be referred to the Supreme Court of Appeal.[99] If the Supreme Court of Appeal finds in favour of the State, the matter can then be referred to the Constitutional Court for review. It is estimated that these various appeals could take up to two years to reach their conclusion.[100] Thus, while 8 December has been pencilled in as a possible start to the trial, it looks increasingly unlikely that this will actually happen.

Needless to say, if the Courts find in favour of Zuma, the trial will not take place at all. In this regard, Zuma is likely to hedge his bets. In his June 2008 application to have the trial dismissed, he stated that, if the Court were to find in favour of the State, he would launch an application for a permanent stay of execution based on his argument that the case against him was part of a larger 'political conspiracy': 'Should the present application not result in a positive outcome in respect of a re-appraisal of the decision to prosecute, a permanent stay application will be brought in which these issues [of a political conspiracy] and the impact on my fair trial rights will be addressed in detail.'[101]

The end result of all this is that, despite the NPA's attempts to secure an agreement on the part of Zuma and his lawyers to start the trial in earnest in April 2009 after sorting out pre-trial matters,[102] it is feasible that Zuma may only come to trial in late 2009 or during 2010; doubtless to take place in the full glare of the international media due to its concurrence with the Soccer World Cup.

That is, of course, if the trial is allowed to take place at all. Indeed, it has been widely speculated in the media that if Zuma does not face his charges before he becomes President, the ANC may force through a constitutional amendment that would prevent any sitting president from being subject to a criminal trial.[103] At this time, it is uncertain whether the

ANC would do this: these rumours are, it must be stressed, pure speculation at this point. However, if the ANC does make such an amendment, it will be the umpteenth time that the ruling party has used its parliamentary majority to prevent an unfettered engagement with what really happened during the Arms Deal.

CHAPTER 9

UNFINISHED BUSINESS AND UNANSWERED QUESTIONS

WHAT'S IN THIS CHAPTER?

- What were the roles of Thabo Mbeki and Chippy Shaik in the corvette deal?
- What happened to Chippy Shaik?
- What happened to the other people who received 'dodgy' 4x4s?
- What has happened to the Scorpions?
- Is the ANC guilty of corruption as an organisation?

KEY DATES FOR THIS CHAPTER

- EARLY 1995 Thabo Mbeki allegedly announces in Germany that the tender for the supply of corvettes is to be reopened, allowing German shipbuilders to retender .
- DECEMBER 1997 The ANC Treasurer-General notes that the ANC is struggling financially as donations to the organisation have dried up.
- NOVEMBER 1998 The GFC's Meko corvette is presented to Cabinet as the preferred bid, although later investigations showed that the GFC's bid was fundamentally flawed.
- MARCH 2001 EADS provides a list of all the people who had received discounted luxury vehicles. The list includes Siphiwe Nyanda (former head of the SANDF) and Llew Swan (Armscor). Vanan Pillay is also on the list and is later fired by the Department of Trade and Industry for receiving a R55 000 discount on a luxury car.
- JANUARY 2002 Chippy Shaik is called to account during a Department of Defence disciplinary hearing. He is given a final warning, but resigns two months later.

- 19 JUNE 2006 German investigators raid the offices of ThyssenKrupp, one of the companies of the German Frigate Consortium which won the tender to supply corvettes. The German authorities are investigating allegations that ThyssenKrupp paid R130m in bribes to South African politicians.

- JULY 2006 Allegations are made in the media (unproven and later suggested to be flawed) that Thabo Mbeki received a bribe from ThyssenKrupp.

- MARCH 2007 Patricia de Lille makes a legal application to be able to prosecute the other 29 recipients of 4x4s from EADS for corruption in her private capacity.

- AUGUST 2007 Justice Minister Brigitte Mabandla announces in Parliament that Chippy Shaik has never been, and currently is not, the subject of a full investigation.

- DECEMBER 2007 The ANC passes a resolution at the National Conference in Polokwane that moves to have the Scorpions scrapped.

- FEBRUARY 2008 Former ambassador Barbara Masekela announces to the media that Mbeki did meet with French arms officials during the Arms Deal. Mbeki had previously claimed that he could not remember if he did.

- FEBRUARY 2008 Chippy Shaik's PhD degree is revoked by the University of KwaZulu-Natal after it is proved that he had extensively plagiarised his thesis.

- MARCH 2008 *Mail & Guardian* runs a story alleging that the ANC might have received money in 1999 from an agent working for ThyssenKrupp.

- APRIL 2008 Cabinet approves the General Law Amendment Bill and the National Prosecuting Amendment Bill, both of which will scrap the Scorpions if passed by Parliament.

- MAY 2008 The Bills to scrap the Scorpions are presented in Parliament and referred to committee.
- JUNE 2008 German prosecutors announce that they have stopped investigations into alleged corruption committed by the German Frigate Consortium in its dealings in South Africa.
- JULY AND AUGUST 2008 The *Sunday Times* runs stories alleging that the German Submarine Consortium was provided with the contract to supply submarines to the South African Navy as a result of a R30m bribe paid to Thabo Mbeki. The allegations are based on a report drawn up by a risk consultancy in the UK. The Presidency responds furiously and reportedly considers taking legal action in response to the article.

After a series of investigations that have resulted in two convictions and one outstanding high-profile trial, one would expect that any dirt surrounding the Arms Deal would have been comprehensively excavated. Indeed, it has been nearly a decade since the Arms Deal was signed; and, importantly, nearly a decade since the first investigations started. The sad reality, however, is that there still exist a number of potentially damning allegations and questions that hover and buzz over the corpse of the Arms Deal. Arguably, it is only once these questions have been answered that the South African public can be considered fully in possession of all the relevant facts. Until then, the Arms Deal will continue to haunt the politics of our new democracy.

THE SELECTION OF THE CORVETTES: WHAT WERE THE ROLES OF THABO MBEKI AND CHIPPY SHAIK?

In December 1999, the South African government signed off the purchase of four Meko A200 corvettes. Each involved two separate products, the ship platform, purchased from the German Frigate Consortium (GFC), and the combat suite to be installed into the ship platform, purchased from the French company, Thomson-CSF (later renamed Thales), which was operating in a joint venture with a local supplier: Schabir Shaik's Nkobi group of companies.[1]

As has been discussed at length in previous chapters, it was the purchase of the combat suites that attracted the most negative attention. This was because the selection of Shaik's ADS was, in effect, wrangled by key players in the acquisition process. A key player in these manoeuvres was Schabir Shaik's brother, Shamin 'Chippy' Shaik. Not only did he refuse to recuse himself from meetings (as shown in the Joint Investigation Report) where his brother's company was discussed, but he might also have provided minutes of these confidential Cabinet meetings to both Thomson and his brother. Indeed, when Schabir Shaik was first arrested in 2001, it was on a charge of being in possession of confidential Cabinet minutes relating to the deal.[2] His inclusion in the deal was of particular concern, as shown in Chapter 7, because his company was not in the initial running to provide its section of the combat suite. Indeed, ADS was only included in the joint venture after some serious strongarming on the part of Schabir Shaik, and, it is alleged, Jacob Zuma.[3]

More recent allegations of corruption and mismanagement, however, have now cast doubt on the integrity of the selection of the entire corvette system (the ship platform and the combat suites). On 19 June 2006, German investigators raided the Dusseldorf offices of ThyssenKrupp, followed by the offices of subsidiary companies in Hamburg and Essien.[4] ThyssenKrupp was one part of the German Frigate Consortium that won the contract to supply the ship platform for the corvettes. The German investigators were looking for some very specific evidence: the tax records of ThyssenKrupp had shown that they had paid an amount totalling roughly R130m to politicians and intermediaries in South Africa, and they were hoping to find out who the money went to.[5] The payment of R130m was known, as the company had actually declared the bribes as a tax write-off under the term 'Useful Expenditure'. Useful Expenditure, until the end of 1999, was legal in Germany, allowing German companies to bribe foreign officials (bribery of German officials was and still is illegal).[6]

Der Spiegel, the German magazine that broke the 'Useful Expenditure' story, was absolutely convinced that ThyssenKrupp's R130m was paid to South African intermediaries and officials. The only question that was outstanding is into whose hands the money flowed. The German investigators, in a letter requesting legal assistance from Swiss authorities, have made some preliminary allegations as to where the money might have gone. According to the letter of request, the investigators allege that a total of $25m was paid in kickbacks 'to achieve the conclusion of the agreement'.[7] It is alleged that $22m of this was paid to a front company in Liberia called Mallar Inc., which then 'directly flowed to South African officials and members of cabinet'.[8] The remaining $3m was allegedly paid to the one man who stood at the centre of the whole corvette deal: Chippy Shaik.[9] Andrew Feinstein has alleged, further, that minutes were kept of the meeting at which it was decided to pay the bribe, and have been recovered; and that a South African investigator has confirmed that they are aware of the location of the funds, which have not been accessed due to concerns over alerting the relevant authorities.[10]

If the allegation is true, then Chippy Shaik would have been involved in unusual dealings with regard to both sections of the corvette deal: the ship platform (through the receipt of the $3m bribe) and the combat suite (by failing to recuse himself from meetings in which the awarding of the contract to his brother's company, ADS, was discussed).

Lurking in the background of all these matters is Thabo Mbeki. As Deputy President of the country from 1994 to 1999, and President thereafter, Mbeki was intimately involved in the Arms Deal and its later investigation. During the period of the acquisitions, Mbeki was part of the Cabinet sub-committee that directed the whole procurement process.

As discussed in Chapter 1, Mbeki played an early role in the corvette selection process. By 1995, the SA Navy had selected two preferred suppliers to provide the corvettes: the Yarrow shipyard (Scotland) and the Bazan shipyard (Spain). However, Mbeki, according to newspaper reports, travelled to Germany in early 1995 and informed his hosts that the deal was still open for tendering.[11] Shortly afterwards, the tender process was scrapped and the whole corvette bid reopened: Bazan, which was seemingly the favourite, would now have to compete once more for the contract. Mbeki's trip to Germany was followed by the deployment, in 1997, of a 'trusted comrade',[12] Mo Shaik (the brother of Chippy and Shabir), to the position of South Africa's Consul General in Hamburg.[13] Hamburg was the hometown of the head office of ThyssenKrupp. When the corvette deal was awarded, the Hamburg Consulate was quietly closed down,[14] suggesting that it had been established purely to act as a contact point between the new South Africa's executive and the Arms Deal company.

Even more worrying are claims that have been made, since 2006, that Mbeki might have met with the French representatives of Thomson-CSF prior to the signing of the combat suite deal. Thomson, remember, was the company awarded the combat suite as part of a joint venture with Shabir Shaik's African Defence Systems. According to Mark Gevisser, the biographer of Thabo Mbeki, there exists 'documentary evidence' that proves that Mbeki attended these meetings. Mbeki, however, has repeatedly denied doing so[15] (or, more accurately, has claimed that he 'honestly can't recall'[16] ever attending a meeting). However, Barbara Masekela, South Africa's former Ambassador to the US and a close Mbeki confidant, confirmed that Mbeki did indeed meet with the French. Masekela, in confirming the meeting, has argued that there was 'nothing wrong with a business wanting to meet people of power' and that there was nothing particularly combustible discussed.[17] Other reports have suggested, instead, that the meeting revolved around the involvement of Shabir Shaik in Thomson's tender: the French, it is alleged, were concerned about whether or not Mbeki was opposed to the inclusion of Shaik's Nkobi as a joint venture (and, presumably, to ADS being included as a subcontractor) and wanted to sound him out about the matter.[18]

Some have also claimed that Mbeki's links to Thomson and the German Frigate Consortium may have been firmed by a golden handshake: a substantial bribe. At this point in time, it is difficult to assess the veracity of this claim. The man who has made the bribery claim against Mbeki,

Nicholas Achterberg, has been alleged to owe ThyssenKrupp a considerable amount of money. Thyssen have suggested, as a result, that Achterberg has made these claims out of malice. Achterberg has also been consistently difficult to contact – on the yacht in the Bahamas on which he now lives – to discuss the claim.[19] The Scorpions, in 2006, claimed further that they had no evidence in their possession that suggested that Mbeki was involved in any improper or corrupt behaviour.[20] In addition, in June 2008, the German Prosecutors Office announced that they had halted their investigations into corruption in the South African deal, and that 'criminally relevant behaviour, in particular acts of bribery, was not established by the German Prosecutors Office'.[21] Even so, the above dealings in the corvette deal raise serious questions about the reasons South Africa signed the corvette deals: more specifically, whether the German victory was based less on their proposal than other, strategic, considerations. Similarly, if true, they also show that the government's oft-stated defence against corruption claims, that they had no role in the selection of subcontractors, is utterly spurious: Mbeki, after all, had allegedly met Thomson-CSF to discuss which subcontractor he would prefer to see included in its bid!

Of course, these claims would have less credence if the choice of systems in the corvette deal had been done entirely by the book. However, in examining the corvette deal, the Joint Investigation Report noted a series of major irregularities in the selection of the German Frigate Consortium as the preferred supplier. In November 1998, the GFC's Meko was presented to Cabinet as the preferred option. During the evaluation process, it was neck and neck with the Bazan in terms of military suitability and cost-effectiveness.[22] Much like the Hawk contract, GFC's bid was chosen as its offset commitments were higher than those of Bazan. However, the Report later found that, in fact, GFC's offset commitments were flaky and incomplete: it 'was nominated the preferred bidder on the basis of the NIP [National Industrial Participation] offer. This is despite the fact that the NIP is not ascertainable in terms of achievability.'[23] The Joint Investigation Team's auditors also found that serious errors had been made in calculating the evaluation scores awarded to the bidders.[24] In addition, what was not properly acknowledged in the evaluation of the offset agreement was that, even though GFC offered the highest total rand amount of offsets, it was lower than Bazan in relation to the contract price. In other words, Bazan offered to provide more offsets per rand spent on the deals than any of the other bidders.[25]

Of greater concern, however, was the fact that GFC was able to bid for the corvettes at all. During the evaluation process, the bidders were asked to provide detailed particulars as to their technical specifications, offset proposals and financing systems. Only one bidder, Bazan, submitted most of what was needed.[26] GFC failed to submit the proper proposals, despite repeated requests. As a result of this, GFC should have been disqualified from further discussions, but it was allowed to proceed to the next round of evaluations and given leeway to submit a more detailed proposal later on in the game. On this point, the Joint Investigation Report was damning in its own particular way, and deserves to be quoted at length:

> The decision to allow the bidders who did not conform with the critical minimum criteria in respect of technical, financing and DIP evaluations was a deviation from the approved value systems. Had this decision not been taken, only Bazan could have been evaluated on two of

the three domains. All the others did not comply with all three and Bazan did not comply with one. This could have resulted in Bazan being the preferred bidder ...

Further observations in the selection process are that:

- Bazan was the only bidder that complied with all the critical minimum criteria in respect of technical and DIP evaluation
- Bazan obtained the highest military value and DIP scores
- Bazan provided the highest percentage of DIP and NIP in relation to the contract price
- Bazan offered the lowest price of the four bidders.[27]

The reality was that the lowest price, that of Bazan, was still considerably higher than it would have been if the corvettes had been purchased in 1995. Remember that Tielman de Waal, the MD of Armscor, provided a breakdown of the cost of four corvettes in 1995, which he estimated to be roughly R1.7bn.[28] Between 1995 and 1999 two things happened to inflate this price: the rand depreciated against most of the major currencies, and the arms industry recovered from a mini-depression that had followed the fall of the Berlin Wall. The result was that South Africa ended up paying just over four times as much as it would have for the entire corvette deal in 1995:[29] an estimated R6.9bn in 1999 terms, or a full R5.2bn more than the estimated price in 1995.[30]

To summarise: Bazan's offer was the cheapest; was the only offer that met the minimum tender requirements at the first stage; and was the bid that offered the largest offset bang-for-its-buck. If the allegations of bribery discussed above turn out to have any merit, it raises key questions as to whether the deal was manipulated to ensure a set out-come that had been swung in favour of GFC by more nefari-ous considerations than technical suitability.

But, even if the allegations of corruption described above turn out to be false, there still exists one key question: how could the government have managed this process so badly?

THE SUBMARINES: ANOTHER QUESTIONABLE DEAL?

The purchase of submarines, although often considered to be unwise considering South Africa's actual strategic needs, has never been subject to sustained suspicion of corrupt ac-tivity. That is, until August 2008. On 3 August 2008, the *Sunday Times* ran an explosive report. In the report, it was alleged that MAN Ferrostaal, a German company that was part of the German Submarine Consortium (GSC) bid, had paid R30m in bribes to Thabo Mbeki, of which R2m was forwarded on to Jacob Zuma and the remaining R28m put into the coffers of the ANC.[31] The allegation was drawn from a report drawn up by an unnamed British risk consultancy after a UK company (also unnamed) was subject to a hos-tile takeover bid by MAN Ferrostaal: the report was drawn up to investigate, the *Sunday Times* claimed, 'the worldwide activities and "questionable business practices" of the ship-builder'.[32]

In addition, the *Sunday Times* report indicated that it had received copies of the draft of the Auditor-General's report into the Arms Deal. The draft, according to the article, had noted that the overall criteria for selection of the submarines had changed to favour GSC; that there were questions raised about the overall score given to GSC's major offsets proposal to build a steel production unit at Coega in the Eastern Cape; and that Tippex had been used to make changes to the working papers used during the evaluation of bidders contrary to instructions, which may have led to the evaluations being unfairly altered to favour GSC.[33] In a second exposé, which followed the 3 August piece, the *Sunday Times* reported that, in fact, MAN Ferrostaal had failed to match nearly all of its offset commitments, raising questions about the propriety of the GSC winning the contract based on its superior offset offers: 'an investigation into Ferrostaal's offsets has uncovered a trail of abandoned and collapsed projects, dubious benefactors and missed deadlines'.[34]

The following week the *Mail & Guardian* filled in some holes in the story. In a multi-page revelation, it revealed the source for the allegation that was included in the risk specialist's report: the ex-spy Mhleli 'Paul' Madaka.[35] Madaka was a former MK soldier, who later worked for the National Intelligence Agency and the Public Service Commission (the body that monitored government spending and watched for corruption in the public service).[36] However, Madaka died on 21 August 2007, his car careening off a highway and, in a grim twist of fate, ploughing into a property owned by MAN Ferrostaal in South Africa.[37] This, in turn, meant that the story could never be effectively corroborated: the only source of the allegations was dead.[38]

The Presidency, along with Ferrostaal, responded furiously to the allegations. Ferrostaal argued, both on its website and during a 702 radio interview with representatives of the company, that its offset projects were a major success. Indeed, the organisation noted that it had created and saved more than 20 000 jobs, and that it had met more than 80 per cent of its offset obligations in a range of industries. At the same time, the company rejected the allegations of bribery and corruption: 'MAN Ferrostaal never made any payments to President Thabo Mbeki, to Jacob Zuma or to any other member of the ANC or to any public official.'[39] They also accused the *Sunday Times* of making a series of factual errors, noting that 'these allegations are wrong and entirely unfounded ... The options of legal action are currently being evaluated.'[40] The Presidency, apparently considering its legal options, released a strongly worded statement that slammed the report: 'This time the *Sunday Times* outdoes itself by placing a spurious allegation in the public domain i.e. President Mbeki received a bribe of R30-million from MAN Ferrostaal. The Presidency would like to place it on record that President Thabo Mbeki has never at any stage received any money from MAN Ferrostaal ... By readily regurgitating known and spurious allegations – supposedly after six months of a laborious investigation – while at the same time concealing easy-to-find information which casts doubt on the credibility of its article, the paper appears to be pursuing an agenda that it only can explain.'[41] Similarly, Alec Erwin, addressing a media briefing, made much the same noises as he made with regard to Scopa, claiming that 'our concern is that very basic homework is not being done by the media, that it's quite possible to check most of these things against documentation that exists in large quantities. So what we're certain about is that our standards of journalism are exceptionally low.'

Certainly, it might be seen by some as somewhat hasty for the *Sunday Times* to have made these claims based on a single source: one, moreover, that could not provide further corroboration. However, it would be considerably easier if, like the corvette deal, the government could claim that the submarine deal was not afflicted with the same issues as affected other procurements: problems that, at the very least, raise questions about how the process was managed.

Four potential bidders were in the running for the submarine contract. These were DCN (France) with the Scorpene; GSC (Germany) with the 209 1400 MOD; Fincantieri (Italy) with the S1600, and Kockums (Sweden) with the Type 192.[42] According to a final evaluation score that was drawn up after taking into account a number of criteria, GSC emerged at the top of the pile, with a normalised score of 100 in terms of its offset commitments, 'military value' and 'financial index', followed by Kockums in second place, Fincantieri in third place and DCN in fourth.[43]

However, the various decisions that went into these final rankings have been criticised by, among others, the Joint Investigation Report. First, the military ranking, which listed the technical suitability of the different models on offer, actually listed GSC as coming last on the list: it was the least technically proficient model on offer. However, this score was then combined, according to a complex calculation, with the costs, to determine the best military value: what would be, in simple terms, the best value for money. Once this was done, GSC emerged as the top contender as it offered the lowest cost to the government. As the Joint Investigation Report noted: 'Although GSC came fourth from an overall performance perspective, the lower costs offered by them in relation to other bidders resulted in the GSC being the overall preferred supplier over all three components evaluated. Costs were therefore a significant factor in the identification of the overall supplier.'[44]

But, and this is where it gets complicated, how cost was determined in terms of value was, itself, very complex. Without going into too much detail, what was important about the way that this was computed was that one specific element of the costing framework, known as the Integrate Logistics Score or ILS (which referred, in fancy language, to how much it would cost to receive logistical support once the submarines had been delivered), dominated the weighting of the index. In fact, the ILS score counted for 67.51 per cent of total cost to value analysis.

What did this mean, in simple terms? It meant that, if a company had a significantly lower ILS cost than a competitor, but was more expensive in the other cost categories, it would still emerge with a higher score. The problem, here, is that GSC had an ILS cost estimate attached to it of USD\$36m, a quarter the size of the offer made by Fincantieri, which had topped the technical evaluation. In fact, the quote was so low that the evaluation team added 75 per cent to its cost in the final evaluation because, as was stated in the submarine evaluation report, 'the logic support package is comprehensive but a large amount of deliverables are offered as options and were not costed into the proposal'.[45] However, the attachment of the 75 per cent additional cost was, according to the Joint Investigation Report, 'arbitrary', and still gave a final cost of \$63m, which was only half of that of Fincantieri and another competitor, DCN.[46] Without full information at its disposal, in other words, the evaluation team had decided to increase the cost of the ILS for GSC, but had done so in a way that still ranked it as offering the lowest cost.

Because of the way the whole index score was weighted, with 67.51 per cent of the final cost to value analysis being made up of the ILS score, having the lowest ILS cost gave GSC a significant advantage. But it is mindboggling that this is actually the case: in a complex calculation that weighed up the total cost and the technical suitability of the various submarines, one small cost factor was given a major weighting. The end result, in simple terms, was that, because of a difference of merely $63m between GSC and other bidders in terms of its ILS, a contract worth over $1bn was awarded to a company that had actually scored the lowest in terms of technical suitability: the actual value for money element of the evaluation, therefore, hinged most materially on the consideration of what amounted to only 10 per cent of the total cost of the submarines! As the Joint Investigation Report noted: 'Therefore, because the denominator for the ILS element in the formulation of the GSC was much less than the other bidders, and because of the impact of the weight factor of 67.51 per cent allocated to the ILS component, the result was the GSC was effectively the preferred bidder in the overall technical evaluation on the basis of the value of US$63m.'[47] GSC, the least technically suitable of the submarines, had therefore been helped on its way to win this cost-value evaluation on the basis of a flimsy technicality.

Of course, the cost to technical value ratio was not the only area in which GSC had triumphed. In particular, GSC had emerged victorious because it offered an absolutely huge offset commitment that dwarfed the proposals of the other competitors: in the ranking of various National Industrial Participation offers, GSC emerged with an indexed score of 100 compared to an indexed score of 14 awarded to its nearest competitor, Kockums.[48] In particular, GSC committed to spend a massive amount of money developing a stainless steel mill at Coega. This formed a huge chunk of GSC's offset commitments. This can be seen by the fact that, in terms of its Defence Industrial Participation score, GSC scored a lowly 25.10, compared to 100 for DCN, 89.6 for Fincantieri, and 88.8 for Kockums.[49] Of course, when the two scores were added up (the DIP and NIP commitments) to form a 'revised total IP' score, GSC came out top because its NIP offer (the stainless steel mill at Coega) was so huge compared to the other offers. Again, in simple terms, what this meant was that GSC came top of the pile in terms of the evaluation of the offset commitments of various bidders, based almost entirely on its plan to build a steel mill at Coega.[50]

This would have been fine, except for one problem: it had already been established that the Coega plan might not be such a good idea after all. To quote from the Joint Investigation Report: 'During a review of files made available by the Department of Finance, two draft reports on the assessment of steel industry projects by Locker Associates Inc and Warburg Dillon Read were identified. These reports were a result of an assessment of the projects ... and reflected that the Coega stainless steel project was risky.'[51] Unfortunately for South Africa, the evaluation was spot-on. Just over six months after the final contracts were signed, GSC pulled out of the Coega plan as it became increasingly clear that it was economically unfeasible.[52] Admittedly, GSC has agreed to find substitution projects to replace the Coega proposal. But, at the time the contracts were signed, GSC had emerged victorious in large part because of the Coega steel mill plan: a plan that was found to be risky by two different independent analysts.

To summarise: GSC had won the tender to supply the submarines even though it was the least technically favoured submarine; it was chosen based on a technicality in the calculation of the value-for-money score; and it had won the evaluation for best offset offer based on an incredibly ambitious offset project, of which the government had already been warned of the risk – an assessment that turned out to be true only a single year later.

Again, much like the corvette deal, even if there was no corruption involved in the selection of GSC as the prime contractor to supply the submarines, we still have to ask the question: how could the government have managed this process so badly?

WHATEVER HAPPENED TO CHIPPY SHAIK?

Despite being found guilty of serious conflicts of interest by the Joint Investigation Report in 2001, Chippy Shaik has faced minimal official sanction. In January 2002, he was hauled before an Armscor disciplinary committee and charged with distributing confidential documents: it was claimed that he had forwarded the draft of the Joint Investigation Report to his lawyers for comment, which he was not entitled to do.[53] The disciplinary committee found Shaik guilty on this count, but decided not to fire him. Instead, he was given what amounted to a slap on the wrist: a final written warning. Three months later, in March 2002, he resigned from Armscor at his own behest.[54] But, despite these hearings, Chippy Shaik was never brought to book over his failure to declare his conflict of interests during the acquisition of the corvette combat suite. He was also never made to answer to the fact that, during the Scopa hearings, he had misled Parliament over the relationship between Thomson and African Defence Systems. As he was a civil servant at the time, he was bound by the rules governing civil servant conduct, and should arguably have been held accountable according to those rules. Repeated requests for this to take place by Andrew Feinstein, amongst others, have been dismissed.[55]

Shaik has never been charged or even fully investigated over his alleged receipt of $3m in bribes from the German

Frigate Consortium. In August 2007, Justice Minister Brigitte Mabandla confirmed in Parliament that he was, indeed, never subject to a fully fledged criminal investigation by the Scorpions. This was the case, according to Mabandla, because the initial Three Agency investigation had found 'no sufficiently credible evidence … to expand this league of the enquiry into a fully fledged criminal investigation.'[56] Furthermore, regardless of the German, British and Swiss investigations into claims of bribery against Shaik, Mabandla also confirmed that 'he is likewise currently not the subject of an investigation by the DSO [Directorate of Special Operations/Scorpions].'[57] This decision has invoked the ire of opposition parties, especially the DA, which responded furiously to Mabandla's confirmation: 'We find it unbelievable that the NPA is not actively pursuing this investigation. A possible explanation is that, should the NPA pursue a case against Mr Shaik, who was intricately involved in the procurement process, he could name names and cause tremendous difficulties at an extremely sensitive period for the ruling party in general.'[58]

But Shaik has faced censure in other areas of his life. In 2003, he was awarded a doctoral degree from the University of KwaZulu-Natal after completing his doctoral thesis entitled 'Development of higher-order theories for the analysis of laminated structures under static and thermal loading'. After receiving a report from Richard Young that the doctoral thesis had been substantially plagiarised,[59] the University conducted its own investigation into the matter. The result was damning: Shaik had plagiarised almost two full chapters of his thesis, taking the material from existing journal reports and books on the subject and even going so far as to translate a text from Russian to English to accomplish the feat. In February 2008, after hearing this evidence, the University's Senate passed a resolution notifying the public that 'the PhD degree awarded to Shamin [Chippy] Shaik, student number 961129282 [has been] withdrawn.'[60]

In response to the breaking of the PhD story, Chippy Shaik threatened to pack his bags and relocate to Australia. As yet, he has not done so. Last heard, he was selling his home in Johannesburg's northern suburb of Fourways and moving to Durban, but denied that he was trying to leave the country.[61]

WHAT ABOUT THE OTHER 4X4S?

When Tony Yengeni received his Mercedes-Benz at a discounted rate in 1998, it quickly emerged that he was not the only figure to benefit from the largesse of Michael Woerfel and European Aeronautic Defence and Space (EADS). When EADS was initially questioned about the matter, they confirmed that over 30 South African VIPs had received discounts on their cars. EADS went so far, in July 2001, as to provide a full list of the VIPs and the discounts that they received.[62]

While Yengeni received the largest discount, the remaining 30 VIPS received discounts ranging from 3,28 per cent to 30,50 per cent of the advertised price.[63] The full list made for intriguing reading, as it emerged that numerous key players in the Arms Deal had received their 4x4s through much the same channels as Yengeni. Included in the list of discount recipients were, amongst others, Siphiwe Nyanda (the Chief of the SANDF at the time of the Arms Deal) who received two cars discounted at a rate of 17.26 per cent and 15.11 per cent; Llew Swan (the former Armscor chief executive) who received a 30,50 per cent discount (the second biggest after Yengeni); and Vanan Pillay (one of the Department of Trade and Industry's representatives during the Arms Deal negotiations) whose 29,02 per cent discount made him the recipient of the third-largest price cut.[64]

As yet, no figure besides Tony Yengeni has been charged with any criminal offence. Michael Woerfel, the man through whom many of the deals were arranged, was freed from criminal prosecution in 2003 when Yengeni submitted his plea-bargain admission of guilt for fraud.[65] As Yengeni's charges had been reduced from corruption to fraud, the State could no longer make a watertight legal case against Woerfel.[66] In Germany, however, Woerfel was less fortunate. Although he was not able to be charged on a count of corruption in Germany due to the matter not yet being illegal according to German law, he still allegedly paid an acknowledgement of guilt fine of DM15 000 (R71 896) for embezzlement.[67]

The only other official who has been inconvenienced as a result of his discounted Merc is Vanan Pillay. In February 2002, Pillay was brought before a disciplinary committee of the Department of Trade and Industry. The committee, after hearing evidence, found that Pillay had contravened the public service's code of conduct in accepting a R55 000 discount on his Mercedes-Benz.[68] In May the same year, Alec Erwin upheld the decision of the DTI on appeal, and Pillay was fired.[69] He has never been charged with criminal misconduct.

Patricia de Lille, in 2007, made it clear that she intended to pursue the matter. In March 2007, she started legal proceedings that aimed to charge the 29 other recipients (excluding Yengeni) of luxury vehicles. De Lille instructed her lawyers to apply for the right to prosecute the 29 individuals in her private capacity: a most unusual motion that would, if successful, mean that the State would have to provide all evidence gathered on the matter by the NPA.[70] As yet, no indication has been given as to whether De Lille has been successful in this application.

WHITHER THE SCORPIONS?

In pursuing their investigations of allegations of widespread corruption around the Arms Deal and other less-than-kosher dealings of the government in power, the Scorpions have become a lightning-rod for conspiracy theories and vicious attacks. These began as early as 2001, when Tony Yengeni decried 'the number of white people' in the Scorpions. 'The guys who persecuted us are in control,' he went on to claim.[71] As a result of these sorts of claims, moves have been made to close the Scorpions down, and to transfer their existing investigators into a new unit under the auspices of the South African Police Service (SAPS).

Most recently, the protracted corruption trial of Jacob Zuma has seen the Scorpions come in for some heavy criticism from the ANC and its alliance partners, Cosatu and the SACP, which have argued for the need to close the unit down. Three mutually reinforcing claims have been advanced to support the scrapping of the Scorpions. First, it is argued that they have been targeting the ANC unfairly in prosecutions and investigations. The most vituperative of these claims came from Gwede Mantashe, the ANC Secretary General, in April 2008. Responding to DA claims that the ANC was trying to close the Scorpions for political reasons, he stated: 'The only thing the DA and the Scorpions have in a common is their persistent hatred of the ANC.'[72] Siphiwe Nyanda similarly argued during a debate at the Institute of Security Studies in 2008 that the Scorpions were 'used to pursue a political agenda and to target certain people in the ANC to the benefit of sectarian and foreign interests'.[73] This, he went on to argue, was shown by the fact that the Scorpions 'were even trying to influence the outcome of Polokwane [the ANC's 2007 National Conference] by issuing statements on Jacob Zuma. All of this amounts to human rights violations.'[74] In the same speech, Nyanda also confirmed what many commentators had noted, that the decision to disband the Scorpions might have been based on a violent reaction to the prosecution of Jacob Zuma: 'It [the ANC's resolution to disband the Scorpions] was informed by the view of how the DSO conducted itself in relation to Jacob Zuma.'[75]

The second argument advanced against the Scorpions, and which is related to the first, is that the Scorpions are pursuing a particular agenda because they are filled with unreconstructed ex-apartheid operatives. This has tied in neatly with Zuma's claims that the charges levelled against him form part of a political conspiracy attempting to prevent his assumption of power. In April 2008, Gwede Mantashe claimed that the Scorpions had been infiltrated by former apartheid operatives who 'hate the ANC'.[76]

The third argument against the existence of the Scorpions is that they are operating in contravention of the Constitution. This argument has been made most forcefully by Mo Shaik, who argued in a February 2008 article that the intended aim of the Constitution was to ensure that any organisation such as the Scorpions would be 'subject to national legislation and the rule of law, to the authority and oversight of Parliament and to the command, control and oversight of the executive'.[77] However, Shaik continued, the Scorpions' jurisdiction and composition has not been properly defined, and, as such, it did not properly report to the relevant political authorities as stipulated by the Constitution. It had, in Shaik's words, come to be 'above' the Constitution.[78] As a result of this, 'the Scorpions have managed, during the decade of their existence, to resist every attempt to subject their activities to constitutional requirements ... Over the years we have witnessed the leakage of information from the Scorpions to influence the public mindset, smear campaigns, an off-the-record briefing of editors, reports of misuse of funding, abuse of authority, the unauthorised disclosure of information, acts of corruption by members of the NPA, selective investigation and prosecutions, and alleged attempts by the Scorpions' senior management to influence political parties.'[79] It has also been argued that the Constitution directs that only a 'single' defence force and a 'single' police force should exist, and that the Scorpions constitute a violation of this constitutional imperative.[80]

There are, however, easy answers to all these complaints. First, it is incredibly doubtful that the Scorpions have directed the majority of their prosecutions against members of the ANC unfairly and selectively. Indeed, the Scorpions, which have had a 90 per cent conviction success rate,[81] have made a series of major arrests and convictions on matters that have little do with the ANC. These have included, as *The Times* reports, 'more than 200 convictions in cases of urban terror, taxi and political violence; more than 2 200 arrests of syndicate bosses and their henchmen; up to R4-billion worth of contraband taken off the streets; contributing more than R160-million to the Criminal Assets Recovery Account (CARA); disrupting more than 100 syndicates involved in smuggling, corruption, violence and rackets.' And this is just the beginning. The Scorpions have also investigated high-level cases of corporate fraud and corruption including the 'collapse of Saambou bank and the health company LeisureNet', as well as claims of corruption in the public service.[82] Compared to the arrest of 2 200 syndicate bosses and 200 convictions in cases of urban terror, the convictions of Tony Yengeni and Shabir Shaik, and the prosecution of Jacob Zuma, pale into insignificance. If anything, the Scorpions might legitimately be accused of having a penchant for arresting criminals.

Secondly, there seems to be little evidence that the Scorpions have been 'infiltrated' by apartheid operatives. According to the NPA, over 95 per cent of all staff members of the Scorpions (or 512 out of 532) had been given security clearances, or were currently being vetted by the National Intelligence Agency.[83]

Lastly, it is still to be determined whether or not the Scorpions' existence violates any section of the Constitution. A case brought against the unit by Mac Maharaj on these grounds has yet to be heard by the Constitutional Court[84] (raising the question of why this matter should not, instead of being pushed hastily through Parliament, await the outcome of the Court's ruling). According to Judge Sisi Khampepe, who was commissioned to investigate the future of the Scorpions, there is no constitutional reason why it should not exist in the form that it does (although she did recommend that oversight of the Scorpions be moved from the Minister of Justice to the Minister of Safety and Security).[85] Her report, which was released in May 2008, two years after its completion, clearly states:

> The rationale for the establishment of the DSO was precipitated by intolerable levels of crime. Despite indications

that crime is dropping, it is my view that organised crime still presents a threat that needs to be addressed through an effective, comprehensive strategy. The argument that the rationale no longer holds since the levels of crime are showing a decline is therefore devoid of merit. For this reason, it is my considered finding that the DSO still has a place in the government's law enforcement plan.

It is my recommendation that, notwithstanding indications that organised crime is being addressed on a concerted basis, the rationale for the establishment of the DSO is as valid today as it was at conception. With regard to the location of the DSO, many endorsed the SAPS argument in favour of locating the DSO within its ranks. But this contention was not supported by cogent constitutional or factual argument.

After careful consideration of the evidence, I am persuaded that no compelling argument has been made to point to the DSO's establishment as unconstitutional. It is my considered conclusion that the location of the DSO within the NPA is constitutional and jurisprudentially sound.[86]

Regardless of these facts, the writing is almost certainly on the wall for the Scorpions. In December 2007, the ANC passed a resolution at its National Conference in Polokwane that 'the constitutional imperative that there should be a single police service should be implemented ... The Directorate of Special Prosecutions [should therefore] be dissolved.'[87] This decision was agreed to by Cabinet, which, at the end of April 2008, approved the General Law Amendment Bill and the National Prosecuting Amendment Bill, both of which combine to scrap the Scorpions and move its investigators into the SAPS, and also give the Minister of

Safety and Security the powers to suspend any investigator considered to be a 'security risk'.[88] The matter still has to be heard in front of Parliament, where the issue will finally be decided. But, considering that the ANC majority has already agreed to the dissolution of the Scorpions during the 2007 Polokwane Conference, it would come as a huge surprise if the ANC's parliamentary majority does not pass the Bills.

The strange thing about these moves is that, even if the Scorpions are scrapped, the most high-profile of the NPA's 'selective prosecutions', the Jacob Zuma trial, will still go ahead. This is because the matter is now before the court, and because it is not the NPA, but the Scorpions itself, that are under review. If, as has been argued by many (and confirmed by the ANC's Siphiwe Nyanda), the scrapping of the Scorpions has been in part motivated by a desire to respond to Jacob Zuma's perceived persecution, why would the ANC bother trying to quash the Scorpions if it did not affect the outcome of the Zuma trial?

WHY IS THE ANC SO CONCERNED?

If anything, the preceding chapters in this book have shown the energy with which the government in power has attempted to cover up and quash any full-on investigation into the Arms Deal. The reaction of the government to the Scopa hearings, as well as the revelations that emerged in the wake of the presentation of the Joint Investigation Report, are only two examples of this.

Explaining this considered attempt to prevent full disclosure of all aspects of the Arms Deal has created somewhat of a problem for outside observers. The idea that the government has tried to quash investigations because it is embarrassed by the extent of mismanagement in the Arms Deal only goes so far. The fact that some government ministers have been accused of corruption has provided another causal explanation, although this, too, can only explain so much. Indeed, considering how well the general South African public responds to righteous crusaders and fighters of corruption (for corruption on the scale of the Arms Deal can only bring pain to the poorest of the poor), it seems strange that the ministers and government officials who have not been accused of corruption have not tried, at all times, to distance themselves from the others who have been accused, and, more importantly, led attempts to clean the government of any potentially (or actually) corrupt politicians.

But there might be a different reason for the ANC's consistent and determined attempts to prevent an unfettered examination of the Arms Deal. Perhaps the ANC, itself, was a beneficiary of corrupt and inappropriate payments. Certainly, this is the opinion of Andrew Feinstein. Writing in 2007, Feinstein recalled how, while he was investigating the Arms Deal, he was warned by a trusted comrade of this possibility:

> '[A] senior member of the ANC's NEC invited me to his house one Sunday. Sitting outside in the sunshine, he explained to me that I was never going to 'win this thing'.
>
> 'Why not?' I demanded.
>
> 'Because we received money from some of the winning companies. How do you think we funded the 1999 election?'
>
> I didn't know what to say. I tried to think of a reason why this comrade might want to mislead me, but couldn't.'[89]

The allegations of broader ANC malfeasance received a somewhat backhanded boost during the trial against Schabir Shaik. As discussed in Chapter 7, Schabir Shaik incorporated a company, Floryn Investments, in June 1994.[90] He toyed with the idea of making the ANC a 'nominal' shareholder in the company: a move that was rejected out of hand by the ANC and, in particular, Thabo Mbeki.[91] But, as Shaik later claimed under oath, Floryn Investments was used to channel donations to the ANC. He noted: 'I first thought of giving the ANC shares in the company, but I had to respect Mbeki's view. At the same time I knew about the ANC's need for funds.'[92] The donations were substantial, and included, as Shaik claimed, roughly R1m paid to the ANC from the accounts of Nkobi Holdings between 1998 and 1999.[93]

This was a remarkable admission, considering the timeframe in which the Arms Deal took place: it was between 1998 and 1999, remember, that the Arms Deal's preferred suppliers were chosen and the deal signed. It was also the period in which Shaik was able to insert his company, Nkobi, as Thomson's joint-venture partner in South Africa (to supply the combat suites for the corvettes), and the period in which Thomson was chosen as the supplier to provide the combat suites for the corvettes. This was done, as is shown above, when other bidders were, in fact, arguably more suitable candidates. Even more perturbing was the fact that none of these donations were ever declared in the financial statements of Floryn Investments,[94] even though Shaik claims that the amounts were paid: suggesting that he had perhaps attempted to ensure that there would be no paper trail linking payments from Floryn Investments to the ANC. The ANC has rejected any idea that the organisation benefited in any way from any deals involving Nkobi or Floryn Investments. In 2003, ANC spokesperson Smuts

Ngonyama argued that 'the ANC has no relationship with Floryn Investments, or with Nkobi Holdings for that matter.' Ngonyama further claimed that any claims of corruption involving the ANC were founded in a malicious desire to smear the organisation: 'We wish to emphasise that the ANC has never benefited from the arms deal, directly or indirectly, and any suggestions to the contrary are nothing more than slander aimed at undermining the integrity of the ANC.'[95] That Shaik might have made these payments to the ANC to influence matters in favour of Thomson and Nkobi is not yet clear, and has, as yet, not been tested in a court of law. But it cannot fail to raise eyebrows.

In March 2008, the *Mail & Guardian* broke another story that suggested that the ANC might have benefited improperly from the Arms Deal. According to the story, which was based on a set of documents 'obtained by the *Mail & Guardian*', ThyssenKrupp (the German company that was part of the GFC, which won the contracts to supply the corvette ship platforms), had written repeatedly to Justice Minister Brigitte Mabandla to 'prevent the seizure of documents and interrogation of witnesses in South Africa'.[96] Part of the reason why ThyssenKrupp has tried to do so, the story alleges, is because of the role played by one Tony Georgiadis (the ex-husband of FW de Klerk's current wife).

Georgiadis's company, Alandis, was raided by the UK's Serious Fraud Office in November 2007 as part of the UK and German investigations into allegations of corruption in the South African Arms Deal.[97] The aim: to investigate whether Georgiades had any role in corrupt activities in South Africa. According to the search warrant used in raiding his property, it is alleged that Georgiades met with representatives of Thyssen as early as 1994, and had entered into an agreement with the company on 26 April 1995. These agreements, it is alleged, were signed as part of an 'agency' or 'commission' agreement with Georgiades, which would see him lobbying for the arms company in South Africa. As part of this agreement, it is claimed, Georgiades received $22m from Thyssen, which was paid into an offshore company, Mallar. These payments, it is alleged, were subsequently channelled 'to South African government officials and Cabinet ministers'.[98] While these claims in themselves are shocking, of even more concern is the allegation that Georgiades paid R500 000 to the ANC (and a further R500 000 to both the Nelson Mandela Children's Fund and a development charity run by Graça Machel in Mozambique) in 1999.[99] If this is true, and if it is true that Georgiades was acting as an agent for Thyssen in South Africa, it will again raise some serious questions as to whether the ANC had benefited from the largesse of a winning bidder in the Arms Deal.

Whatever the reality of the above allegations, what is certain is that, in the years after the ANC assumed power, it faced a constant financial struggle. At the 49th National Conference, held in Bloemfontein in December 1994, this was candidly admitted as a concern: 'ANC structures are having to operate in an environment where foreign funding has dwindled to a trickle. The years of illegality have bred a dependence on external funding which the ANC is finding difficult to escape from. No comprehensive plans have been developed – at national, provincial and branch level – to make the ANC financially self-sufficient.'[100] It later emerged during the Shaik trial that, by 1995, the ANC 'was facing a debt of R40 million to its bankers'.[101] Indeed, as the Treasurer-General of the ANC admitted in December 1997: 'by April 1995 we were in the "black" (out of the "red"). But by June we were already deep in the red again. This in and out of red was to characterize our period in office.'[102] This was because, among other factors:

> The ANC had largely depended on friendly countries and institutions for it's [sic] funds. Most of these donors were in foreign lands. The 1994 elections created the perception or expectation that a ruling Party had access to the country's resources. Also, the purpose for which we were funded, to defeat apartheid, had been accomplished. So our erstwhile donors were reluctant or unable to continue funding us. Our members' contributions were and are negligible. In many ways we had become dependent on the President's initiatives and those of some officials for income.[103]

Even more worrying, the TG noted in the same address, was the fact that many of the initiatives that the party had launched had 'failed to yield dividends'.[104] The result was, the TG argued, an untenable situation: 'An organization which does not have the resources to sustain itself cannot hope to survive. It does not matter how noble an organization's ideals and policies are, these remain meaningless for as long as they cannot be implemented. Implementation largely depends on funds.'[105]

And yet, scarcely a year later, with no improvement expected in the ANC's balance sheets, it was able to contest a costly and high-profile national election. Just how this was achieved and whether its path was smoothed by the largesse of arms companies, is still, and will probably remain for some time, one of the many unanswered questions of the new South Africa.

APPENDICES

APPENDIX A

WHO'S WHO AND WHAT'S WHAT IN THE ARMS DEAL

THE PEOPLE

Achterberg, Nicholas: A relatively unknown quantity, Achterberg has allegedly claimed that he has proof that Thabo Mbeki received a bribe from ThyssenKrupp.

Agent RS452: The name of an apartheid security force agent. Bulelani Ngcuka was accused in 2003 of being Agent RS452, which led to the establishment of the Hefer Commission of Enquiry tasked with investigating the claim. It emerged that Agent RS452 was actually Vanessa Brereton (q.v.)

Baqwa, Selby: Former Public Protector who served from 1995 to 2002. Baqwa formed one prong of the Three Agency investigation that presented its report, known as the Joint Investigation Report, to Parliament in November 2001.

Brereton, Vanessa: an Eastern Cape human rights lawyer who worked for the apartheid security forces during 'Operation Crocus', which attempted to follow the activities of the white left in the Cape. Brereton tearfully admitted in 2003 to being Agent RS452 in an attempt to move on from her past.

Charter, Richard: Charter, now deceased, was alleged by the Serious Fraud Office (UK) to have received R27m as covert commission for his work as British Aerospace's registered agent in SA, and a further R350m in covert commissions from the company. Charter chaired the Airborne Trust, which facilitated BAe's R4.5m donation to the MK Military Veterans Association, of which Joe Modise was Honorary President.

Chiba, Laloo: An ANC stalwart who had served time on Robben Island. He served as an ANC representative on Scopa and worked together with Andrew Feinstein and Gavin Woods in attempting to uncover suspected malfeasance in the arms deal.

Crawford-Browne, Terry: A high-profile critic of the arms deal, and the South African chairman of Economists Allied For Arms Reduction (ECAAR). He published a book, *Eye on the Money*, to detail his experiences of fighting against the Arms Deal. He attempted to have the Arms Deal cancelled in a series of high-profile trials, but failed in his attempts.

Delique, Sue: Former secretary to Alain Thetard, the head of operations for the arms company Thomson-CSF. During Schabir Shaik's trial, she testified that she had typed up a handwritten version of the infamous 'encrypted fax' and faxed it to Thomson's head office in France.

De Lille, Patricia: The fiery parliamentarian who at first represented the Pan Africanist Congress, then formed her own party, the Independent Democrats (ID). De Lille broke the story of Arms Deal corruption in 1999 when she presented a document signed by 'concerned ANC MPs' to Parliament that alleged widespread corruption.

De Waal, Tielman: Former MD of Armscor. In 1995 he argued that purchasing four navy corvettes (which he estimated would cost R1.7bn) would generate a huge inflow of cash for the country through offset commitments.

Erwin, Alec: Minister of Trade and Industry. Erwin was part of the group of four Ministers who gave a press briefing in January 2001 in which they claimed that Scopa and the Auditor-General did not understand the Arms Deal. Erwin was also part of the Cabinet sub-committee tasked with overseeing the arms procurement process.

Esterhuyse, HD: Former General Manager for acquisitions of aeronautic and marine supplies for Armscor. Esterhuyse was noted for his recollection that, as early as March 1997, UK's Defence Export Organisation was inappropriately wooing SA officials.

Fakie, Shauket: Auditor-General from 2000 to 2007, whereafter he moved to head MTN's business risk management. Fakie's submitted two key reports in the Arms Deal saga. The first, released in 2000, noted serious concerns about the rectitude of the Arms Deal. The second, submitted as part of the Joint Investigation Report into the Arms Deal, was released in November 2001. Fakie's role in writing the reports was subject to severe controversy after he admitted that he had submitted a draft of the Joint Investigation Report to the executive for comment. He was taken to court by Richard Young and forced, as a result, to provide all documents (including drafts of the Joint Investigation Report) to Richard Young or face contempt of court. The documents released to Richard Young show that the final Joint Investigation Report was heavily edited before it was published. Fakie admittedto Parliament that the Report was edited, but claimed there were no major changes to its contents or findings.

Feinstein, Andrew: ANC MP and former leader of the ANC Study Group that formed the ANC component on Scopa. Together with Gavin Woods, Feinstein strongly criticised the Arms Deal and argued for the need for it to be investigated by a 'super-team' of investigators, including Judge Willem Heath. Feinstein came under strong pressure from the ANC leadership to stop his criticism of the Arms Deal, and, when he refused, was demoted from his position as head of the ANC component on Scopa. He resigned from Parliament in August 2001 after being taken to task for refusing to vote with the ANC in a motion of support of Parliamentary Speaker Frene Ginwala. Feinstein recently published a warts-and-all account of the Arms Deal, *After the Party*, which is highly recommended reading for anyone interested in the Arms Deal.

Georgiades, Tony: Ex-husband of FW de Klerk's current wife. In 2008, it was alleged by German and British authorities that Georgiades had acted as agent for ThyssenKrupp and may have funnelled a portion of $22m in bribes to SA ministers through his company, Mallar. Georgiades is also alleged to have made three R500 000 donations to the ANC, Nelson Mandela Children's Fund and Graça Machel's Mozambique development charity in 1999. However, as the German investigation was stopped by German authorities, these remain untested allegations and, as such, should be treated with caution.

Ginwala, Frene: Speaker of the National Assembly from 1994 to 2004. Ginwala has attracted criticism for her alleged role in neutering Scopa's controversial 14th Report. In 2007, she was appointed by Thabo Mbeki to conduct an enquiry into the National Director of Public Prosecutions, Vusi Pikoli, as to whether he is fit to hold office.

Heath, Willem (Judge): A high-profile judge who headed the Special Investigating Unit, also known as the Heath Unit. In 2000, Scopa recommended that Heath be included in an investigating team tasked with examining malfeasance in the Arms Deal. However, his inclusion was blocked by President Thabo Mbeki. Heath's Unit had wide-ranging powers, including the legal right to cancel contracts if they were found to have been subject to corruption.

Hefer, Joos (Judge): The judge who presided over the Hefer Commission of Enquiry formed to investigate whether Bulelani Ngcuka was an apartheid spy. In his judgment, he found that Ngcuka was probably not a spy, but attacked Ngcuka's unit for persistent leaks to the media about ongoing investigations undertaken by the NPA and the Scorpions.

Hlongwane, Fana: Former advisor to Joe Modise. The UK's Serious Fraud Office has alleged that Hlongwane received a substantial commission for 'work done on the Gripen project'. The matter is still under investigation.

Hlophe, John (Judge): Judge President of the Cape High Court. In May 2008, judges of the Constitutional Court laid a complaint against Judge Hlophe with the Judicial Services Commission. The complaint alleged that Hlophe had attempted to improperly influence the outcome of the Constitutional Court's pending decision over appeals lodged by Jacob Zuma and Thint to have search warrants used to seize evidence be declared unconstitutional. Hlophe rejects the allegations, and claims that the complaint was motivated by an 'ulterior motive': to ensure that he can no longer hold office. The matter is still to be heard by the Judicial Services Commission.

Kasrils, Ronnie: Former Deputy Minister of Defence, and a former member of MK's High Command in exile. Kasrils gave vocal support to the Arms Deal in the mid-1990s, and famously argued that the offsets that would flow from the Arms Deal would 'delight the Minister of Finance'. He currently serves as Minister for Intelligence Services.

Khampepe, Sisi (Judge): High-profile judge appointed by Thabo Mbeki in September 2006 to investigate whether or not the Scorpions should be scrapped based on constitutional concerns. Her report was only released to the public in May 2008 after the DA had successfully petitioned the government under the terms of the Promotion of Access to Information Act. Khampepe found that there was no constitutional reason for the Scorpions to be disbanded or moved from the NPA into the South African Police Service.

Kleuver, Henry: Former Auditor-General; replaced by his former deputy, Shauket Fakie, in 2000.

Lekota, Mosiuoa 'Terror': Minister of Defence, appointed in 1999. Lekota was part of the group of four Ministers who gave a press briefing in January 2001 in which they claimed that Scopa and the Auditor-General did not understand the Arms Deal. He also defended the Arms Deal against claims of corruption by arguing that the State could only be held liable for negotiations undertaken in signing primary contracts and could not take responsibility for any corruption in the selection of sub-contractors.

Mabandla, Brigitte: Current Minister of Justice and Constitutional Development, appointed in 2004. In 2007, she confirmed in Parliament that Chippy Shaik was not subject to any investigations regarding allegations of corruption levelled against him.

Maharaj, Mac: A hero of the liberation struggle who headed one of the ANC's most successful underground campaigns in the 1980s, Operation Vula. In 2003, he supported claims that Bulelani Ngcuka was an apartheid spy. Maharaj was subject to an investigation by the Scorpions into alleged corruption. However, he has never been charged and the company for which he worked at the time, Discovery Holdings, released a report clearing him of any wrongdoing. Maharaj is currently contesting the constitutional validity of the Scorpions.

Manuel, Trevor: Minister of Finance from 1996 to date. On 3 December 1999, Manuel signed the loan agreements that provided the means by which SA could undertake the Arms Deal.

Maqhubela, Ntobeko: A former ANC and MK operative in the Durban area in the 1980s. After a seeming setup, he was arrested and sentenced to 20 years in prison for seditious activities by the apartheid government. During the Hefer Commission of Enquiry, Maqhubela testified that there was no way that Ngcuka could have been an apartheid spy or sold out his Durban comrades.

Masekela, Barbara: SA's former ambassador to the US and a close Mbeki confidant. In 2008, she confirmed that Mbeki had met with French arms officials, which Mbeki has claimed he cannot remember.

Mbeki, Thabo: Deputy President of SA from 1994 to 1999, and President of SA from 1999 to date. Mbeki chaired the Cabinet sub-committee that oversaw the arms procurement process. He became increasingly unpopular after he dismissed Jacob Zuma as Deputy President in 2005, and was defeated by him in the election to become President of the ANC at the Polokwane National Conference in December 2007. It has been alleged that Mbeki received a kickback from a winning arms company. Mbeki has responded furiously to any claims of corruption in the Arms Deal, arguing that these claims are motivated by racism. In 2008, the *Sunday Times* alleged that Thabo Mbeki had received a R30m bribe from MAN Ferrostaal, German company that formed part of the GSC. The Presidency vehemently denied the allegations and was considering its legal options. Ferrostaal also denied the allegations. A subsequent *Mail & Guardian* report found that the allegations were drawn from a single source – an ex-spy, Mhleli 'Paul' Madaka, who died in 2007 following a car accident, meaning that the claims could not be corroborated.

Meiring, George (General): Former head of the SANDF. General Meiring, along with General Pierre Steyn, was a vocal opponent of awarding the contract to supply LIFT to BAe's Hawk.

Modise, Joe: Minister of Defence from 1994 to early 1999. Modise has been persistently linked to allegations of corruption for his role in the Arms Deal. Most famously, he urged the Arms Deal selection team to ignore cost as a criterion when assessing whether or not to purchase BAe's Hawk. He was criticised for taking a position as a director of Conlog, a company that was slated to receive a substantial contract flowing from BAe's offset commitments. Modise died in November 2001.

Mushwana, Lawrence: Public Protector from 2002 to date. In May 2004, after receiving a complaint from Jacob Zuma regarding Bulelani Ngcuka's claim that there was a *prima facie* case of corruption against Zuma, Mushwana tabled a biting report that found that Ngcuka had infringed on Zuma's constitutional rights by making the statement. Mushwana's report courted massive controversy, although the parliamentary sub-committee tasked with discussing it later only 'noted' rather than 'accepted' it, meaning that it would not take any action based on Mushwana's report.

Motlanthe, Kgalema: Former Secretary-General of the ANC, elected as Deputy President of the organisation during the 2007 ANC National Conference in Polokwane. It has been widely speculated that, if Jacob Zuma is found guilty of corruption in his upcoming trial, Motlanthe may be put forward by the ANC as its presidential candidate in 2009.

Moynot, Jean-Pierre Robert: Moynot was listed as the representative of Thint Holdings and Thint Pty in both the corruption indictments served on Thint and Zuma. He was a director of both companies at two different stages (see Appendix C).

Moyses, Bill: The magistrate who presided over Tony Yengeni's case. After Yengeni had admitted to fraud in 2003, Moyses sentenced Yengeni to four years in prison, noting that: 'I regret to say that the example you set as Chief Whip of the ANC is shocking.'

Munusamy, Ranjeni: Former *Sunday Times* journalist who leaked Mo Shaik's intelligence report alleging that Bulelani Ngcuka was an apartheid spy to *City Press*.

Naidoo, Jay: Former Minister with no Portfolio in charge of the government's Reconstruction and Development Programme, and former Minister for Posts, Telecommunications and Broadcasting. It was claimed in 1995 that Naidoo was a vocal critic of any arms purchases. He is not to be confused with Jayendra Naidoo.

Naidoo, Jayendra: The chief negotiator for the SA government during the arms procurement process. In 2000, Jayendra Naidoo, along with Chippy Shaik, admitted that arms companies only faced a 10 per cent penalty if they failed to deliver on their offset commitments.

Ngcuka, Bulelani: Former National Director of Public Prosecutions, appointed to the position in July 1998. Ngcuka resigned from the position in July 2004 following the presentation of the Mushwana report and the fallout that ensued. Ngcuka was a high-profile figure in the Arms Deal, and most famously made the comment that there was a *prima facie* case of corruption against Jacob Zuma. In 2003, he was accused of being an apartheid spy, but was cleared of the charge by the Hefer Commission of Enquiry.

Nkobi, Thomas: Former Treasurer-General of the ANC, and inspiration for the name of Schabir Shaik's Nkobi group of companies.

Nyanda, Siphiwe: Former Chief of the SANDF, who resigned from the position in 2005. It has been alleged that Nyanda received a discounted luxury vehicle from EADS, a winning contractor in the Arms Deal.

Pahad, Essop: Current Minister in the Presidency, a position to which he was appointed in 1999. Pahad is seen as very close to Thabo Mbeki. Andrew Feinstein has claimed that Essop Pahad was sent to bring the ANC component of Scopa into line following the presentation of Scopa's 14th Report.

Pikoli, Vusi (Advocate): The man who was appointed to replace Bulelani Ngcuka as the National Director of Public Prosecutions in 2005. In June 2005, he authorised the NPA to lay charges of corruption against Jacob Zuma. He was suspended by Thabo Mbeki in 2007. Mbeki claimed that this was because of an irreconcilable breakdown in the relationship between Pikoli and Justice Minister Brigitte Mabandla. Pikoli has, in turn, claimed that he was suspended because he attempted to prosecute Jackie Selebi, the National Commissioner of the SAPS, against the wishes of Thabo Mbeki. The matter has been referred to an enquiry headed by Frene Ginwala, which is still to present its findings.

Pillay, Vanan: A representative of the Department of Trade and Industry who took part in Arms Deal negotiations. He was fired from the Department of Trade and Industry in 2002 for accepting a R55 000 discount on a Mercedes-Benz purchased through DASA, a company that had successfully bid for a contract arising from the Arms Deal.

Radebe, Jeff: Former Minister of Public Enterprise from 1999 to 2004, and current Minister of Transport. Radebe was part of the group of four ministers who gave a press briefing in January 2001 in which they claimed that Scopa and the Auditor-General did not understand the Arms Deal.

Shaik, Mo: former head of ANC intelligence in SA, Shaik claimed in 2003 that Bulelani Ngcuka had acted as an apartheid spy, a charge that was dismissed by the Hefer Commission of Enquiry. He admitted under testimony during the Hefer hearings that he had made the allegations against Ngcuka in order to protect the honour of Jacob Zuma. He is brother to Schabir, Chippy and Yunis Shaik.

Shaik, Schabir: Jacob Zuma's former financial advisor. Shaik was found guilty in 2005 on two counts of corruption, and one count of fraud, for having a corrupt relationship with Jacob Zuma. He was sentenced to 15 years in prison. Shaik's appeals against the charges have failed at every attempt and he is currently serving his 15 year sentence. He is brother to Mo, Chippy and Yunis Shaik.

Shaik, Shamin 'Chippy': A key mover-and-shaker in the Arms Deal. Chippy Shaik was appointed as the Chief of Acquisitions for the Department of Defence in 1998, and was a key player in the evaluation process that led to the eventual selection of the preferred suppliers in the Arms Deal. In 2001, the Joint Investigation Report slammed Shaik for failing to recuse himself from meetings at which the selection of Schabir Shaik's African Defence System as a subcontractor to supply the information management system for the corvettes was discussed. He has subsequently been alleged to have received $3m from a successful bidder in the Arms Deal, but has never been charged on any count of corruption. In 2008, Shaik's PhD degree was withdrawn by the University of KwaZulu-Natal after it emerged that he had substantially plagiarised from other sources in writing the thesis. He is brother to Schabir, Mo and Yunis Shaik.

Sigcau, Stella: Former Minister of Public Enterprise who served on the Cabinet sub-committee tasked with overseeing the arms procurement process.

Simpson-Anderson, Robert (Vice Admiral): Former head of the SA Navy. From 1993 to 1995, he was a key player in supporting the purchase of four corvettes at a cost of R1.7bn.

Singh, Bianca: Former Secretary to Schabir Shaik. Singh testified during his corruption trial that he had frequently turned to Jacob Zuma for help in business and that money had frequently been transferred from Shaik's account to Zuma's. She resigned as Shaik's assistant after personal conflict during a trip to meet Thomson-CSF representatives in Mauritius.

Squires, Hilary (Judge): The judge who presided over the case of corruption lodged against Schabir Shaik. Squires delivered his judgment on 31 May 2005, finding Shaik guilty on two counts of corruption and one count of fraud. His decision was subsequently upheld by two further courts of appeal.

Swan, Llew: Former Chief Executive of Armscor. According to a list released by DASA of discount cars provided to South African 'VIPs', Swan was allegedly a recipient of a 30.5 per cent discount on a luxury vehicle. Independent Democrat leader Patricia de Lille subsequently petitioned for the right to privately prosecute Swan, among other recipients, for receiving the discounts. No indication has been given as to whether De Lille's request has failed or succeeded.

Steyn, Pierre (General): The former Secretary of Defence. Steyn testified during the Joint Investigation hearings into the Arms Deal that he felt that the selection of BAe's Hawk had been predetermined by Minister Joe Modise, even though the Hawk was not the Air Force's first choice of trainer jet. Steyn attempted to block the Hawk being presented to Cabinet as a possible candidate, but was overruled by Joe Modise. Steyn resigned from his position in 1998 over the Hawk scandal, which he explained in 2007: 'as secretary of defence, I was going to have to account for the costs to Parliament, which I couldn't do'.

Taljaard, Raenette: Was DA Spokesperson on Finance, now Director of the Helen Suzman Foundation. She has been an outspoken critic of corruption in the Arms Deal. In 2003, she submitted questions to Zuma in Parliament asking whether he had met Shaik and Thetard in Durban on 11 March 2000 or on any date to discuss the alleged bribe paid to Zuma. In Zuma's second indictment, served in December 2007, Zuma was charged with fraud for lying to Parliament in response to Taljaard's question.

Thetard, Alain: Former Chief Executive of Thales/Thomson's SA subsidiary, Thint. During Judge Hilary Squires' judgment on the corruption charges faced by Schabir Shaik, it was accepted that Thetard had authored the famous 'encrypted fax' that stated that Jacob Zuma was to receive a R500 000 a year retainer from the arms company in return for protection from investigation. Squires found that, in all likelihood, Thetard had sent the fax to Thomson's head office in France. Thetard was never charged with corruption. Instead, the charges were withdrawn in return for him submitting an affidavit admitting to writing the fax. He later submitted a second affidavit that contradicted the first.

Van der Walt, Johan: The auditor employed by the State to track and monitor the finances of Schabir Shaik and Jacob Zuma. During Shaik's trial, Van der Walt spent days in the witness box outlining how Shaik had made corrupt payments to Zuma.

Woerfel, Michael: The man in charge of marketing for DASA, who is alleged to have provided 30 discounted luxury vehicles to various SA VIPs in suspicious circumstances. Woerfel organised Tony Yengeni's vehicle discount, and was initially charged with corruption along with Yengeni. After Tony Yengeni pleaded guilty to fraud, but not corruption, the charges were dropped against Woerfel. However, it has been alleged that he has subsequently paid an admission of guilt fine in Germany for embezzlement.

Woodburne, Lambert 'Woody' (Vice Admiral): Former head of the SA Navy, replaced by Robert Simpson-Anderson in 1992. Woodburne retired from the Navy after suffering personal problems, but also severely criticised the funding cuts suffered by the Navy from 1989 onwards.

Woods, Gavin: The former IFP member of Scopa. Together with Andrew Feinstein, Woods established the *modus operandi* of Scopa, and led its investigation into the Arms Deal. Woods was frustrated after Feinstein's resignation from Parliament by the ANC's partisan approach to Scopa politics. After writing two scathing reports on the neutering of Scopa, Woods resigned in 2002.

Yengeni, Tony: The ANC MP who served as Chief Whip in Parliament, as well as the Chairman of the Joint Standing Committee of Defence. In 2001, Yengeni was arrested and charged with fraud, perjury and corruption in relation to his receipt of a discounted luxury Mercedes-Benz 4x4 from Michael Woerfel. He subsequently pleaded guilty to a reduced charge of fraud and was sentenced to four years in prison. He appealed this sentence until 2006, when he was finally sent to prison. He spent less than four months in prison before being released on parole. Since then, he has risen up the ANC ranks, and is currently a member of the ANC's National Working Committee, a 20-person council that is arguably the most important and powerful structure in the ruling party.

Young, Richard: Director of C^2I^2, the company that lost the bid to provide the information management systems for the corvettes to Schabir Shaik's African Defence Systems. Young has consistently claimed that this was the result of fraudulent or corrupt activity. In 2003, he successfully took Auditor-General Shauket Fakie to court to compel him to release all the documents in possession gathered during his investigation into the Arms Deal. In 2007, Young complained to the University of KwaZulu-Natal about plagiarism in the PhD thesis of Chippy Shaik. As a result of the complaint, Schaik's thesis was reviewed by the University and withdrawn. Young has remained a critical opponent of the arms deal and currently runs the best website on the deal: www.armsdeal-vpo.co.za.

Zuma, Jacob: Deputy President of SA from 1999 to 2005. He was dismissed by Thabo Mbeki from this position after his financial advisor, Schabir Shaik, was found guilty by Judge Hilary Squires on two counts of corruption and one of fraud. Included in the charges against Shaik (for which he was found guilty) was the claim that he had helped Zuma solicit a R500 000 per year payment from Thomson-CSF. Zuma was charged with corruption in 2005, but the case was struck off the role after Judge Herbert Msimang found that the State had taken too long to present its case. In 2007, he was elected President of the ANC during the National Conference at Polokwane. However, in 2008, he was charged once again by the NPA on counts including corruption and racketeering.

THE COMPANIES AND INSTITUTIONS

Aeromacchi: The Italian arms manufacturer whose jet, the MB339, was rejected in favour of BAe's Hawk.

African Defence Systems (ADS): The company that was selected to provide the information management system used in the corvettes purchased by the SA government. The Joint Investigation Report found that the selection of ADS might have been flawed as Chippy Shaik, the brother of Schabir, had failed to recuse himself from meetings discussing the selection of ADS. Schabir Shaik owned a shareholding in ADS through the company Thomson (Pty) (South Africa), in which his Nkobi Holdings had a minority shareholding.

Armscor: The SA defence giant. The arms procurement process was conducted according to Armscor's guidelines and regulations.

Bazan: The Spanish shipyard that seemed to set to win the contract to supply corvettes to the SA Navy in 1995. However, they were forced to resubmit their tender after it was decided to re-start the tendering process. Their ship was rejected in favour of GFC's Meko Corvette, even though the Joint Investigation Report showed that Bazan's bid was the only one that met the minimum specified criteria.

British Aerospace (BAe): the British Arms manufacturer that won the tender to supply both the Gripen and Hawk jets to the SAAF. It has been consistently linked to allegations of corruption by the UK's Serious Fraud Office, which has alleged that the company paid substantial amounts of money to SA politicians and figures of influence in order to secure the Hawk and Gripen contracts.

Conlog: A SA firm specialising in 'prepayment' services. Eyebrows were raised when Joe Modise was appointed a director of the company after he had retired from office, since Conlog had been slated to receive a considerable contract arising from BAe's offset obligations.

DaimlerChrysler Aerospace (DASA): A subsidiary of Daimler-Chrysler. DASA was shown to have ordered a car for Tony Yengeni at a substantially reduced rate. DASA was incorporated into European Aeronautic and Defence (EADS) in 1999. EADS owned 33 per cent of Reutech Radar Systems, which won a contract to supply tracking radars for the corvettes.

Defence Export Services Organisation (UK): An investment and lobbying arm of the UK government. In 1997, DESO presented a procurement package to the SA government that would see SA purchasing Hawks and Gripens from the UK's BAe.

Der Spiegel: The German magazine that has published a number of allegations of corruption that have emerged as a result of the investigation into the Arms Deal undertaken by German authorities.

European Aeronautic Defence and Space (EADS): EADS incorporated DASA in 1999. EADS owned 33 per cent of Reutech Radar Systems, which won a contract to supply tracking radars for the corvettes.

Ferrostaal: A German company, part of the German Submarine Consortium (GSC). In August 2008, the *Sunday Times* alleged that the company had paid a R30m bribe to Thabo Mbeki. The allegation was denied by both the Presidency and Ferrostaal. Ferrostaal listed a steel mill at Coega as its single most important offset proposal in tendering for the submarine contract. However, during the evaluation process, reports by two independent analysts determined that the Coega mill was a risky proposition. The Coega steel mill project was scrapped in 2000, barely six months after the final contracts were signed, as it was economically unviable. The company agreed to institute substitute projects to replace the scrapped proposal. Ferrostaal claimed, in August 2008, that its offset projects were still on track and that the company would meet its offset obligations.

Floryn Investments: One of Schabir Shaik's numerous companies. During Shaik's corruption trial, he claimed that he had used Floryn Investments as a vehicle by which he made substantial donations to the ANC.

German Frigate Consortium: A consortium of companies, including ThyssenKrupp, which won the contract to supply the ship platforms for the corvettes purchased for the SA Navy.

German Submarine Consortium: A consortium of companies that was selected to provide three submarines to the SA Navy.

Joint Standing Committee on Ethics and Members' Interests: A parliamentary watchdog committee tasked with overseeing that MPs did not have any conflict of interest and to monitor the declaration of members' interests. The Committee, in 2001, decided not to investigate the Tony Yengeni saga, although the opposition parties on the Committee rejected the decision.

Joint Investigating Team: The three-pronged team, made up of the Auditor-General's Office, the National Prosecution Authority and the Public Protector, that investigated the Arms Deal between 2000 and 2001, and presented their findings to Parliament in 2001. Their report found substantial problems with the Arms Deal, but was largely considered a whitewash. It later emerged that the report had been substantially edited.

MK Military Veterans Association: An association formed to provide assistance to MK soldiers returning to post-apartheid SA. The association, of which Joe Modise was Honorary President, signed a memorandum of understanding with BAe and the Airborne Trust, according to which the Association was to receive a R4.5m donation from BAe to build a training and agri-business unit on land donated to the Association by the ANC.

Nkobi Holdings: The parent company directed by Schabir Shaik, who holds a majority shareholding. In 1996, Nkobi and Thomson-CSF signed an agreement that ensured that Thomson was bound to conduct its business in SA through Thomson (Pty) (South Africa). Nkobi Investments (a subsidiary of Nkobi Holdings) held a minority shareholding in Thomson (Pty) South Africa. This, in effect, meant that Thomson-CSF was a joint-venture partner with Nkobi in all its SA ventures.

Nkobi Investments: One of Schabir Shaik's subsidiary companies, initially owned entirely by himself. Ownership was later transferred to Nkobi Holdings. Nkobi Investments initially had a minority shareholding in Thomson Holdings (South Africa). It also had a 30 per cent shareholding in Thomson (Pty) (South Africa).

SAAB: A Swedish industrial giant, selected as part of a joint contract with BAe to supply Gripens to the SAAF.

The Scorpions: The crack investigating team that has led most of the investigations and prosecutions arising from the arms deal. Their activities have attracted the ire of the ANC which, in 2007, voted to have the unit scrapped or moved to the SAPS.

Serious Fraud Office (UK): An investigative unit based in the UK. The SFO is currently investigating allegations of corruption made against BAe for its role in the SA arms deal. The SFO has submitted a request for assistance to SA authorities to help with its investigation.

Special Investigating Unit (SIU): Also known as the Heath Unit, under Judge Willem Heath. The Unit had wide-ranging powers, including the legal right to cancel any contract shown to have been conducted corruptly. Scopa recommended that the SIU be included in any investigation of the arms deal: a suggestion that was rejected by the SA government, and Thabo Mbeki in particular.

Thales: See Thomson-CSF International (France)

Thomson-CSF (France): The mammoth French holding company that acts as the parent company for Thomson-CSF International. Thomson-CSF was later renamed Thales. Thomson-CSF was awarded the contract to supply the combat suites for the corvettes purchased by the SA government. Thomson-CSF was bound to conduct its business in SA with Schabir Shaik's Nkobi Holdings according to an agreement reached between the two in 1996.

Thomson-CSF International (France): The French subsidiary of Thomson-CSF. It was later renamed Thales International.

Thomson-CSF Holdings (Southern Africa): The SA subsidiary of Thomson-CSF that was incorporated in SA in 1996 to promote the development of SA industry by entering into joint ventures. Schabir Shaik was a director of the company from 1996 until his resignation in September 1999. Alain Thetard was appointed as a director in April 1998. Nkobi Holdings and Thomson-CSF International (France) were joint shareholders of the company until September 1999, when all shares were transferred to Thomson-CSF International (France)

Thomson (Pty) (South Africa): Another Thomson company. It was also incorporated in July 1996 to promote SA industry by entering into joint ventures. Nkobi Investments (a subsidiary of Nkobi Holdings) and Thomson-CSF Holdings (South Africa) were joint shareholders in the company, with Nkobi possessing 30 per cent of the shares until September 1999, after which it was reduced to 25 per cent. Schabir Shaik was a director of the company from its inception, and Alain Thetard was appointed as a director on 1 April 1998.

'Three Agencies': see Joint Investigating Team

ThyssenKrupp: A German company, part of the GFC consortium that won the contract to supply ship platforms for the corvettes. It has been alleged that ThyssenKrupp paid substantial kickbacks to both Thabo Mbeki and Chippy Shaik. The investigation into this claim was abandoned by German investigators in 2008. According to a statement issued by ThyssenKrupp, the investigation was abandoned as no evidence was found to support the claims. The allegation has been furiously denied by the Presidency and ThyssenKrupp.

Yarrow: The Scottish shipyard that was selected as one of the two preferred suppliers (along with Bazan) to supply corvettes to the SA Navy in 1995.

APPENDIX B

THE ONLY ARMS DEAL TIMELINE YOU'LL EVER NEED

The SADF suffers severe budget and staff cuts.

March
It is announced that the SA Navy is looking to purchase four new warships, the corvettes.

Late 1993
Foreign arms companies begin inundating the SANDF with enquiries regarding arms purchases.

April–May
After SA's first democratic elections, Joe Modise is appointed Minister of Defence. In the same year, Modise authorises the Navy to begin tendering for corvettes.

December
The ANC's Treasurer-General delivers a report at the Annual

Conference in Bloemfontein. He notes that the party's foreign funding has dried up and no plans have been made to achieve financial self-sufficiency.

1995

6–14 January
Thabo Mbeki travels to Germany, where he allegedly tells the German Foreign Minister that 'the race is still open' for companies to submit tenders for the corvettes.

February
The SA Navy announces that it has narrowed down the tenders for corvettes to the Bazan shipyard in Spain and the Yarrow shipyard in Scotland. The tenders from both shipyards promise massive investment and job creation.

27 February
Schabir Shaik registers Nkobi Holdings as a holding company with himself initially as sole shareholder.

June
The corvette deal is scrapped after intense public criticism. Any new purchases would only be made after a substantial review of the SANDF's military requirements

October
The Air Force completes an analysis of its needs. It is decided that only the Cheetah trainers need to be replaced in the short to medium term.

1 October
Zuma receives the first of his payments from Schabir Shaik, which Shaik later claimed formed part of a pattern of loans to Zuma.

1996

May–August
Thomson-CSF sets up its local branches in SA by incorporating Thomson-CSF Holding (Southern Africa) and Thomson (Pty). Thomson and Nkobi enter into a complicated agreement, the result of which is to make Nkobi the joint venture partner in all of Thomson's business in SA.

May
The Department of Defence presents a White Paper before Parliament that urges for a balance to be struck between the obligations of the RDP and the need to prepare the country for any military eventuality.

1997

March
The SANDF, after receiving bids from 23 suppliers for the provision of a fighter/trainer jet, chooses four bidders to enter the next stage of evaluation. Neither the Hawk nor the Gripen, two of BAe's jets, make the list.

18 June
Cabinet approves the Defence Review, which finds that SA needs to undertake extensive purchases to maintain SANDF capability.

July
Mo Shaik is appointed to the position of SA's Consul General to Hamburg. Hamburg is the home town of Blohm and Voss, one part of the German Frigate Consortium.

August
Parliament approves the Defence Review, paving the way for the Arms Deal to start.

2 October

Thabo Mbeki announces that SA is to re-open tenders for the purchase of arms. Total cost is estimated at R12bn.

October

Standard Bank institutes legal action against Michigan Investment for R443 618, 52. Michigan Investment is the company in whose name Zuma's loan for his Killarney home had been opened. (The amount is settled in February 1998 by a number of cheques deposited into Standard Bank.)

October

SAAF Command Council meets to decide on the force structure to be used. Apparently on the strict instructions of Joe Modise, it decides to adopt a 'three-tier' system. As a result, BAe's Gripen and Hawk can be resubmitted for evaluation. By the end of the month, three preferred suppliers for the supply of the ALFA are chosen. At first, the Gripen is the lowest rated of all the choices on offer due to its cost.

December

The ANC Treasurer-General presents his report to the ANC National Conference. He notes the parlous financial state of the ANC, 'in and out of the red', and that they have become 'dependent on the President's initiatives and those of some officials for income'.

1998

March

According to Tony Yengeni's later admission of guilt, he undertakes a tour of DaimlerChrysler's assembly plant in Brazil with Michael Woerfel, and becomes interested in a new Mercedes-Benz 4x4. When Yengeni returns to SA, he approaches Woerfel and asks him to organise a discount on one.

March

BAe allegedly commits to make a donation to the MK Military Veterans Association worth R4.5m. Joe Modise, Life President of the Association, intervenes a month later to ensure that BAe's Hawk remains a contender in the evaluation process for the Lead-in Fighter Trainers.

17 March

According to the court's accepted version of events, Schabir Shaik writes to the head of Thomson-CSF, Jean-Paul Perrier, telling him that Zuma wants to discuss Thomson's seeming uncertainty about including Nkobi as a partner in Thomson/ADS's bid for the corvettes. The letter is copied to Thabo Mbeki.

April

The SANDF commits to purchasing 24 Lead-in Fighter Trainers. In total, 20 proposals from international companies are received, which are whittled down to four. This list includes BAe's Hawk and Aeromacchi's MB339FD. The MB339FD is the SAAF's favoured choice.

14 April

Thomson-CSF purchases shares in Altech Defence Systems, which will be renamed African Defence Systems). ADS is the company that wins the tender to supply the information management system to be used in the corvette combat suites.

30 April

Joe Modise instructs the team evaluating the purchase of LIFT aircraft to adopt a 'visionary' approach to selecting the planes. He orders that two separate evaluations be drawn up, one of which is to exclude cost as a criterion. Even according to this new evaluation, BAe's Hawk still lies in second place behind the MB339FD.

13 May

According to the court's accepted version of events, Shaik sends another note to Perrier asking for a meeting to discuss the potential exclusion of Nkobi from the Thomson/ADS contract as Perrier has failed to answer the 17 March 1998 letter.

June
The Department of Trade and Industry receives a report that BAe's offset proposals were radically inflated during the evaluation process. The Joint Investigation Report notes that, at this stage, BAe's offset proposals are a load of hot air.

July
General Pierre Steyn, who later resigns over the purchase of BAe's Hawk, tries to stop Cabinet being presented with an evaluation that excludes cost criteria in choosing the LIFT. He is overruled by Joe Modise.

9 July
It is alleged that Chippy Shaik meets with representatives of Thomson-CSF (Bernard de Bollaidre and Alain Thetard). He allegedly informs them that he could help facilitate Thomson's bid if Thomson's joint venture partners were to his liking (read: Schabir Shaik and Nkobi). Shaik allegedly tells the representatives that 'he would otherwise make things difficult' for Thomson's bid.

31 August
At a Cabinet briefing meeting on the Arms Deal, attended by Thabo Mbeki, Ronnie Kasrils, Joe Modise, Stella Sigcau and Pierre Steyn, Chippy Shaik presents two options for the purchase of the LIFT (the costed and non-costed options). According to Pierre Steyn, no decision is made at the meeting, but minutes drawn up by Chippy Shaik show that the meeting decided to select BAe's Hawk. Steyn complains and another set of minutes are drawn up and allegedly sent to Modise. But nothing comes of the complaint and the Hawk is selected.

October
Health Minister Nkosazana Dlamini-Zuma states that the government cannot roll out anti-retrovirals to Aids patients in SA

as it would be too expensive. It was established in August 2003 that it would have cost the government R5.6bn to provide ARVs to all those in need by 2008, which would have deferred the deaths of 1,721,329 people.

October
Woerfel orders a Mercedes-Benz ML320 for Yengeni. Woerfel orders it as a staff car and intends to sell the car to Yengeni at a 50 per cent discount. Yengeni registers the car in his name on 22 October.

18 November
Mbeki announces that Cabinet has approved the R30bn Arms Deal and given Mbeki and the Cabinet sub-committee in charge of the deal the authorisation to negotiate and finalise the deals with the primary contractors. It is announced that the deal will produce offset benefits worth R104bn and create 65 000 jobs.

18 November
According to the court's accepted version of events, Jacob Zuma, Schabir Shaik and representatives of Thomson-CSF meet in Durban. As a result of the meeting, at which Zuma is alleged to have acted as mediator, Nkobi is given a share in ADS.

November
Deputy Auditor-General Shauket Fakie identifies the Arms Deal as 'high risk' from an audit point of view. He requests the right to investigate the matter.

25 November
Mbeki defends the Arms Deal while in Sweden, arguing: 'the idea that money that you are using to acquire defence equipment is necessarily money that is being diverted from housing is emotionally appealing, but it is wrong'.

1999

19 February
Thomson-CSF takes over the remaining shares in ADS, becoming the sole shareholder.

March
Modise, in his final address to Parliament, defends the Arms Deal. He claims that it will only cost the taxpayer R500m a year for 15 years.

May
Yengeni enters into a finance arrangement with DaimlerChrysler financial services to pay for his 4x4, a full seven months after he had taken receipt of the car. He allegedly only enters into the agreement after it becomes clear that rumours were being spread that he had received the car as a gift from an arms company.

June
ANC wins a landslide election victory. Thabo Mbeki is appointed President while Jacob Zuma is appointed Deputy President. Zuma is also appointed the Leader of Government Business in Parliament.

28 June
Auditor-General Henry Kleuver asks Mbeki to obtain permission for the Auditor-General's office to audit the Arms Deal. The matter is referred to the Ministry of Defence.

July
Gavin Woods is appointed chairperson of the Standing Committee on Public Accounts (Scopa).

August
The Office for Serious Economic Offences (which later becomes the Scorpions) is created by an act of Parliament.

August
The Department of Finance presents an affordability study of

the Arms Deal which raises serious concerns, including the pos-sibility of currency fluctuations and a severe impact on the gov-ernment's attempts to cut down on the budget deficit.

9 September
Patricia de Lille announces the 'De Lille Dossier', requesting that the government institute a full judicial investigation into the Arms Deal on the basis of the allegations of corruption in-cluded in the dossier.

9 September
The Office of the Presidency releases a statement that defends Zuma against any involvement in 'shady Arms Deals'.

15 September
Thomson-CSF transfers its shares in ADS to Thomson Pty and FBS Holdings. Thomson Pty is part-owned by Shabir Shaik's company, Nkobi Investments. FBS stands for Futuristic Busi-ness Solutions, which is allegedly part-owned by members of Joe Modise's extended family.

20–21 September
Shauket Fakie (now Auditor-General) writes to Defence Minis-ter Lekota urging the need to meet so that the Arms Deal can begin to be audited. Lekota responds the following day giv-ing the Auditor-General's office *carte blanche* to investigate the Arms Deal.

27 September
Reversing Lekota's 21 September decision, General Keith Snow-ball writes to Fakie informing him that Lekota's earlier letter was invalid. Attached is a new letter from Lekota stating that the Auditor-General needs to clear the 'terms of reference' of the investigation with the Executive.

November
Patricia de Lille hands over her dossier and supporting docu-ments to Judge Willem Heath. Heath heads the SIU, which has wide-ranging legal powers giving it almost unfettered power to

investigate the Arms Deal. The unit also has the legal power to cancel any contract it finds is corrupt.

6 November
Joe Modise gives an interview to *The Star* admitting to being the director of Conlog and dismisses claims that this is improper. Conlog, a pre-payment specialist, is slated to receive a considerable contract arising from the offset commitments of BAe, which has received the biggest slice of the Arms Deal.

29 November
An Audit Steering Committee is formed to 'steer' the Auditor-General's investigation. Chippy Shaik is allegedly included in the Committee.

3 December
The government finalises the Arms Deal by signing the final loan and purchase agreements. It is estimated to cost R30bn.

2000

February
The Office for Serious Economic Offences admits that it has begun its own investigation into the Arms Deal.

February–March
Jacob Zuma starts building his homestead in Nkandla, planned to cost over R1m.

10/11 March
Jacob Zuma, Alain Thetard and Schabir Shaik meet in Durban. According to the court's accepted version of events, the meeting is to discuss the payment of a R500 000-a-year bribe to Zuma in return for protection against any investigation into Thomson's potentially corrupt activity in getting its Arms Deal contract.

17 March
According to the court's accepted version of events, the famous

'encrypted fax' which gave details of the above meeting is faxed to Thomson by Alain Thetard's secretary.

15 August
Auditor-General Shauket Fakie releases the first official report of his investigation into the Arms Deal. The report raises serious questions about the rectitude of the acquisition process and recommends further investigation. In the same month, the Public Protector, Selby Baqwa, announces that his office has also begun a preliminary investigation into the Arms Deal.

9 October
The Heath Unit lodges an official request to be granted a presidential proclamation giving it the right to investigate the Arms Deal.

11 October
Scopa conducts its public hearing into the Arms Deal and questions Chippy Shaik (head of acquisitions for the Department of Defence in the Arms Deal) and Jayendra Naidoo (the government's chief negotiator in the Arms Deal). They admit that the cost of the Arms Deal has spiralled to R43.8bn. They also admit that Arms Deal companies only face a 10 per cent penalty on the original contract price if they fail to meet their offset obligations. Chippy Shaik claims that he recused himself from meetings involving discussions about ADS, in which his brother had a stake: this is later found to be false by the Joint Investigating Team.

16 October
According to the court's accepted version of events, Zuma receives a R2m cheque from Mandela, which he deposits into his personal bank account. R1m is transferred to the Jacob Zuma Education Trust, while the other half is a gift from Mandela to help Zuma over his financial hump so that he can do his job as Deputy President properly. Of the R1m in Zuma's account R900 000 is left after erasing Zuma's overdraft.

18 October

According to the court's accepted version of events, noticing that Zuma has R900 000 in his bank account, Shaik uses his cash-focus internet banking to transfer the money from Zuma's account into a fixed deposit account of one of his companies, Floryn Investments. (A good portion of this is transferred out of the Floryn account in November 2000, when over R700 000 is transferred into the cheque accounts of Floryn and Kobitech Transport Systems, while a further R100 000 is used to reduce the overdraft of Kobitech.) The following day, Shaik instructs that construction of Zuma's Nkandla residence be stopped, but Zuma overrules the decision as he presumably still believes he has R900 000 in his account.

30 October

Scopa releases its now-famous '14th Report' into the Arms Deal. The Report urges the government to form a 'super-investigating' team to investigate the Arms Deal. Scopa explicitly argues that the team should include the Heath Unit.

1 November

According to the court's accepted version of events, Shaik fills in a form to apply for a 'service provider agreement' with Thomson, which the State found was cover for the bribe to Zuma. The agreement stipulates that the fee owed to Nkobi is R1m, which is the amount of Zuma's bribe payment.

3 November

Scopa's '14th Report' is presented to Parliament, where it is approved.

27 December

The Speaker of Parliament, Frene Ginwala, wades into the Scopa row. She claims that she was not aware 'of any resolution of Parliament of the National Assembly instructing the President to issue any proclamation regarding the work of the Heath Commission.'

2001

1 January
Nkobi/Shaik and Thomson sign the final version of the 'service provider agreement'.

6 January
ANC spokesperson Smuts Ngonyama states on radio that the ANC doesn't want the Heath Unit to be part of the probe.

12 January
Mail & Guardian runs its first report on the role of Schabir Shaik in the Arms Deal. It notes that he has been a director of the SA branch of Thomson from 1996, and that Thomson/ADS has earned nearly R400m from arms contracts.

12 January
Alec Erwin, Trevor Manuel, Jeff Radebe and Mosiuoa Lekota hold a press conference at Johannesburg International Airport. They defend the procurement process, noting that cost has increased to R43bn because of inflation; also that procurement did not deal with secondary contracts, distancing the government from potential corruption. But most important, they accuse Scopa and the AG of not understanding the Arms Deal.

19 January
A day of action for the Arms Deal. Mbeki writes to Willem Heath telling him that he is not going to grant Heath the right to investigate the Arms Deal. In the letter, he claims that Heath was just desperately 'touting' for work. On the same day, Jacob Zuma sends a letter to Gavin Woods of Scopa explaining the decision to exclude Heath from the Arms Deal investigation. Judge Hilary Squires later found that the letter seemed to relish rubbing Scopa's nose in the decision and served as evidence that Zuma was not supportive of the Arms Deal investigation. Lastly, Mbeki appears on TV to explain to the country why he has excluded Heath. He argues: 'It is also clear that we cannot allow the situation to continue where an organ appointed by

and accountable to the Executive refuses to accept the authority of the Executive. This situation of ungovernability will not be allowed to continue.'

23 January
The ANC component of Scopa releases a statement claiming that Scopa never directly asked for Heath to be part of the investigating team. Andrew Feinstein is forced to read the statement to the press. However, after seeing a crestfallen Gavin Woods, he approaches the media and retracts the statement.

29 January
Feinstein, who had pushed for a full investigation of the Arms Deal, is demoted from his position as ANC spokesperson on Scopa. He is replaced by Geoff Doidge, who was Tony Yengeni's deputy.

9 February
R250 000 is deposited by Thomson (Mauritius) into the bank account of Kobitech. (Squires would note that this was 'plainly' the first payment of the anticipated R1m.)

24 February
According to the court's accepted version of events, a R250 000 cheque is drawn from the account of Kobitech and paid into the account of Development Africa. Shaik draws up a further three post-dated cheques, each for R250 000 (making a total of R1m), for Development Africa. But, in April, he orders his bank to cancel the cheques: the suggestion being that he could not honour these amounts as no further amount was forthcoming from Thomson.

26 February
Ministers Manuel, Erwin and Lekota appear before Scopa. They make repeated claims distancing the government from the subcontracts involved in the Arms Deal, claiming that the government had no role in the selection of subcontractors. Erwin states: 'I have to stress again and again we are not prepared to

take responsibility for subcontracts. How the primary contractor and sub-contractor got together is their business.'

28 February
ANC uses majority in Scopa to push through a statement that the original Scopa 14th Report had not 'provided for the definite' inclusion of Heath in the investigating team.

25 March
The *Sunday Times* breaks the story that Tony Yengeni had received a discounted luxury 4x4 through DaimlerChrysler Aerospace, which had a stake in the Arms Deal.

March
Speaking before Parliament, Tony Yengeni claims that he did not need to register the 4x4 as a 'gift' in the Declaration of Members' Interests as he had paid for the car.

28 March
Feroza Mohamed, the Parliamentary Registrar, is given the go-ahead from the Joint Committee on Ethics and Members' Interests to request that Yengeni fully explain why he did not declare the 4x4 as a gift.

18 April
Yengeni responds, arguing that the 4x4 did not constitute a gift. Mohamed rejects the explanation and requests that JCEMI begin a full-scale investigation into the matter.

9 May
ANC uses majority in Parliamentary Joint Standing Committee on Ethics and Members' Interests to force through resolution that states that Yengeni does not need to appear before the Committee to answer questions related to claims that he had received his 4x4 via corrupt channels.

17 May
ANC uses its majority on Scopa to force through a resolution that completely exonerates the Executive from any wrongdo-

ing in the Arms Deal. Opposition parties draw up a second report that comes to the opposite conclusion.

8 June
Vote in support of a motion of confidence in Frene Ginwala is held in Parliament. ANC uses its majority to support Ginwala, although Feinstein abstains from voting.

12 June
ANC members on Scopa claim that Scopa is 'too busy' to continue investigating the Arms Deal. They note that other members of Scopa could continue their investigations, but the statement essentially marks the end of Scopa's investigation.

2 July
The *Cape Times* publishes a list provided by EADS which shows that 30 SA politicians and VIPs (including defence chief Siphiwe Nyanda and Armscor's Llew Swan) received discounts on luxury vehicles from DaimlerChrysler.

15 July
Yengeni takes out a full-page advertisement, which cost roughly R250 000, in *Sunday Independent*. Yengeni rejects all the claims made against him and argues that the allegations made against him amount to a witch-hunt.

30 August
Feinstein resigns from his position as an ANC MP after being taken to task for abstaining in a vote to support a motion of confidence in Ginwala moved by the ANC.

3 October
Yengeni is arrested and charged with fraud, perjury and forgery. Woerfel, the man from DaimleryChrysler Aerospace who wrangled Yengeni's 4x4, is also charged. The following day, Yengeni resigns from his position as ANC Chief Whip.

5 October
Yengeni lashes out at the Scorpions for being filled with white

people who were 'the same guys who persecuted us'.

9 October
The Scorpions raid properties in France, Mauritius and SA as part of their investigation into the Arms Deal. Schabir Shaik's Durban home and the Durban offices of Nkobi are included in the raid.

17 October
News reports emerge that Auditor-General Shauket Fakie had forwarded his original AG report (released in August 2000) into the Arms Deal to Cabinet for review. It later emerges that a paragraph directly implicating Chippy Shaik in improper activities had been edited to clear Shaik.

15 November
The Joint Investigation Report is presented to Parliament. The report fingers Joe Modise and Chippy Shaik for irregular activities in the Arms Deal, but clears the government of any wrongdoing. It also notes Modise's irregular behaviour regarding the purchase of equipment from BAe, but claims that though 'undesirable' it was not 'irregular'. Opposition parties slam the Report as a cover-up.

16 November
Schabir Shaik is arrested and charged with theft of state documents. He had been found to be in possession of Cabinet minutes during the raids on his home and office. On the same day, Mbeki writes a stinging column on *ANCToday* attacking naysayers who claimed the Joint Investigation Report was a cover-up. Mbeki argues that they are working from the assumption that 'Africans ... are naturally prone to corruption, venality and mismanagement'.

19 November
Chippy Shaik is suspended from the Department of Defence for leaking classified information related to the Arms Deal.

26 November
Joe Modise dies at home.

20 January
Chippy Shaik is found guilty by the Department of Defence of leaking confidential documents relating to the Arms Deal. A week later, he is punished with a final written warning, considered by many to be a slap on the wrist.

25 February
Gavin Woods resigns as the chairperson of Scopa in protest at the way it handled the Arms Deal investigation, and in hope that his resignation would force other members of Scopa to rethink their approach to the investigation.

28 March
Chippy Shaik resigns from the Department of Defence.

30 May
Vanan Pillay, fingered along with Yengeni in accepting a discounted car from DaimlerChrysler, is fired by the Department of Trade and Industry. Pillay had bought a car for R141 000 in July: the car's actual value was R196 000.

13 August
Parliament agrees to adopt all committee findings relating to the Arms Deal. This essentially means that the issue can no longer be debated in Parliament.

29 November
The *Mail & Guardian* breaks the story that Zuma is being investigated in connection with corruption charges linked to Thales and Schabir Shaik. It is alleged that Zuma solicited a R500 000 a year payment from Thales for his favourable input into the Arms Deal.

December
Mo Shaik reconstructs an ANC intelligence report dating from 1989 in which it is claimed that Ngcuka was an apartheid spy.

10 December
Senior members of the ANC rally around Jacob Zuma. Much as they will for the following four years, they claim that allegations of corruption had been levelled in order to discredit Zuma ahead of the ANC National Conference to take place in Stellenbosch the following week and to undermine his push for presidency.

16 December
Zuma is re-elected unopposed as Deputy President of the ANC. At the same time, Yengeni is elected as a member of the 60 member NEC. He came in at 43rd place with 2 047 out of 3 000 delegates voting in his favour.

2003

13 February
Yengeni enters into a plea bargain with the State in which he admits to fraud in wrangling his 4x4 through DaimlerChrysler Aerospace/EADS. He is sentenced to four years. Yengeni's lawyers appeal the sentence for the next three years. As a result of the plea bargain, the charges against Woerfel are dropped.

13 March
Auditor-General drops appeal against a November judgment in favour of Richard Young. This means that the AG has to release the documents requested by Young, including drafts of the Joint Investigation Report. Extracts of these drafts are given to the media and show that the Report had been heavily edited to reflect more favourably on the government and key players in the Arms Deal.

30 May

In the wake of the release of documents from the Auditor-General to Richard Young and the media furore that followed, Mbeki writes his second column on the Arms Deal on *ANC-Today*. He claims that anti-African stereotypes underpinned the claims of corruption in the Arms Deal.

June

Patricia Hewitt, the British trade minister, admits in UK's House of Commons that BAe had definitely paid commissions to agents to help secure the BAe deal. The UK's SFO later alleges that roughly £112m in covert commissions were paid out by BAe.

30 June

New scandal erupts after the UK newspaper *The Guardian* runs a story alleging that British Aerospace had paid over R2bn in illegal commissions to agents in SA.

25 July

NPA launches a formal investigation into a smear campaign against Bulelani Ngcuka after a two-page email claims that he had been abusing his office for political reasons.

30 July

ANC suspends Yengeni's membership for five years.

August

Joint Health and Treasury Task Team finds that it would cost the government R5.7bn a year to roll out anti-retrovirals to everybody in SA who needed them. This would have 'deferred' the death of 1 721 329 people and the orphaning of 860 000 children.

14 August

Mac Maharaj resigns from Discovery Holdings pending a formal investigation into claims that he received a R500 000 bribe from Schabir Shaik while in office at the Department of Transport. He is later cleared by Discovery Holdings of any wrongdoing but agrees to resign from his position. Maharaj has never faced charges regarding these claims.

23 August
NPA head Bulelani Ngcuka states that the NPA is about to charge Schabir Shaik for fraud and corruption. He also notes that there is a *prima facie* case of corruption against Jacob Zuma, but that the NPA has decided not to charge Zuma on this basis. On the same day, Mac Maharaj gives Thabo Mbeki an ANC intelligence report that found that Ngcuka was an apartheid spy.

25 August
Schabir Shaik is provided with a full charge sheet outlining the charges against him.

6 September
City Press runs an article that questions whether Bulelani Ngcuka was an apartheid spy. The article notes that in 1989 an ANC intelligence report had fingered Ngcuka for being the apartheid spy with the name Agent RS452.

19 September
Mbeki appoints the Hefer Commission to investigate claims that Ngcuka was an apartheid spy.

16 October
Judge Hefer begins his hearings: over the course of the next two months, testimonies are heard from a range of sources including Mac Maharaj and Mo Shaik. The testimonies of Maharaj and Shaik show that the only source of the information was Mo Shaik's intelligence report from 1989, which was factually flawed on a number of levels. During the hearings, former Eastern Cape human rights lawyer, Vanessa Brereton, announces that she had actually been Agent RS452.

6 November
Jacob Zuma lays a complaint with the Public Protector, Lawrence Mushwana, that Ngcuka had abused his position of power in claiming that there was a *prima facie* case against him.

2004

20 January

Hefer finds that Ngcuka probably never acted as an agent for the pre-1994 government security service. However, he attacks Ngcuka's office for persistent media leaks about on-going investigations, and laments the effect that this has had on Mac Maharaj in particular.

3 March

The Cape High Court finds in favour of the government in legal battle with Terry Crawford-Browne of the Economists Allied for Arms Reduction. Crawford-Browne had undertaken legal action in an effort to have the Arms Deal scrapped as unconstitutional.

28 May

Appearing before Parliament, Public Protector Lawrence Mushwana raps Ngcuka and Maduna over the knuckles in connection with the Zuma affair. Mushwana found that Ngcuka's statement that there was a *prima facie* case against Zuma was 'unfair and improper'.

25 June

The ad hoc Parliamentary Committee tasked with examining Mushwana's report makes a compromise decision, 'noting' Mushwana's report rather than accepting it, which means that Parliament does not have to decide whether or not to fire Ngcuka. The Committee is divided along party lines, with the ANC and NNP wanting to focus only on the report and the rest of the opposition parties arguing that Ngcuka should be called to give his side of the story.

24 July

Bulelani Ngcuka resigns from his position as head of the NPA.

10 August

Auditor-General Shauket Fakie is found to be in contempt of court for failing to provide all the documents owing to Richard

Young in terms of Young's application according to the Promotion of Access to Information Act. Fakie is given 30 days to hand over the material or face arrest. He eventually does so, and Young finally receives all the documents requested from Fakie, including full drafts of the Auditor-General's report.

11 October
Schabir Shaik's trial begins. Judge Hilary Squires hears evidence for nearly six months. The trial begins in earnest on 14 October when the State and Defence present their cases, and the first witness, Professor Sono, is called for the State.

2005

1 April
Judge Sisi Khampepe is tasked with investigating the case for and against the abolition of the Scorpions by Thabo Mbeki. (The report is held back and only released in May 2008 after the Democratic Alliance forces the government to disclose the report under the Promotion of Access to Information Act.)

31 May–2 June
Judge Hilary Squires presents his judgment in the Schabir Shaik case. He finds Shaik guilty on two counts of corruption: one for soliciting a R500 000-a-year bribe for Jacob Zuma from French arms company Thomson, and another for having a corrupt relationship with Zuma. He is also found guilty of fraud.

8 June
Shaik is sentenced to 15 years in prison. His lawyers move to appeal.

14 June
Thabo Mbeki fires Jacob Zuma from his post as Deputy President.

29 June
Jacob Zuma makes a short appearance in court for the first time.

He is charged with corruption on the basis of having a 'generally corrupt' relationship with Schabir Shaik and for having accepted a bribe from Thomson in return for his protection against any investigations into the company.

1 July
Defying Thabo Mbeki, ANC delegates decide at a national gathering to keep Jacob Zuma as the party's Deputy President.

18 August
Zuma's Johannesburg house is raided by the Scorpions. Also raided are his Nkandla home and the offices of his attorneys. The legality of these raids is contested in court for the next three years, but is eventually cleared by the Constitutional Court.

11 October
Zuma appears in court for a second time and is formally indicted on two counts of corruption. His trial is slated to start on 31 July 2006.

6 December
Zuma is formally charged with raping a 31-year old HIV-positive woman. The following day, the ANC requests that he stops making statements on behalf of the ANC but retains him as the organisation's Deputy President.

2006

13 February
Zuma appears in court on the rape charge. His lawyers demand that Judge Bernard Ngoepe recuse himself as he had previously issued search warrants in the Zuma corruption investigation. The lawyers are successful and Judge Willem van der Merwe is appointed to replace Ngoepe in March.

15 February
Durban High Court rules that the search warrants used to effect the raids on Zuma's house and his attorney's offices were illegal

and that the documents seized must be returned.

3 April
Zuma takes the stand in his rape trial. He admits during his testimony that he had unsafe sex with his rape accuser but claims that it was consensual. His testimony infuriates a range of public health and gender equality advocates, as he admits that he knew that the woman had HIV/Aids but thought that he would not contract the disease as he had a shower directly afterwards. He also claims that he knew that she wanted to have sex with him because she was wearing a short traditional wrap-around, and that it was not part of Zulu culture to refuse sex with an aroused woman.

8 May
Jacob Zuma is found not guilty on charges of rape. However, the Judge lambastes Zuma for having sex with a woman when Zuma was aware that the woman had Aids. In his judgment, Judge Van Der Merwe states: 'Had Rudyard Kipling known of this case at the time he wrote his poem If, he might have added the following: "And if you can control your body and your sexual urges, then you are a man, my son."'

May
ANC votes to reinstate Zuma in his party duties.

June
Mail & Guardian reports that the UK's Serious Fraud Office has lodged a request for legal assistance with SA authorities. The application allegedly makes mention of a number of South Africans the SFO would like to investigate who may have received corrupt payments from BAe. This, allegedly, includes Fana Hlongwane, formerly advisor to Joe Modise.

19 June
German investigators raid the offices of ThyssenKrupp, one of the companies that formed the German Frigate Consortium which had won the tender to supply the corvettes. They are

searching for evidence to support the allegation that the company had illegally paid R130m to SA agents and politicians. Both Thabo Mbeki and Chippy Shaik are alleged to have received bribes from Thyssen. The allegations are denied by the Presidency and ThyssenKrupp. The investigation is later halted by German authorities (see below).

31 July
The State argues for a postponement in the Zuma trial. Zuma's legal team reject the request and submit an affidavit in support of a motion for a permanent stay of prosecution. The affidavit argues that the case against Zuma was lodged as part of a political conspiracy against him, and that the delays in the presentation of the trial prejudiced him in his personal and political life.

14 August
The State files six affidavits rejecting the claims made in Zuma's affidavit. The affidavits are written by Penuell Maduna, Bulelani Ngcuka, Leonard McCarthy, Vusi Pikoli, Advocate Johan du Plooy and Advocate Billy Downer.

21 August
Zuma responds with a second affidavit calling for a stay of prosecution. He argues that the State's affidavits materially failed to answer any of the charges raised by his first affidavit.

29 August
The State submits a further affidavit relating to Zuma's motion for a stay of prosecution. The affidavit, written by Leonard McCarthy, warns that Zuma could not rely on the findings of Lawrence Mushwana's investigation of whether Ngcuka had abused his office in making the *'prima facie'* statement in August 2003. McCarthy argues that Mushwana's probe had no legal basis to challenge the NPA's decisions and that Mushwana had acted in bad faith by misleading both the NPA and the Presidency.

21 August
The Supreme Court of Appeal rejects Yengeni's pleas for a reduction in his sentence of four years for fraud. He is ordered to report to Pollsmoor prison in 72 hours.

20 September
Zuma's trial on charges of corruption is struck from the roll. Presiding judge, Judge Herbert Msimang, responds angrily to the State's request to postpone the trial to further prepare. He finds that the State's case had limped from 'one disaster to another' and that the State had erred in deciding to include evidence still under appeal.

September
Defence Minister Lekota admits in Parliament that only 13 000 of the 65 000 jobs promised by offsets have been created.

6 November
The Bloemfontein Supreme Court of Appeal upholds Squires' decision in finding Schabir Shaik guilty of two counts of corruption and one count of fraud. The Court also rejects decreasing Shaik's sentence.

11 December
In a move with international implications, Tony Blair moves to block the UK's Serious Fraud Office from investigating allegations that BAe bribed officials during the late-1980s Saudi Arabia Arms Deal. He declares that it is in the interests of national security to do so. However, SFO quickly confirms that it is still investigating SA corruption related to BAe.

2007

January
After spending four months in prison, Tony Yengeni is released on parole from Pollsmoor. He is received by a cavalcade of ANC leaders from the Western Cape.

March

Major-General Otto Schur, the Defence Department's chief director of acquisitions, notes in an interview with Scopa that the SAF was barely using the Hawk and Gripen jets. They are likely only to be flown for 100 hours a year, as there is no conventional need for them to be used.

March

Patricia de Lille announces that she has started legal proceedings to obtain the right to privately prosecute the other 29 recipients of discounted vehicles from DaimlerChrysler/EADS.

August

Justice Minister Brigitte Mabandla confirms in Parliament that Chippy Shaik had never been and currently is not under investigation for corruption in the Arms Deal.

October

The Constitutional Court rejects Schabir Shaik's final appeal against his charges and sentence. However, Shaik is given leave to appeal the seizure of his assets ordered by Judge Hilary Squires.

19 October

The Department of Justice confirms that it has received a request for mutual legal assistance from German investigators looking into alleged corruption in the GFC deal.

8 November

The National Prosecuting Authority wins a major victory when the Supreme Court of Appeal overturns an earlier decision that had declared illegal the search and seizure warrants used to search the homes of Zuma and the offices of his attorneys. This means that the NPA can now submit those documents seized as evidence, which allegedly include details of all payments made by Shaik up until the raid in August 2005 (Shaik had, allegedly, continued paying Zuma even as the case against Shaik was being heard). The NPA is also given the legal right to approach

Mauritian authorities for the handover of documents in their possession.

28 November

Zuma's legal counsel submits an application to the Constitutional Court to have the judgment delivered by the Supreme Court of Appeal declared invalid. If successful, the documents seized during the August 2005 raids will be declared inadmissible in court.

December

Reports emerge in the media that the Navy does not have the capacity to run the three submarines purchased as part of the Arms Deal due to staff shortages. It is rumoured that the Navy will mothball two of the submarines, leaving one operational.

18 December

Jacob Zuma is elected President of the ANC at the Polokwane National Conference. This means that Zuma will most likely become the next President of SA in 2009. Convicted fraudster Tony Yengeni is elected to the 21st place on the ANC's 80-member National Executive Committee. He is later chosen to serve on the 20-member National Working Committee, perhaps the most powerful organ in the ANC.

20 December

State prosecutors note that there is enough evidence to charge Zuma for corruption and that a case will be lodged against him soon. Reeling from the claim, the ANC at the Polokwane National Conference votes to disband the Scorpions.

27 December

Scorpions Investigating Director Aubrey Mngwengwe signs off a new indictment to be delivered to Zuma. According to the new indictment, he is to be charged on two counts of corruption, one of racketeering, one of money laundering and 12 of fraud: 16 charges in total. Zuma is presented with the indictment on 29 December, and the NPA announces that the trial will commence on 4 August 2008.

2008

According to the 2008 budget, SA has, up to 2008, spent R43.09bn on the Arms Deal, with a further R4.3bn to be spent by 2011.

13 February
Barbara Masekela, former SA Ambassador to the US, claims that Mbeki did meet with French arms officials during the Arms Deal acquisition process.

13 February
It is confirmed that Zuma is in Mauritius with his legal team, contesting the State's application for the documents used in the Shaik trial to be given over to the National Prosecuting Authority to be used in the Zuma trial. He alleges that the documents were initially handed to the State by illegal means. Presenting his argument to the Mauritian courts, Zuma claims that he is a victim of a political conspiracy – which is strongly denied by the State. Zuma argues that there was 'carefully orchestrated, politically inspired and driven strategy to exclude me from any meaningful political role ... It suffices to say that certain individuals deployed in established institutions both inside and outside the ANC are strongly opposed to my stewardship of the ANC and the country.'

29 February
The University of KwaZulu-Natal withdraws Chippy Shaik's PhD thesis after it finds that the thesis had been extensively plagiarised.

March
Mail & Guardian publishes a story that alleges that German and UK authorities are jointly investigating allegations that ThyssenKrupp illegally paid Tony Georgiades a commission of $22m. The story notes that the investigators are also investigating the allegation that a portion of this $22m was channelled to SA officials and government ministers. It also claims that Georgiades

had made a R500 000 donation to the ANC. However, as the German investigation has subsequently been stopped by German authorities, these remain allegations and have not been proven.

2 March

Britain's *Sunday Telegraph* reports that the UK's Serious Fraud Office is intensifying its investigation of corruption involving BAe in SA.

13 March

The Constitutional Court hears the cases for and against the submission of the documents seized by the Scorpions' 2005 raids on Zuma and his attorneys. The Court reserves judgment; it has not, as yet, reached a decision.

20 March

Mail & Guardian reports that the Scorpions have 'recently registered an investigation into SA's multi-billion rand purchase of jet trainers and jet fighters from British arms giant BAe systems and Sweden's Saab.'

April

ANC Secretary-General Gwede Mantashe makes the following combustible statement: 'The only thing the DA and the Scorpions have in common is their hatred of the ANC.'

18 April

The State presents its argument in the Mauritius Supreme Court contesting Zuma's legal argument. They reject with contempt Zuma's claims that his prosecution is based on a political conspiracy.

20 April

The British High Court overturns Tony Blair's December 2006 decision to stop the SFO from investigating corruption relating to the Saudi Arms Deal. It is declared a major victory for the anti-bribery pressure groups Corner House Research and Campaign Against Arms Trade, which led the legal application to have the investigation restarted.

End April

The Cabinet approves the General Law Amendment Bill and the Prosecuting Amendment Bill. Both, if passed by Parliament, would scrap the Scorpions and move its investigators into a new unit in the SAPS.

May

The Khampepe Report is finally released. Written by Judge Sisi Khampepe, it argued that there was no constitutional reason for disbanding the Scorpions although it noted that that the Scorpions should report to the Minister of Correctional Services rather than the Minister of Justice.

30 May 2008

Judges of the Constitutional Court lay a complaint against Judge John Hlophe with the Judicial Services Commission. The Constitutional Court judges allege that Hlophe had contacted two Constitutional Court judges in an attempt to 'improperly' influence the outcome of the Zuma and Thint search warrant appeals. Hlophe rejects the allegations and claims that they are motivated by an 'ulterior motive' held by Chief Justice Pius Langa and Deputy Chief Justice Dikgane Moseneke to remove him from office at all costs. The matter is still to be heard by the Judicial Services Commission.

June 2008

German prosecutors announce that they have stopped investigations into alleged corruption committed by the German Frigate Consortium in its dealings in South Africa, led by ThyssenKrupp. ThyssenKrupp release a media statement claiming that the investigation had been stopped as the investigators had found no evidence of corruption.

June 2008

Jacob Zuma's legal team submit an application to have the charges against him dismissed. Zuma's team claim that the NPA had violated his constitutional right to be included in a 'review' of the decision to prosecute him reached in 2005.

30 June

The Supreme Court of Mauritius rejects Jacob Zuma's application to prevent documents seized by Mauritian authorities being given to South African authorities. The original copies of the documents are reportedly to be used in the upcoming corruption trial of Jacob Zuma. Photocopies of the documents had been submitted as evidence during the Schabir Shaik trial.

31 July 2008

The Constitutional Court rejects the appeals launched by Jacob Zuma and Thint to have the search warrants used to raid the properties of Zuma, Thint and others declared illegal. This allows the State to include the 93 000 documents seized during the August 2005 raids in Zuma's upcoming corruption trial.

3 August

The *Sunday Times* runs a story that alleges that German company MAN Ferrostaal had paid a R30m bribe to Thabo Mbeki, and that Mbeki had passed R2m of this bribe to Jacob Zuma and the remainder to the ANC. The Presidency strongly rejects the allegations and is currently considering its legal options. MAN Ferrostaal also reject the allegations.

4–8 August 2008

After filing a responding affidavit to Zuma's appeal to have his case dismissed, the State, along with Zuma's legal team, lead their heads of argument in the High Court over the application. High Court Judge Chris Nicholson, hearing the arguments, notes that he will deliver his judgment in September 2008. However, it is rumoured that Zuma will appeal if he loses the application. According to Zuma's founding affidavit, he intends to submit a further application for a permanent stay of prosecution in September 2008 if the application to have the case dismissed fails.

THE ARMS-DEAL COMPANIES[1]

Company name: AFRICAN DEFENCE SYSTEMS (ADS)
Country in which incorporated: South Africa
Major shareholders: Initially held by Thomson-CSF (France) and Allied Technologies, until Thomson-CSF took over all shares on February 1999. After a series of permutations, Allied Technologies' portion of the shares (10 per cent of the total) were transferred to Thomson (Pty) (80 per cent) and FBS Holdings (Pty) (20 per cent)
Directors of note: Jean-Pierre Robert Moynot
Moynet represented accused Nos 2 and 3 in both Zuma trials
Relationship with other companies: The company that was at the centre of most of the complaints noted by the Joint Investigation Report regarding the Thomson contract. ADS won the tender to supply information management systems for the combat suites for the corvettes. It was employed as a subcontractor by Thomson-CSF, which had won the right to supply the entire combat suite for the corvettes.

At first Shaik was prevented from holding any shares in the company, but, after some serious wrangling, was able to get a minority shareholding when a portion of the shares were transferred to Thomson (Pty), of which Shaik's Nkobi Investments owned 30 per cent (later reduced to 25 per cent).

Company name: THOMSON-CSF
Country in which incorporated: France
Major shareholders: n/a
Directors of note: n/a
Relationship with other companies: The major company that acted as the holding company for all the other Thomson companies.

Company name: THOMSON-CSF (INTERNATIONAL)
Country in which incorporated: France
Major shareholders: Thomson-CSF
Directors of note: Jean-Paul Perrier
Relationship with other companies: A subsidiary company owned by the Thomson-CSF parent company.

Company name: THOMSON-CSF HOLDING (SOUTHERN AFRICA) later renamed THINT HOLDING (SOUTHERN AFRICA) *Accused No. 2 in both Zuma trials*
Country in which incorporated: South Africa (1996
Major shareholders: Nkobi Holdings and Thomson-CSF (International) until September 1999, when all shares were transferred to Thomson-CSF (International)
Directors of note: Schabir Shaik. Alain Thetard. Jean-Marie Robert Moynot (from 1996 to 1 April 1998, and then from October 2002).
Moynet represented accused Nos 2 and 3 in both Zuma trials
Relationship with other companies: This company was the SA subsidiary of Thomson-CSF. It was through this company that Thomson would conduct all its business in SA. It was partially owned by Nkobi Holdings (Shaik) until September 1999.

Company name: THOMSON (PTY) later renamed THINT (PTY) *Accused No. 11 in the Shaik trial. Accused No. 3 in both Zuma trials.*
Country in which incorporated: South Africa (July 1996)

Major shareholders: Nkobi Investments with 30 per cent (later reduced to 25 per cent) and Thomson-CSF Holdings
Directors of note: Schabir Shaik, Alain Thetard, Jean-Marie Robert Moynot (from 1996 to April 1998, and from 16 January to October 2004)
Moynet represented both accused No. 2 and 3 in both Zuma trials.
Relationship with other companies: Yet another Thomson subsidiary. This company was partially owned by Nkobi Investments, of which Nkobi Holdings was the majority shareholder. This company, and the one above, were the vehicles through which Shaik's Nkobi companies owned shares in Thomson and ADS as a whole.

Company name: NKOBI HOLDINGS
Accused No. 2 in the Shaik trial
Country in which incorporated: South Africa
Major shareholders: a) Star Corp SA (wholly owned by Schabir Shaik)
b) Clanwest Investments (partially owned by Schabir Shaik)
c) Floryn Investments
d) Workers College
Directors of note: Schabir Shaik
Relationship with other companies: Schabir Shaik's parent company, which held shares in Thomson Holdings and Thomson Pty (through Nkobi Investments).

Company name: NKOBI INVESTMENTS
Accused No. 3 in the Shaik trial
Country in which incorporated: South Africa
Major shareholders: Initially wholly owned by Schabir Shaik, but by 20 August 1998, wholly owned by Nkobi Holdings.
Directors of note: Schabir Shaik.
Relationship with other companies: A subsidiary of Shaik's Nkobi parent company, which owned a share in Thomson (Pty).

Company name: KOBIFIN (PTY) LTD
Accused No. 4 in the Shaik trial
Country in which incorporated: South Africa.
Major shareholders: Nkobi Holdings.
Directors of note:
Relationship with other companies: Subsidiary of Shaik's Nkobi parent company.

Company name: KOBITECH (PTY) LTD
Accused No. 5 in the Shaik trial
Country in which incorporated: South Africa
Major shareholders: Nkobi Holdings
Directors of note:
Relationship with other companies: Subsidiary of Shaik's Nkobi parent company

Company name: PROCONSULT (PTY) LTD
Accused No. 6 in the Shaik trial
Country in which incorporated: South Africa.
Major shareholders: Nkobi Holdings.
Directors of note:
Relationship with other companies: Subsidiary of Shaik's Nkobi parent company.

Company name: PRO CON AFRICA (PTY) LTD
Accused No. 7 in the Shaik trial
Country in which incorporated: South Africa.
Major shareholders: Nkobi Holdings.
Directors of note:
Relationship with other companies: Subsidiary of Shaik's Nkobi parent company.

Company name: KOBITECH TRANSPORT SYSTEM (PTY) LTD
Accused No. 8 in the Shaik trial.
Country in which incorporated: South Africa.
Major shareholders: Nkobi Holdings.

Directors of note:
Relationship with other companies: Subsidiary of Shaik's Nkobi
parent company.

Company name: CLEGTON (PTY) LTD
Accused No. 9 in the Shaik trial.
Country in which incorporated: South Africa.
Major shareholders: Schabir Shaik.
Directors of note:
Relationship with other companies: A company wholly owned
by Schabir Shaik.

Company name: FLORYN INVESTMENTS
Accused No. 10 in the Shaik trial
Country in which incorporated: South Africa.
Major shareholders: Schabir Shaik.
Directors of note:
Relationship with other companies: A company wholly
owned by Schabir Shaik, which owns 10 per cent of Nkobi
Holdings. During his trial, Shaik claimed that he used Floryn
Investments as a vehicle to donate money to the ANC.

NOTES

CHAPTER 1

1 Engelbrecht, L. 'South Africa's multi-billion arms programme revisited (Part One)', *Defence Systems Daily*, 15 October 2001.

2 Crawford-Browne, T. *Eye on the Money*, p 125.

3 Engelbrecht, L. 'South Africa's multi-billion arms programme revisited (Part One)', *Defence Systems Daily*, 15 October 2001.

4 'Pocket power', *Leadership SA*, 31 May 1992.

5 'Navy sells 'tired' ships: one to scrap', *Cape Times*, 19 December 1992.

6 'You're in the navy now', *Sunday Star*, 19 March 1992.

7 'Adrift on uncertain seas', *Pretoria News*, 9 March 1993.

8 '"Don't sink the navy," beg experts', *Weekend Argus*, 20 February 1993, and 'Navy chief lashes out at shortage of funds', *Sunday Times*, 16 August 1992.

9 'Pocket power', *Leadership SA*, 31 May 1992.

10 'Unions seek to scuttle corvette bid', *Weekend Argus*, 28 May 1995.

11 'Fewer babies and not corvettes will save SA', *Weekend Argus*, 7 May 1995.

12 'Trimmed navy setting sail for a bright, rosy future – weather permitting', *Weekend Argus*, 21 March 1993.

13 'Adrift on uncertain seas', *Pretoria News*, 9 March 1993.

14 'Staying out in front', *The Argus*, 10 September 1993.

15 'French warship may visit Cape', *Sunday Tribune*, 2 January 1994.

16 'Guns vs. butter? Corvettes decision looms for new SA', *Weekend Argus*, 26 February 1995.

17 'Pretoria becoming top armaments trade centre', *The Argus*, 12 April 1995.
18 'Guns vs. butter? *Weekend Argus*, 26 February 1995.
19 'An undimmed capacity for intrigue', *Sunday Times*, 21 May 1995.
20 'Cabinet weighs RDP against military needs', *Weekend Star*, 23 April 1995.
21 Gumede, W. M. 2005. *Thabo Mbeki and the Battle for the Soul of the ANC*. Zebra, Cape Town, p 138.
22 'Bengu pledge on national loan scheme', *Business Day*, 23 February 1995, and 'Students march to seek funding for education', *The Argus*, 23 February 1995.
23 'Navy corvettes sail into Cabinet storm', *Sunday Times*, 14 May 1995.
24 'Unions seek to scuttle corvette bid', *Weekend Argus*, 28 May 1995.
25 *Sowetan*, 21 April 1995.
26 'A greater priority than new ships', *Cape Times*, 28 March 1995.
27 'Newest hawk on the block', *Weekly Mail & Guardian*, 12 April 1995.
28 'Support corvette deal, says Kasrils', *The Citizen*, 31 March 1995.
29 'Newest Hawk on the Block', *Weekly Mail & Guardian*, 12 April 1995.
30 'Buying of warships defended', *Cape Times*, 1 March 1995.
31 Crawford-Browne, T. *Eye on the Money*, p. 129
32 *Ibid*.
33 'Coal for corvettes?', *City Press*, 19 March 1995.
34 'Guns vs. Butter? *Weekend Argus*, 26 February 1995.
35 'Steaming to safety', *Daily News*, 26 May 1995.
36 'Corvettes – Thabo all at sea', *Weekend Argus*, 20 May 1995.
37 "Ships Anchored", *Financial Mail*, 16 June 1995
38 'Defence in a Democracy: White Paper on National Defence for the Republic of South Africa', May 1996, www.dod.mil.za.
39 See *South African Defence Review*, 1998, Chapter 3.
40 *Strategic Defence Packages: Joint Report*, 2001, Chapter 3. Available at www.info.gov.za.
41 'Modise takes military begging bowl to Mbeki after no joy from Manuel', *Sunday Independent*, 25 May 1997.
42 Address by the Deputy Minister of Defence, Mr Kasrils: The Defence Review Debate, National Assembly, 20 August 1997. Available at www.info.gov.za.
43 *Ibid*.

44 'SA to call for military equipment tenders by year-end, says Mbeki', *Business Day*, 3 October 1997.

CHAPTER 2

1 Crawford-Browne, T. *Eye on the Money*, p 135.
2 Parliamentary briefing by Mr RF Haywood, Executive Chairperson of Armscor, on proposed armament procurements, 3 August 1998. Available at: www.info.gov.za.
3 *Strategic Defence Packages: Joint Report*, Chapter 3, paragraphs 3.1.1.4–3.1.1.5, 2001. Available at: www.info.gov.za.
4 *Ibid.*
5 Modise, J. 'Realising our hopes', Address by the Minister of Defence on the Defence Budget Vote, 9 March 1999.
6 'Arms bonanza for SA', *Pretoria News*, 19 November 1998; and 'Cabinet OK to huge Arms Deal', *The Star*, 19 November 1998.
7 'R30bn Arms Deal finalised', *Business Report*, 4 December 1999.
8 Extrapolated by the author from: 'Strategic Defence Packages: Joint Report', 2001, available at www.info.gov.za; 'The Arms Deal for Dummies', *Cape Argus*/Helen Suzman Foundation, 27 March 2003; and 'South Africa's Multi-Billion Arms Deal Programme Revisited (Part One)', *Defence Systems Daily*, 15 October 2001.
9 'Newest hawk on the block', *Weekly Mail & Guardian*, 12 April 1995.
10 'The hardware', *SABC Special Report*. Available at www.armsdeal-vpo.co.za.
11 Crawford-Browne, T. *Eye on the Money*, p 130.
12 'The hardware', *SABC Special Report*. Available at www.armsdeal-vpo.co.za.
13 www.gripen.com.
14 'The hardware', *SABC Special Report*. Available at www.armsdeal-vpo.co.za.
15 *Ibid.*
16 'A significantly inferior product', *The Citizen*, 7 January 2004.
17 'The hardware', *SABC Special Report*. Available at www.armsdeal-vpo.co.za.

18 Address by the Deputy Minister of Defence, Mr. Kasrils: The Defence Review Debate, National Assembly, 20 August 1997. Available at: www.info.gov.za.

19 Modise, J. 'Realising our hopes', Address by the Minister of Defence on the Defence Budget Vote, 9 March 1999.

20 'File on Four', Radio Documentary broadcast on BBC Radio 4, 2003. The transcript is available for download from www.armsdeal-vpo.co.za.

21 Engelbrecht, L. 'South Africa's multi-billion arms programme revisited (Part One)', *Defence Systems Daily*, 15 October 2001.

22 Crawford-Browne, T. *Eye on the Money*, p 135.

23 World Trade Organisation Agreement on Government Procurement, Article XVI. Available at: www.wto.org. South Africa joined the WTO on 1 January 1995.

24 Gevisser, M. *Thabo Mbeki: The Dream Deferred*, p 681.

25 Cooper, N. 1999. 'Offsets information website', cited in Batchelor, P. and Dunne, P. 'Industrial participation, investment and growth: the case of South Africa's defence related industry', February 2000. Available at: www.ipocafrica.org.

26 'From arms broker to arms boss', *Mail & Guardian*, 1 February 2002.

27 Feinstein, A. *After the Party*, p 163.

28 *Ibid.*

29 Crawford-Browne, T. *Eye on the Money*, pp 152-153.

30 Minutes: Joint Standing Committee on Defence, Joint Investigation Report into Strategic Defence Packages (Question Formulation), 29 November 2001. Available at: www.pmg.org.za.

31 'More Arms Deal lies', *Business Day*, 8 September 2006. Also see: 'Proceedings of the National Assembly', 6 September 2006, Parliamentary Hansard, NA060906. Available at: www.parliament.gov.za.

32 'The Arms Deal: the shadows lengthen', *Business Day*, 20 September 2006.

33 'Arms Deal brings in R850m for SA firms', *Cape Argus*, 6 November 2007.

34 'Offset scheme spins R11.4bn in investments', *Business Report*, 2 September 2007.

35 'Arms Deal brings in R850m for SA firms', *Cape Argus*, 6 November 2007.

36 *Ibid.*

37 Feinstein, A. *After the Party*, p 162.
38 *Ibid.*
39 'Highs and lows of the Arms Deal … in rands and sense', *Business Report*, 25 July 2004.
40 Crawford-Browne, T. *Eye on the Money*, p 151.
41 Feinstein, A. *After the Party*, p 162.
42 '2008 Estimates of National Expenditure, Vote 19: Defence', p 379. Available at: www.treasury.gov.za.
43 GEAR was adopted in 1996 and committed South Africa to a policy of strict financial conservatism. Social spending would be reduced while the country tried to decrease the foreign debt that had been accrued during the apartheid period. It attracted considerable criticism from the left wing, including Cosatu and the SACP, who criticised the policy as a neo-liberal sellout to the 'Washington consensus'.
44 'Offsets and the affordability of the Arms Deal', Economists Allied For Arms Reduction, 2002. Available at: www.ecaar.org.
45 'The litmus test has not yet been passed', *Mail & Guardian*, 23 November 2001; and 'Strategic Defence Packages: Joint Report', 2001. Available at: www.info.gov.za.
46 'Mbeki quizzed about plans to buy war planes', *Daily News*, 26 November 1998.
47 'Full roll out on the cards?', *Focus*, No 32, November 2003.
48 'Full Report of the Joint Health and Treasury Task Team Charged with Examining Treatment Options to Supplement Comprehensive Care for HIV/Aids in the Public Health Sector', 8 August 2003, paragraph 4.4, p 56. Available at: www.info.gov.za.
49 Extrapolated by the author from the 'National Estimates of Expenditure' for Housing, Defence, Health and Education for the years 1999, 2004 and 2008. All available at: www.treasury.gov.za.
50 The R15 000 housing subsidy figure is taken from: 'People of PE to get 3845 new houses', *Eastern Province Herald*, 20 May 1999; and 'Housing: some DIY required', *The Star*, 18 January 1999. The housing backlog was estimated to stand at roughly 2.3m in November 2007: 'Absa injects money to cut housing backlog', *Mail & Guardian*/SAPA, 26 November 2007. Available at: www.mg.co.za.
51 The above figures for number of categories of employees and their average annual salary is taken from Seidman-Makgetla, N. 'A new labour policy for the public service', *Indicator SA*, Vol 17, No 4,

December 2000. Available at: www.naledi.org.za.

52 According to a 2007 report provided by Eskom, a station the size of Lethabo would have cost roughly R30bn to build in 2007. See: 'Electricity: cost and benefits', *Generation Communication*, 4 May 2007, available at: www.eskom.co.za. The generation capacity of Lethabo is taken from 'Factbox – S. African power crisis: Eskom's generating capacity', Reuters, 18 March 2008. Available at: www. reuters.com. The current shortfall in electricity provision is estimated at 3000 MW/hours, which takes the country below the 'reserve margin' of generation safety. This figure is taken from 'National response to South Africa's electricity shortage', January 2008. Available at: www.info.gov.za.

53 '2008 Estimates of National Expenditure, Vote 19: Defence', p 379. Available at: www.treasury.gov.za.

54 Gevisser, M. *Thabo Mbeki: The Dream Deferred*, p 683.

55 'SA's R13,7bn fighter jets turn into an expensive folly', *Business Day*, 12 March 2007.

56 'Arms Deal sub lies idle', *Cape Argus*, 5 December 2007.

57 'More Arms Deal lies', *Business Day*, 8 September 2006.

CHAPTER 3

1 'More of a cock-up than a conspiracy', *Mail & Guardian*, 16 November 2001.

2 'Deputy President tried to keep arms investigation away from Heath's unit', *Cape Times*, 27 August 2003.

3 'Executive had power to influence arms probe', *Mail & Guardian*, 30 November 2001.

4 *Ibid*, p 10.

5 'De Lille in push for arms probe', *IOL*, 9 September 1999; 'De Lille demands independent arms probe', *IOL*, 12 September 1999.

6 'ANC arms scandal a smear – Lekota', *Saturday Star*, 10 September 1999.

7 'Executive had power to influence arms probe', *Mail & Guardian*, 30 November 2001.

8 *Ibid.*

9 'Mbeki thought to have used apartheid legislation to vet investigator's report', *Mail & Guardian*, 16 November 2001.

10 *Ibid.*

11 'Executive had power to influence arms probe', *Mail & Guardian*, 30 November 2001. For information on Pillay, see: 'Arms Deal participant fired', *Business Day*, 30 May 2002.

12 *Special Review by the Auditor-General of the Selection Process of Strategic Defence Packages for the Acquisition of Armaments at the Department of Defence*, RP161/2000, 15 September 2000, paragraph 3.2. Available at: www.armsdeal-vpo.co.za.

13 *Ibid*, paragraph 3.3.

14 *Ibid*, paragraph 3.1.

15 *Ibid*, paragraph 4. Also see: 'AG recommends probe into certain Arms Deals', *IOL*, 20 September 2000; and 'AG finds flaws in R30bn Arms Deal', *Mail & Guardian*, 21 September 2000.

16 A short history of the Directorate of Special Prosecutions can be found at www.npa.gov.za.

17 'Heath, OSEO probing R30-b Arms Deal', *IOL*, 7 February 2000.

18 *Ibid.*

19 'Baqwa launches Arms Deal investigation', *IOL*, 29 September 2000. A history and description of the powers of the Public Protector's Office can be found at www.publicprotector.org.za.

20 Feinstein, A. *After the Party*, p 157.

21 *Ibid.*

22 *Ibid*, p 159.

23 *Ibid*, p 161.

24 *Ibid*, p 165.

25 'What's a combat suite (and why should we care?)', *Noseweek*, December-January 2003.

26 Feinstein, A. *After the Party*, p 165.

27 'What's a combat suite (and why should we care?)', *Noseweek*, December-January 2003.

28 See: *Strategic Defence Packages: Joint Report*, Chapter 11 – Allegations/complaints by C²I² Systems (Pty) Ltd, 2001. Available for download from www.info.gov.za. When Schabir Shaik was first arrested in 2001 it was on the basis of being in possession of confidential Cabinet documents, suggesting that Schabir had been given minutes relating to the Arms Deal. See: 'Shaik 'had cabinet

minutes and state letters'', *Cape Argus*, 16 November 2001.

29 As is shown later in this chapter, the draft version of the Joint Investigation Report included a section, later excluded, entitled 'Inaccuracies in the presentation to Scopa', which detailed the various ways in which Shaik had misled the committee. See: 'Mystery of Tippex unmasked as entrepreneur battles for justice', *Business Day*, 7 January 2005.

30 Feinstein, A. *After the Party*, pp 166–172.

31 Standing Committee on Public Accounts: *Special Review of Strategic Arms Purchases – SANDF, 30 October 2000*. Available at: www.pmg. org.za.

32 'Summary of background information on the Strategic Defence Procurement Package', issued on behalf of the Government of South Africa by the Ministers of Defence, Finance, Public Enterprises and Trade and Industry, Government Communication Information Systems, 12 January 2001. Available at: www.info.gov.za.

33 A full background of Heath's SIU can be found at www.siu.org.za.

34 'Blacked out to please the state', *Mail & Guardian*, 28 July 2000.

35 'Heath applies for formal probe into Arms Deal', *Mail & Guardian*, 9 January 2000.

36 'Blacked out to please the state', *Mail & Guardian*, 28 July 2000

37 'Heath rejects blackmail claim', *SABCNews*, 11 January 2001.

38 Letter from Thabo Mbeki to Judge Willem Heath, 19 January 2001. Available at: www.info.gov.za.

39 'Mbeki organogram mystery solved', *News24*, 22 January 2001.

40 'Public broadcast on the issue of the strategic defence acquisition programme', Government Communication and Information Service, 19 January 2001. Available at: www.info.gov.za.

41 'Report (A) from the Director of Public Prosecutions Western Cape, Advocate FW Kahn SC, and Advocate J Lubbe SC, to the Minister of Justice and Constitutional Development, PM Maduna', 18 January 2001. Available at: www.info.gov.za.

42 *Sunday Independent*, 21 January 2001, quoted in Feinstein, A. *After the Party*, p 188.

43 'Muddled Maduna missive misses mark on Heath Unit', *Business Day*, 17 January 2001.

44 Feinstein, A. *After the Party*, p 175.

45 *Ibid*, p 176.

46 *Ibid*.

47 Letter to President Mbeki from the Minister of Justice and
   Constitutional Development Dr P Maduna, 15 January 2001.
   Available at www.info.gov.za. Also see: Minutes: Standing
   Committee on Public Accounts, 29 May 2001: Defence
   Procurement Package Investigation (Second Committee Report),
   available for download from www.pmg.org.za
48 Letter from Frene Ginwala to Hon. Jacob Zuma, 29 January 2001.
   Submitted as Appendix 1 during Special Review of *Strategic Arms
   Acquisition: Standing Committee on Public Accounts*, Briefing by Dr
   Frene Ginwala, 29 January 2001. Available at: www.pmg.org.za.
49 This letter was used in the State's evidence against Schabir Shaik
   to show that Zuma had attempted to block the probe into the
   Arms Deal. Thabo Mbeki, however, later admitted that he had
   authorised the letter. Jacob Zuma has claimed that Mbeki did more
   than just authorise the letter: he has claimed that Mbeki actually
   wrote it. See: 'I authorised Zuma's letter to Woods – Mbeki', *Sunday
   Argus*, 26 February 2006; 'Arms-deal letter pivotal in Zuma's battle',
   Business Day, 29 August 2006 and 'Arms Deal returns to haunt
   ANC', *Mail & Guardian*, 11 February 2007.
50 Letter from the Deputy President, Mr. Jacob Zuma, to the
   Chairperson of the Parliamentary Standing Committee on Public
   Accounts, Dr Gavin Woods, 19 January 2001. Available at:
   www.info.gov.za.
51 See: Feinstein, A. *After the Party*, p 191.
52 *Ibid*, p 192.
53 'ANC cracks whip in watchdog committee', *Sunday Independent*,
   3 February 2001.
54 Feinstein, A. *After the Party*, p 204.
55 *Ibid*, p 207.
56 'Scopa "too busy" for arms probe', *News24*, 12 June 2001.
57 'Gavin Woods resigns', *News24/SAPA*, 25 February 2002.
58 'The last rites have been read', *Mail & Guardian*, 7 March 2002.
59 See: *Strategic Defence Packages: Joint Report*, Chapter 11 –
   Allegations/complaints by C^2I^2 Systems (Pty) LTD, 2001. Available
   at: www.info.gov.za.
60 *Ibid*, Chapter 10, paragraph 10.5.4.
61 *Ibid*, Chapter 11, paragraphs 11.6.9.8 and 11.6.9.10.
62 See: 'How Modise wrangled SA's fighter jet deal', *Mail & Guardian*,
   3 November 2001.

63 *Strategic Defence Packages: Joint Report*, Chapter 14, paragraph 14.1.7. Available at: www.info.gov.za.
64 'German arms probe fingers late Modise', *Sowetan*, 26 March 2008.
65 *Strategic Defence Packages: Joint Report*, Chapter 14, paragraph 14.1.25. Available at: www.info.gov.za.
66 'Defence chief says his conscience is clear', *Mail & Guardian*, 18 July 2001.
67 *Strategic Defence Packages: Joint Report*, Chapter 14, paragraph 14.1.13. Available at: www.info.gov.za.
68 *Ibid*, paragraph 14.1.1.
69 Mbeki, T. 'Truth stands in the way of Arms Deal accusers', *ANC Today*, 16 November 2001. Available at: www.anc.org.za.
70 'Chippy Shaik meddled in arms probe', *Mail & Guardian*, 23 November 2001.
71 *Ibid*.
72 *Ibid*.
73 'Arms Deal report was 'heavily edited'', *Mail & Guardian*, 21 May 2003.
74 'Mystery of Tippex unmasked as entrepreneur battles for justice', *Business Day*, 7 January 2005
75 Feinstein, A. *After the Party*, p 212.
76 *Ibid*, p 214.
77 *Ibid*.
78 *Ibid*, p 215.
79 'Mystery of Tippex unmasked as entrepreneur battles for justice', *Business Day*, 7 January 2005.
80 'How state "edited" arms report to Parliament', *Business Day*, 21 May 2003.
81 *Ibid*.
82 'Parliament must unravel arms-deal mess', *Sunday Independent*, 23 January 2005.

CHAPTER 4

1 'In the matter between the State and Tony Sithembiso Yengeni (Accused No. 1) and Michael Joseph Worfel (Accused No. 2),

Accused No.1's Plea of Guilty', Case No. 14/09193/01, 2003.
Available at: www.armsdeal-vpo.co.za.

2 'Tony Yengeni, the 4x4 and the R43bn arms probe', *Sunday Times*, 25 March 2001.

3 'My car feels like flying a jet – Yengeni', *The Argus*, 26 March 2001.

4 *Ibid.*

5 'The De Lille Dossier', 1999. Available at: www.armsdeal-vpo.co.za.

6 'This is a story about a 4x4, one of the most powerful men in Parliament and how they got bogged down in the R43bn Arms Deal controversy', *Sunday Times*, 25 March 2001.

7 *Ibid.*

8 *Ibid.*

9 *Ibid.*

10 'Now it's Tony three-Mercs', *Sunday Times*, 29 April 2001.

11 'This is a story about a 4x4, one of the most powerful men in Parliament and how they got bogged down in the R43bn Arms Deal controversy', *Sunday Times*, 25 March 2001.

12 'In the matter between the State and Tony Sithembiso Yengeni (Accused No. 1) and Michael Joseph Worfel (Accused No. 2), Accused No.1's Plea of Guilty', Case No. 14/09193/01, 2003. Available at: www.armsdeal-vpo.co.za.

13 *Ibid.*

14 'Car allegations are hogwash, says Yengeni', *The Star*, 25 March 2001.

15 'Statement by Tony Yengeni regarding media reports', July 2001. Available at: www.armsdeal-vpo.co.za.

16 'A round to Yengeni', *Business Day*, 7 September 2001.

17 'Statement by Tony Yengeni regarding media reports', July 2001. Available at: www.armsdeal-vpo.co.za.

18 *Ibid.*

19 *Ibid.*

20 'Tony comes out swinging', *Mail & Guardian*, 1 April 2001.

21 'Statement by Tony Yengeni regarding media reports', July 2001. Available at: www.armsdeal-vpo.co.za.

22 'Buddies coughed up for "facts" on Yengeni 4x4', *City Press*, 22 July 2001.

23 *Sowetan*, 18 July 2001.

24 'Registrar urges Yengeni probe', SAPA/*News24*, 8 May 2001.

25 'Minutes: Joint Committee on Ethics and Members' Interests:

Yengeni Ethics Enquiry', 22 May 2001. Available at: www.pmg.org.
za.
26 'Appendix 1: Report No 1 to the Joint Committee on Ethics and
Members' Interests with regards to the complaint against Tony
Yengeni' in 'Minutes: Joint Committee on Ethics and Members'
Interests: Yengeni Ethics Enquiry', 22 May 2001. Available at:
www.pmg.org.za.
27 *Ibid.*
28 All above taken from: 'Appendix: Interim Report of the Joint
Committee on Ethics and Members' Interests with regard to
the complaint against Mr T S Yengeni MP' in 'Minutes: Joint
Committee on Ethics and Members' Interests: Yengeni Ethics
Enquiry', 29 May 2001. Available at: www.pmg.org.za.
29 'ANC lets Yengeni off the hook', *Business Day*, 10 May 2001.
30 'Yengeni charged with fraud, perjury, forgery', *Mail & Guardian/*
SAPA, 3 October 2001; and 'I'm stepping down, says Yengeni', *IOL/*
SAPA, 4 October 2001.
31 'Yengeni stung by Scorpions', *Pretoria News*, 6 October 2001.
32 'Tony Yengeni found guilty of fraud', *Mail & Guardian/*SAPA,
13 February 2003; and 'State withdraws case against German
businessman', *SAPA*, 19 March 2003.
33 'In the matter between the State and Tony Sithembiso Yengeni
(Accused No. 1) and Michael Joseph Worfel (Accused No. 2),
Accused No.1's Plea of Guilty', Case No. 14/09193/01, 2003.
Available at: www.armsdeal-vpo.co.za.
34 Taken from: 'Statement by Tony Yengeni regarding media reports',
July 2001, available at: www.armsdeal-vpo.co.za; and 'Tony comes
out swinging', *Mail & Guardian*, 1 April 2001.
35 'In the matter between the State and Tony Sithembiso Yengeni
(Accused No. 1) and Michael Joseph Worfel (Accused No. 2),
Accused No.1's Plea of Guilty', Case No. 14/09193/01, 2003.
Available at: www.armsdeal-vpo.co.za.
36 'Yengeni's ANC membership suspended', *Business Day*, 30 July
2003; and 'Yengeni bows to pressure', *Natal Witness*, 6 March
2003.
37 'Magistrate slams Yengeni's "shocking example"', *Cape Times*,
20 March 2003.
38 *Ibid.*
39 'Yengeni has "72 hours to report to Pollsmoor"', *IOL/*SAPA,

21 August 2006.

40 'ANC leaders flock to Yengeni's release', *Mail & Guardian*,
15 January 2007.

41 'Yengeni's warm jail memories', *The Witness*, 12 January 2007.

42 'From hero to zero … to hero', *The Star*, 8 January 2008.

43 'Back with a Zuma', *Mail & Guardian*, 19 January 2007.

44 *Ibid;* and 'Outcry at Yengeni release "disgrace"', *Business Day*,
16 January 2007.

CHAPTER 5

1 'Soldiering ahead in business', *Saturday Star*, 6 November 1999.

2 *Ibid*; and 'How Modise wrangled SA's jet fighter deal', *Mail &
Guardian*, 3 November 2001.

3 'BAe and the Arms Deal: Part 1', *Moneyweb*, 14 August 2007.
Available at: www.moneyweb.co.za.

4 *Ibid.*

5 *Strategic Defence Packages: Joint Report*, 2001, Chapter 4, paragraphs
4.1.12–4.1.13. Available at: www.info.gov.za.

6 *Ibid.*

7 'BAe and the Arms Deal: Part 1', *Moneyweb*, 14 August 2007.
Available at: www.moneyweb.co.za.

8 *Ibid.*

9 *Ibid.*

10 *Ibid.*

11 The Joint Investigating Report notes that in a workshop prior to
the three-tier system being decided on, it was reported that 'the
2-tier system was not acceptable to the Minister of Defence'. See:
Strategic Defence Packages: Joint Report, 2001, Chapter 4, paragraph
4.3.1.4. Available at www.info.gov.za.

12 *Ibid.*

13 'BAe's Hawks more like albatrosses', *The Star*, 13 January 2007.

14 'Strategic Defence Packages: Joint Report', 2001, Chapter 4,
paragraph 4.3.1.6. Available at: www.info.gov.za.

15 *Ibid.*

16 'BAe and the Arms Deal: Part 1', *Moneyweb*, 14 August 2007.

Available at: www.moneyweb.co.za.

17 *Strategic Defence Packages: Joint Report*, 2001, Chapter 4, paragraph 4.3.6.3. Available at: www.info.gov.za.

18 'Strategic Defence Packages: Joint Report', 2001, Chapter 4, paragraph 4.5.1.10. Available at: www.info.gov.za.

19 'BAe and the Arms Deal: Part 2', *Moneyweb*, 15 August 2007. Available at: www.moneyweb.co.za.

20 *Ibid*.

21 *Ibid*.

22 *Strategic Defence Packages: Joint Report*, 2001, Chapter 4, paragraph 4.5.1.10. Available at: www.info.gov.za.

23 *Ibid*, paragraphs 4.5.3.6–4.5.3.7.

24 'BAe and the Arms Deal: Part 2', *Moneyweb*, 15 August 2007. Available at www.moneyweb.co.za.

25 *Strategic Defence Packages: Joint Report*, 2001, Chapter 4, paragraph 4.5.5.2. Available at: www.info.gov.za.

26 *Ibid*, paragraph 4.5.5.3.

27 *Ibid*.

28 *Ibid*.

29 *Ibid*.

30 'Pierre Steyn speaks out about the Arms Deal', *Mail & Guardian*, 2 February 2007.

31 *Ibid*; and 'BAe and the Arms Deal: Part 2', *Moneyweb*, 15 August 2007. Available at: www.moneyweb.co.za.

32 *Ibid*.

33 'BAe and the Arms Deal: Part 2', *Moneyweb*, 15 August 2007. Available at: www.moneyweb.co.za.

34 *Ibid*.

35 *Ibid*.

36 *Ibid*.

37 *Ibid*.

38 *Ibid*.

39 *Strategic Defence Packages: Joint Report*, 2001, Chapter 4, paragraph 4.12.1. Available at: www.info.gov.za.

40 *Ibid*, paragraph 4.12.2.

41 *Ibid*.

42 See: www.conlog.co.za.

43 Feinstein, A. *After the Party*, p 155. Also see: 'Modise was bought', *Noseweek*, December 2003.

44 'Soldiering ahead in business', *Saturday Star*, 6 November 1999.

45 Feinstein, A. *After the Party*, p 210.

46 'BAE denies it paid for Modise's cars', SAPA, 7 March 2003.

47 'BAE rubbishes Arms Deal claims", *Mail & Guardian*/SAPA, 16 December 2003.

48 See: 'Another export success for the SA economy", 11 May 2007, www.abbptt.co.za/news/.

49 'National industrial participation (NIP), Defence Summary: Project Description', September 1999. Available at: www.info.gov.za/ issues/procurement/background/nip.html.

50 'Memorandum of Understanding MKMVA', http://www.anc.org.za/ ancdocs/pr/1998/pr0325.html.

51 'MK Veterans Receive R4.5m Aerospace Lift', http://www.anc.org. za/ancdocs/pr/1998/pr0325.html.

52 Mashike, L. and Mokalobe, M. 2003. 'Reintegration into Civilian Life: The Case of Former MK and APLA Combatants', *Track Two*, Vol. 12, Nos 1 and 2, September.

53 'Veterans Inc', *Mail & Guardian*, 20 September 2007.

54 'BAe denies it paid for Modise's cars", *Mail & Guardian*, 3 July 2003.

55 'File on Four', Radio Documentary broadcast on BBC Radio 4, 2003. Transcript available at: www.armsdeal-vpo.co.za.

56 Feinstein, A. *After the Party*, pp 177-178.

57 'BAe and the Arms Deal: Part 1', *Moneyweb*, 14 August 2007. Available at: www.moneyweb.co.za.

58 'BAe's web of influence in South Africa', *Mail & Guardian*, 12 January 2007.

59 *Ibid.*

60 *Ibid.*

61 'BAE Systems, the Hawks and the role of the British', *Business Report*, 8 October 2006.

62 'BAe and the Arms Deal: Part 1', *Moneyweb*, 14 August 2007. Available at: www.moneyweb.co.za.

63 'Comment from Campaign Against Arms Trade on the draft corruption legislation', August 2003. Available at: www.caat.org. uk.

64 '"Billions paid to SA agents" in Arms Deal', *Cape Times*, 1 July 2003.

CHAPTER 6

1 'Chippy Shaik blasted in arms report', *Mail & Guardian*,
   16 November 2001.
2 *Ibid.*
3 'Scorpions grab Arms Deal proof', *Beeld*, 9 October 2001; and
   'Scorpions raid France, Mauritius, SA', *Business Day*, 10 October
   2001.
4 'Shaik "had Cabinet minutes and state letters"', *Cape Argus*,
   16 November 2001.
5 'Shaik to appear in Durban court', *IOL*, 20 January 2002.
6 *Ibid.*
7 'Arms bidder in court over minister's minutes', *IOL*, 27 May 2002.
8 *Ibid.*
9 'Scorpions probe Jacob Zuma', *Mail & Guardian*, 29 November
   2002.
10 'Scorpions grill Shaik for seven hours', *Mail & Guardian*, 30 July
   2003.
11 'Maharaj's words come back to haunt him', *Business Day*, 31 July
   2003.
12 'Thumbs up for Mac's decision', *News24*, 14 August 2003.
13 O'Malley, P. 2008. *Shades of Difference: Mac Maharaj and the Struggle
   for South Africa*, Penguin: Johannesburg, p 416.
14 *Ibid.*
15 'Press statement by Bulelani Thandabantu Ngcuka, National
   Director of Public Prosecutions on the decision on whether
   to prosecute after the completion of the investigation against
   Deputy President, Mr Jacob Zuma, Schabir Shaik and others',
   23 August 2003. Available at: www.armsdeal-vpo.co.za.
16 *Ibid.*
17 *Ibid.*
18 'Was Ngcuka a spy?', *City Press*, 6 September 2003.
19 *Ibid.*
20 *Ibid.*
21 *Ibid.*
22 'Masters of political diversion do SA's revolution no favours',
   Business Day, 11 September 2003.
23 'Spy claim just a sign of desperation', *The Star*, 12 September 2003.
24 'Mo: I went public for Zuma', *The Star*, 21 November 2003.

25 O'Malley, P. 2008. *Shades of Difference: Mac Maharaj and the Struggle for South Africa*, Penguin: Johannesburg, p 416.

26 *Ibid.*

27 'Judge names auditor for spy probe's work', *Business Day*, 3 October 2003.

28 'Evidence row rocks spy probe', *The Star*, 16 October 2003.

29 '"I am Agent RS452"', *The Star*, 21 October 2003.

30 *Ibid.*

31 'The truth should make Ngcuka's accusers hang heads in shame', *Business Day*, 23 October 2003.

32 *Ibid.*

33 'Ngcuka a spy? Impossible, says Maqhubela', *Daily News*, 22 October 2003.

34 *Ibid.*

35 *Ibid.*

36 'The truth should make Ngcuka's accusers hang heads in shame', *Business Day*, 23 October 2003.

37 *Ibid.*

38 'Ngcuka a spy? Impossible, says Maqhubela', *Daily News*, 22 October 2003; and 'Who is Mr X?', *Cape Times*, 24 October 2003.

39 'Maharaj on the attack', *Cape Times*, 18 November 2003.

40 *Ibid.*

41 'Mac: All I have is my integrity', *IOL*/SAPA, 18 November 2003.

42 'Hefer Report: NDPP's office filled with leaks', *The Star*, 21 January 2004.

43 'Grilled Mac fingers Mo', *The Star*, 18 November 2003.

44 'Tide turns on Maharaj as spy claims fall apart', *Business Day*, 19 November 2003.

45 'How Mac caved under fire', *Cape Times*, 20 November 2003.

46 'Mo: I went public for Zuma', *The Star*, 21 November 2003.

47 'How Mac and Mo came apart', *Sunday Times*, 23 November 2003.

48 'Mo Shaik close to tears at Hefer', *Mail & Guardian*, 20 November 2003.

49 'Mo: I went public for Zuma', *The Star*, 21 November 2003.

50 'Ngcuka cleared on spy charges', *Cape Times*, 20 January 2004.

51 'Hefer Report: NDPP's office filled with leaks', *The Star*, 21 January 2004.

52 *Ibid.*

53 'Zuma lodges complaint with Public Protector over Ngcuka and "malicious" probe', *Cape Times*, 7 November 2003

54 'Public Protector raps Ngcuka', *News24*, 28 May 2004.

55 *Ibid.*

56 'First meeting of Scorpions committee', *Sunday Argus*, 6 June 2004.

57 'Public Protector a "liar" and "sad case"', *Mail & Guardian*, 30 May 2004.

58 'Ngcuka sorry, but says he'll fight Mushwana', *Cape Times*, 4 June 2004; and 'Ngcuka defies the ANC', *City Press*, 5 June 2004.

59 'Public Protector changed tune', *Sunday Times*, 27 June 2004.

60 *Ibid.*

61 'Mushwana findings on Zuma "flawed"', *Cape Argus*, 30 August 2006.

62 NPA questions Mushwana's ambit on Zuma report, *The Star*, 30 August 2006.

63 'Zuma chose own "jury"', *Mail & Guardian*, 18 June 2004.

64 *Ibid.*

65 *Ibid.*

66 'MPs divided over Ngcuka finding', *City Press*, 19 June 2004.

67 *Ibid.*

68 'The lion that mewed', *Mail & Guardian*, 24 July 2004.

69 'Mission accomplished', *Sunday Times*, 1 August 2004.

CHAPTER 7

1 Squires, H. Judgment in the matter between the State and Schabir Shaik *et al*. Case No. CC27/04, 31 May 2005. Available at: www.armsdeal-vpo.co.za.

2 In the High Court of South Africa (Durban and Coastal Local Division) in the matter between the State and Schabir Shaik and Others: Indictment. Available at: www.armsdeal-vpo.co.za.

3 *Ibid*, paragraphs 20–24.

4 *Ibid*, paragraph 20.

5 *Ibid*, paragraph 25.

6 *Ibid*, paragraph 28.

7 *Ibid*.

8 In the High Court of South Africa (Durban Coastal and Local Division) in the matter between the State and Schabir Shaik and Others: Summary of Substantial Facts in terms of Section 144(3)(a) of Act 51 of 1977, paragraph 26. Available at: www.armsdeal-vpo.co.za.

9 *Ibid.*

10 *Ibid.*

11 *Ibid.*

12 In the High Court of South Africa (Durban and Coastal Local Division) in the matter between the State and Schabir Shaik and Others: Indictment, paragraph 28. Available at: www.armsdeal-vpo.co.za.

13 In the High Court of South Africa (Durban Coastal and Local Division) in the matter between the State and Schabir Shaik and Others: Summary of Substantial Facts in terms of Section 144(3)(a) of Act 51 of 1977, paragraphs 38–45. Available at: www.armsdeal-vpo.co.za.

14 *Ibid.*

15 See: 'Modise quizzed in arms probe', *Dispatch*, 5 October 2001; 'Arms and empowerment – cadres cash in', *Financial Mail*, 4 May 2001; Feinstein, A. *After the Party*, p 143. In his judgment on the Shaik trial, Judge Hilary Squires noted that FBS was 'an acceptable black empowerment partner to the Government'. Also see: In the matter between the State and Schabir Shaik *et al*. Case No. CC27/04, 31 May 2005. Available at: www.armsdeal-vpo.co.za.

16 In the High Court of South Africa (Durban Coastal and Local Division) in the matter between the State and Schabir Shaik and Others: Summary of Substantial Facts in terms of Section 144(3)(a) of Act 51 of 1977. Available at: www.armsdeal-vpo.co.za.

17 *Ibid.*

18 *Ibid.*

19 *Ibid.*

20 *Ibid.*

21 *Ibid.*

22 *Ibid*, paragraphs 54–55.

23 In the High Court of South Africa (Durban and Coastal Local Division) in the matter between the State and Schabir Shaik and Others: Indictment. Available at: www.armsdeal-vpo.co.za.

24 In the High Court of South Africa (Durban Coastal and Local

Division) in the matter between the State and Schabir Shaik and
Others: Summary of Substantial Facts in terms of Section 144(3)(a)
of Act 51 of 1977, paragraphs 92–125. Available at: www.armsdeal-
vpo.co.za.

25 *Ibid.*

26 *Ibid.*

27 *Ibid.*

28 *Ibid.*

29 *Ibid.*

30 *Ibid*, paragraphs 126–158.

31 *Ibid.*

32 All above taken from *Ibid*

33 *Ibid.*

34 In the High Court of South Africa (Durban and Coastal Local
Division) in the matter between the State and Schabir Shaik and
Others: Indictment. Available at: www.armsdeal-vpo.co.za.

35 In the High Court of South Africa (Durban Coastal and Local
Division) in the matter between the State and Schabir Shaik and
Others: Summary of Substantial Facts in terms of Section 144(3)(a)
of Act 51 of 1977, paragraphs 92–125. Available at: www.armsdeal-
vpo.co.za.

36 'State outlines case', *Daily News*, 14 October 2004.

37 '"I'm not guilty; he's just a good friend"', *Cape Argus*, 13 October
2004.

38 *Ibid.*

39 *Ibid.*

40 *Ibid.*

41 *Ibid.*

42 *Ibid.*

43 'The big showdown', *The Star*, 14 October 2004.

44 *Ibid.*

45 'Zuma did meet Thetard, Shaik claims', *Business Day*, 25 February
2005.

46 'Shaik "boasted of links with Zuma"', *Mail & Guardian*, 14 October
2004.

47 *Ibid.*

48 *Ibid.*

49 *Ibid.*

50 *Ibid.*

51 *Ibid.*
52 *Ibid.*
53 'Witness illustrates Shaik deal strategy', *Sunday Times*, 28
    November 2004; '"Zuma used clout to promote Shaik"', *Cape
    Times*, 26 November 2004; '"Shaik used Zuma to quash plans
    for ecotourism school"', *Business Day*, 26 November 2004;
    'Shaik "used influence with Zuma to stop eco tourism school"',
    SAPA, 25 November 2004; and 'Scottish professor testifies about
    correspondence', SAPA, 25 November 2004.
54 *Ibid.*
55 *Ibid.*
56 *Ibid.*
57 *Ibid.*
58 *Ibid.*
59 'Quote unquote', *The Star*, 11 December 2004.
60 'Zuma finances "dealt with daily"', *Cape Argus*, 18 October 2004.
61 *Ibid.*
62 *Ibid.*
63 'Shaik's assistant spills the beans', *Mail & Guardian*, 18 October
    2004.
64 *Ibid.*
65 *Ibid.*
66 'Shaik's call to Zuma for help', News24/SAPA, 15 October 2004.
67 *Ibid.*
68 In the High Court of South Africa (Durban and Coastal Local
    Division) in the matter between the State and Schabir Shaik and
    Others: Indictment.' Available at: www.armsdeal-vpo.co.za .
69 'Shaik sought Arms Deal damage control – Singh', News24,
    18 October 2004.
70 *Ibid.*
71 *Ibid.*
72 Squires, J. 'Judgment on Admissibility: 17 February 2005, in the
    High Court of South Africa (Durban and Coastal Local Division) in
    the matter between the State and Schabir Shaik and Others,' Case
    No: CC27/04. Available at: www.armsdeal-vpo.co.za.
73 'Encrypted Zuma fax sees light', *SAPA*, 19 October 2004.
74 *Ibid.*
75 'Secretaries have their day', *Sunday Times*, 24 October 2004.
76 'Hi-tech explanation lends weight to encrypted fax', *SAPA*,

26 November 2004.

77 *Ibid.*

78 *Ibid.*

79 *Ibid.*

80 'Witnesses who made Shaik trial worth watching', *The Star,*
10 December 2004.

81 *Ibid.*

82 'And our Mampara of the Year is ... Jacob Zuma!', *Sunday Times,*
21 December 2004.

83 'Zuma owes Shaik "half his pension"', *Mail & Guardian,* 15
November 2004.

84 'A poor deputy president', *Mail & Guardian,* 22 October 2004.

85 'The witnesses that made the Shaik trial worth watching', *The
Star,* 10 December 2001; and 'Partner gave the go-ahead for R1,2m
write-off', *The Star,* 23 November 2004.

86 *Ibid.*

87 'Heaven help SA – Shaik bookkeeper', *Cape Argus,* 17 November
2004.

88 'Shaik cooked books to hide Zuma bribes', *Business Day,*
17 November 2004.

89 'Heaven help SA – Shaik bookkeeper', *Cape Argus,* 17 November
2004.

90 'Zuma letter alarming, says MP', *Daily News,* 1 December 2004.

91 Squires, H. 'Judgment in the matter between the State and Schabir
Shaik *et al.*' Case No. CC27/04, 31 May 2005. Available at: www.
armsdeal-vpo.co.za.

92 *Ibid.*

93 *Ibid.*

94 *Ibid.*

95 *Ibid.*

96 *Ibid.*

97 *Ibid.*

98 *Ibid.*

99 *Ibid.*

100 *Ibid.*

101 *Ibid.*

102 *Ibid.*

103 *Ibid.*

104 *Ibid.*

105 *Ibid.*

106 Extrapolated from: Squires, H. 'Judgment in the matter between the State and Schabir Shaik *et al.*' Case No. CC27/04, 31 May 2005. Available at: www.armsdeal-vpo.co.za.

107 'Allegations of Involvement of Deputy President Jacob Zuma in Arms Deals', Office of the Presidency, 9 September 1999. Available at: www.armsdeal-vpo.co.za.

108 Squires, H. 'Judgment in the matter between the State and Schabir Shaik *et al.*' Case No. CC27/04, 31 May 2005. Available at: www.armsdeal-vpo.co.za.

109 'Shaik granted leave to appeal', *SAPA*, 29 July 2005.

110 *Ibid.*

111 *Ibid;* and 'Shaik wins some, loses most', *Sunday Times*, 31 July 2005.

112 *Ibid.*

113 This was a controversial statement. The phrase was initially attributed to Squires, but he later pointed out that he never used the term. In fact, it was the prosecution that used the term, but, due to consistent errors in media reportage, it was assumed that this was, indeed, the term that Squires had used in reaching his judgment. Nevertheless, it was an accurate portrayal of the essential case against Shaik, and has, with due cause, entered into the popular vocabulary as the gist of the case against Shaik and Zuma on this first charge. The trial judges at the Supreme Court of Appeal also made use of the phrase. See 'Judgment in the Supreme Court of Appeal of South Africa in the matter Between Schabir Shaik and Others', Case No. 62/06, 6 November 2006, paragraph 8. Available at: www.armsdeal-vpo.co.za.

114 'S Shaik and 10 Others vs. The State (Criminal Appeal) and S Shaik and 4 Others v The State (Civil Appeal)', Judgment Summary, paragraphs 6–7 in 'Judgment' in the Supreme Court of Appeal of South Africa in the matter between Schabir Shaik and Others, Case No. 62/06, 6 November 2006. Available at: www.armsdeal-vpo.co.za.

115 *Ibid*, paragraph 8.

116 *Ibid,* paragraphs 11-12.

117 See 'Judgment, in the Supreme Court of Appeal of South Africa in the matter between Schabir Shaik and Others', Case No. 62/06, 6 November 2006, paragraph 223. Available at: www.armsdeal-vpo.co.za.

118 'Guilty! Guilty! Guilty!', *The Star*, 2 October 2007.
119 'Bleak day for Shaik', IAfrica/SAPA, 29 May 2008.
120 *Ibid.*

CHAPTER 8

1 Mbeki, T. Statement at the Joint Sitting of Parliament on the Release of Hon Jacob Zuma from his Responsibilities of Deputy President, 14 June 2005. Available at: www.info.gov.za.
2 'Heath in Zuma firestorm', *The Star*, 29 June 2005.
3 'Zuma case struck off roll', *SAPA*, 20 September 2006.
4 'Zunami rules', *Sowetan*, 19 December 2007.
5 See: 'Zuma to fight charges', *Mail & Guardian/SAPA*, 15 May 2008.
6 'Indictment: In the High Court of South Africa (Durban and Coastal Local Division) in the matter between the State and Jacob Zuma, Thint Holding and Thint (Pty)'; and 'Summary of Substantial Facts In Terms of Section 144(3)(a) of Act 51 of 1977 in the High Court of South Africa (Durban and Coastal Local Division) in the matter between the State and Jacob Zuma, Thint Holding and Thint (Pty)'. Both available at: www.armsdeal-vpo. co.za.
7 *Ibid.*
8 *Ibid.*
9 'State seeks to put Zuma trial on hold', *Business Day*, 21 July 2006.
10 'Zuma's lawyers tackle Scorpions', *Sunday Times*, 28 August 2005.
11 'Round 1: Scorpions 0 Zuma 1', *News24/SAPA*, 9 September 2005.
12 'Zuma on offensive against Scorpions' raids and seizures', *Business Day*, 26 September 2005.
13 'Zuma goes for the KO', *Mail & Guardian*, 17 February 2006.
14 'Raids by Scorpions were legal, says judge', *IOL*, 5 July 2006.
15 *Ibid.*
16 *Ibid.*
17 *Ibid.*
18 *Ibid.*
19 'Complaint led against Hlophe for interfering in Zuma appeal', 30 May 2008, Statement issued by Constitutional Court judges.

Available at: www.politicsweb.co.za.

20 'Statement in support of complaint to the Judicial Services
Commission by the Judges of the Constitutional Court made on
30 May 2008', 17 June 2008, in Letter to Justice CT Howie, Judicial
Services Commission, from Chief Justice Pius Langa, 17 June 2008.
Available at: www.armsdeal-vpo.co.za.

21 *Ibid.*

22 *Ibid.*

23 Hlophe, M.J. 'Response to the statement of Chief Justice Langa
filed on behalf of the Constitutional Court Judges, 30 June 2008',
2 July 2008. Available at: www.politicsweb.co.za.

24 *Ibid.*

25 *Ibid.*

26 Langa, P. 'Statement in response to complaint made to the Judicial
Service Commission by Hlophe JP made on 10 June 2008', in
Letter to Justice CT Howie, Judicial Services Commission from
Chief Justice Pius Langa, 17 June 2008. Available at: www.
armsdeal-vpo.co.za.

27 *Ibid.*

28 Langa, C. 2008. Judgment in the Constitutional Court of South
Africa, Case CCT89/07 and Case CCT91/07 in the matter of
Thint vs. National Director of Public Prosecutions and Others
and Jacob Zuma and Michael Hulley vs. National Director of
Public Prosecutions and Others, 31 July. Available at: www.
constitutionalcourt.org.za and www.armsdeal-vpo.co.za.

29 Judgment in the Constitutional Court of South Africa, Case
CCT89/07 and Case CCT91/07 in the matter of Thint vs. National
Director of Public Prosecutions and Others and Jacob Zuma and
Michael Hulley vs. National Director of Public Prosecutions and
Others, 31 July. Available at: www.constitutionalcourt.org.za and
www.armsdeal-vpo.co.za. Also Media summary of judgment in the
Constitutional Court of South Africa, Case CCT89/07 and Case
CCT91/07 in the matter of Thint vs. National Director of Public
Prosecutions and Others and Jacob Zuma and Michael Hulley
vs. National Director of Public Prosecutions and Others, 31 July.
Available at: www.constitutionalcourt.org.za and www.armsdeal-
vpo.co.za.

30 Media Summary of judgment in the Constitutional Court of
South Africa, Case CCT89/07 and Case CCT91/07 in the matter

of Thint vs. National Director of Public Prosecutions and Others and Jacob Zuma and Michael Hulley vs. National Director of Public Prosecutions and Others, 31 July. Available at: www. constitutionalcourt.org.za and www.armsdeal-vpo.co.za.

31 *Ibid*.

32 *Ibid*.

33 'Nzimande "not surprised" by Zuma judgment', SAPA, 31 July 2008.

34 'Political hand behind Zuma judgment: SASCO', SAPA, 31 July 2008.

35 'Cosatu "respects" Concourt ruling', SAPA, 31 July 2008.

36 Jacob Zuma vs. The Hon. Attorney General and Others, in the Supreme Court of Mauritius, 30 June 2008, Record No. 240/08. Available at: www.npa.org.za.

37 *Ibid*.

38 Sole, S. 'Legally lush, factually sparse', *Mail & Guardian*, 4 August; and 'Zuma drags President into the fray', *The Star*, 2 August 2006.

39 *Ibid*.

40 *Ibid*.

41 'COSAS "will down pens" if Zuma case is postponed', *Cape Times*, 27 July 2006.

42 'E Cape Cosatu considers strike over Zuma trial', *Mail & Guardian*, 24 July 2006.

43 'Crooks hide at NPA, young communists claim', *IOL/SAPA*, 28 July 2006.

44 Sole, S. 'Legally lush, factually sparse', *Mail & Guardian*, 4 August; and 'Zuma drags President into the fray', *The Star*, 2 August 2006.

45 'First Accused's Answering Affidavit, in the High Court of South Africa Natal Provincial Division in the matter between the State and Jacob Gedleyihlekisa Zuma and Others', Case No. CC358/2005, paragraph 20.

46 *Ibid*, paragraph 32(a).

47 *Ibid*, paragraphs 86–87.

48 *Ibid*, paragraph 62.

49 *Ibid*, paragraph 28–30.

50 *Ibid*, paragraph 47.

51 Sole, S. 'Legally lush, factually sparse', *Mail & Guardian*, 4 August; and 'Zuma drags President into the fray', *The Star*, 2 August 2006.

52 'First Accused's Answering Affidavit, in the High Court of South

Africa Natal Provincial Division in the matter between the
State and Jacob Gedleyihlekisa Zuma and Others', Case No.
CC358/2005, paragraph 66.

53 *Ibid*, paragraph 66.

54 *Ibid*.

55 *Ibid*, paragraph 55.

56 'Affidavit of Mr Ngcuka in the High Court of South Africa
Natal Provincial Division in the matter between the State and
Jacob Gedleyihlekisa Zuma and Others', Case No. CC358/2005.
Emphasis in the original. Available at: www.armsdeal-vpo.co.za.

57 'The empire strikes back', *Mail & Guardian*, 16 August 2006; and
'Prosecutors slam Zuma in court papers', *IOL/SAPA*, 18 August
2006.

58 'Affidavit of Dr Maduna in the High Court of South Africa Natal
Provincial Division in the matter between the State and Jacob
Gedleyihlekisa Zuma and Others', Case No. CC358/2005. Available
at: www.armsdeal-vpo.co.za.

59 'Zuma ridicules Pikoli's story', *Star*, 23 August 2006; and 'Zuma
stands by his conspiracy theory', *Pretoria News*, 24 August 2006.

60 *Ibid*.

61 'NPA questions Mushwana's ambit on Zuma report', *The Star*, 30
August 2006.

62 *Ibid*

63 'Case against Zuma "was doomed from the start"', *Cape Argus*, 21
September 2006.

64 'Zuma case struck off roll', *SAPA*, 20 September 2006.

65 The State never directly admitted to including the seized
documents in the evidence to be used in a reformulated
indictment of Zuma and Thint. This was claimed to be the case by
Zuma and Thint; this claim was 'not denied by the defence'. See:
Msimang, H. 2006. Judgment in the High Court of South Africa
(Natal Provincial Division) in the matter between the State and
Jacob Gedleyihlekisa Zuma, Thint Holdings (Southern Africa) (Pty)
Ltd and Thint (Pty) Ltd. Available at: www.saflii.org.

66 Msimang, H. 2006. Judgment in the High Court of South Africa
(Natal Provincial Division) in the matter between the State and
Jacob Gedleyihlekisa Zuma, Thint Holdings (Southern Africa) (Pty)
Ltd and Thint (Pty) Ltd. Available at: www.saflii.org.

67 'Jubilation as Zuma case struck from the roll', *SAPA*, 20 September 2006.

68 *Ibid.*

69 'JZ fans revelling in court victory should keep an eye on the big picture', *Cape Argus*, 26 September 2006.

70 'Zuma lays into the Scorpions', *Mail & Guardian*, 21 September 2006.

71 *Ibid.*

72 'The Zuma super charges', *Mail & Guardian*, 4 January 2008.

73 'Schedule to Indictment and Summary of Facts: Payments made by Shaik and Nkobi Group to and on behalf of Zuma', prepared by KPMG. Available at: www.armsdeal-vpo.co.za.

74 *Ibid.*

75 *Ibid.*

76 'Indictment in the High Court of South Africa (Natal Provincial Division) in the matter of the State versus Jacob Gedleyihlekisa Zuma, Thint Holding (Southern Africa) and Thint (PTY)'. Available at: www.armsdeal-vpo.co.za.

77 *Ibid.*

78 *Ibid.*

79 *Ibid.*

80 Annexure A to Indictment and Summary of Facts. Available at: www.armsdeal-vpo.co.za.

81 *Ibid.*

82 'Indictment in the High Court of South Africa (Natal Provincial Division) in the matter of the State versus Jacob Gedleyihlekisa Zuma, Thint Holding (Southern Africa) and Thint (PTY)'. Available at: www.armsdeal-vpo.co.za.

83 *Ibid.*

84 *Ibid.*

85 *Ibid*, paragraphs 137–139.

86 *Ibid*, paragraphs 140–148.

87 *Ibid*, paragraphs 149–150.

88 *Ibid*, paragraph 151.

89 *Ibid*, paragraph 152.

90 'State seeks Zuma court date', *Cape Times*, 5 August 2008.

91 Zuma, J. 2008. Affidavit submitted to High Court, 17 June. Available at: www.saflii.org.za.

92 *Ibid.*

93 *Ibid.*

94 *Ibid.*

95 Du Plooy, J. 2008. Answering affidavit filed in the High Court of South Africa (Natal Provincial Decision) in the matter between the State and Jacob Gedleyihlekisa Zuma and Others, Case No. 273/07 (8652/08), 11 July, paragraph 143.

96 *Ibid*, paragraphs 144–145.

97 'Zuma hits out at media', *IOL*/SAPA, 5 August 2008.

98 'Political rhetoric or real warning?', *IOL*, 4 August 2008.

99 'Why Zuma will walk', *IOL*, 2 August 2008.

100 *Ibid*.

101 Zuma, J. 2008. Affidavit submitted to High Court, 17 June. Available at: www.saflii.org.za.

102 'State seeks Zuma court date', *Cape Times*, 5 August 2008.

103 'Why Zuma will walk', *IOL*, 2 August 2008.

CHAPTER 9

1 See: *Strategic Defence Packages: Joint Report*, 2001, Chapter 7 – Selection of Prime Contractors: Corvettes. Available at: www.info.gov.za.

2 'Shaik "had Cabinet minutes and State letters"', *Cape Argus*, 16 November 2001.

3 See: 'How the case against Shaik implicated Deputy President', *Sunday Times*, 31 August 2003. This was also addressed at length during Judge Hilary Squires' judgment on the case against Schabir Shaik. See: 'In the matter between the State and Schabir Shaik *et al.*' Case No. CC27/04, 31 May 2005. Available at: www.armsdeal-vpo.co.za.

4 'The corvettes, the R130m "expenses" and Thabo Mbeki', *Sunday Times*, 16 July 2006.

5 *Ibid;* and 'Excellent connections', *Der Spiegel*, 3 July 2006.

6 *Ibid*.

7 'On German kickbacks and the corvette contract', *politicsweb*, 7 April 2008. Available at: www.politicsweb.co.za.

8 *Ibid*.

9 *Ibid*.

10 Feinstein, A. *After the Party*, p 226.

11 'On German kickbacks and the corvette contract', *politicsweb*,
   7 April 2008. Available at: www.politicsweb.co.za; 'Corvettes "bias"
   claim probed', *The Argus*, 14 June 1995; 'Corvettes – Thabo all at
   sea', *Weekend Argus*, 20 May 1995.

12 Gevisser, M. *Thabo Mbeki: The Dream Deferred*, p 677.

13 'Mo's ready for great Shaiks in Germany', *The Star*, 15 July 1997.

14 Feinstein, A. *After the Party*, p 226.

15 Gevisser, M. *Thabo Mbeki: The Dream Deferred*, p 677.

16 '"Mbeki did meet with arms company"', *The Star*, 13 February
   2008.

17 *Ibid*.

18 See: 'Mbeki's secret French connection', *Noseweek*, June 2006.

19 See: 'Mbeki, the MacGuffin, Bazan, and the scuppering of the
   original corvette contract', *everfasternews*, 12 July 2006. Available
   at: www.ever-fasternews.com. Also see: 'Arms deal: focus on
   Mbeki', *Mail & Guardian*, 7 July 2006.

20 'Mbeki in clear about arms deal report', IOL/SAPA, 9 July 2006.

21 'German industrial giant cleared in arms-deal probe', *Mail &
   Guardian Online*, 18 June 2008.

22 See: 'On German kickbacks and the corvette contract (II)',
   politicsweb, 8 April 2008. Available at: www.politicsweb.co.za.

23 *Strategic Defence Packages: Joint Report*, 2001, Chapter 7, paragraph
   7.3.5.4 (i). Available at: www.info.gov.za.

24 *Ibid*, paragraph 7.3.5.4(a).

25 *Ibid*, paragraph 7.3.5.4(i).

26 *Ibid*.

27 *Ibid*.

28 'Guns vs. butter? Corvettes decision looms for New SA', *Weekend
   Argus*, 26 February 1995.

29 See: 'On German kickbacks and the corvette contract', *politicsweb*,
   7 April 2008. Available at: www.politicsweb.co.za.

30 *Strategic Defence Packages: Joint Report*, 2001. Available at: www.
   info.gov.za. Also see *The Arms Deal for Dummies, Cape Argus/Helen
   Suzman Foundation*, 27 March 2003, and 'South Africa's multi-
   billion arms deal programme revisited (Part One)', *Defence Systems
   Daily*, 15 October 2001.

31 'The R30m bombshell that points fingers at both Mbeki and his
   former Deputy: Special Investigation', *Sunday Times*, 3 August
   2008.

32 *Ibid.*
33 *Ibid.*
34 'The big con', *Sunday Times*, 10 August 2008.
35 'The spy who fingered Mbeki', *Mail & Guardian*, 8 August 2008.
36 *Ibid.*
37 *Ibid.*
38 *Ibid.*
39 'Mistakes, inaccuracies and omissions contained in the "Secret Report" underlying the Sunday Times allegations', letter sent to the *Sunday Times*, 24 August 2008. Available at www.manferrostaal. com.
40 'Arms dealer requests correction', *Cape Times*, 10 August 2008.
41 'Presidencies guns fire at Sunday Times', *Mail & Guardian*/SAPA, 3 August 2008.
42 *Strategic Defence Packages: Joint Report*, 2001, Chapter 6 – Selection of Prime Contractors: Submarines. Available at: www.info.gov.za.
43 *Ibid*, paragraph 6.1.6.
44 *Ibid*, paragraph 6.4.8.9.
45 *Ibid*, paragraph 6.4.8.10.
46 *Ibid.*
47 *Ibid.*
48 *Ibid*, paragraph 6.1.6.
49 *Ibid*, paragraph 6.4.6.13.
50 *Ibid.*
51 *Ibid*, paragraph 6.4.5.7.
52 *Ibid*, paragraph 6.4.5.8.
53 'Shamin Shaik guilty of "disclosing information"', *Mail & Guardian*/SAPA, 20 January 2002.
54 'Chippy Shaik resigns', *Sunday Times*, 28 March 2002.
55 Author's personal communication with Andrew Feinstein, 9 May 2008.
56 'No credible evidence on Chippy – Mabandla', *Cape Argus*, 3 August 2007.
57 *Ibid.*
58 *Ibid.*
59 Letter from RM Young to Professor Eduard Eitelberg, 17 April 2007. Available at: www.armsdeal-vpo.co.za.
60 'Resolution and reasons for withdrawal of S. Shaik's PhD thesis', 29 February 2008. Available at: www.armsdeal-vpo.co.za.

61 'Chippy's packing, but denies it's for Australia', *The Times*,
   23 March 2008.
62 'The full list of vehicles supplied by EADS', *Cape Times*, 2 July 2001.
63 *Ibid*.
64 *Ibid*. Also see: 'More Mercs pop up, defence chief to answer why',
   SABC News, 24 June 2001; 'Chief of SANDF also got Merc', *Sunday
   Times*, 24 June 2001; and 'VIP car list makes for interesting
   reading', *IOL*, 2 July 2001.
65 'State withdraws charges against German businessman', SAPA,
   19 March 2003.
66 *Ibid*.
67 'Chippy Shaik shock', *The Citizen*, 6 February 2007.
68 'Pillay found guilty after Merc probe', *IOL*, 15 February 2002.
69 'Arms deal participant fired', *Business Day*, 30 May 2002.
70 'De Lille in rare move over arms-deal accused', *The Star*, 23 March
   2003; and 'Arms deal: ID president Patricia de Lille initiates
   process to be able to privately prosecute the other South Africans
   who received massive luxury car discounts', Press statement,
   22 March 2007. Available at: www.id.org.za.
71 'Yengeni stung by Scorpions', *Pretoria News*, 6 October 2001.
72 'Scorpions, DA "hate the ANC"', *News24*, 15 April 2008.
73 '"Zuma case influenced decision"', *Mail & Guardian*, 11 April 2008.
74 *Ibid*.
75 *Ibid*.
76 'Animal Farm', *Business Day*, 17 April 2008.
77 'The Scorpions versus the Constitution', *Sunday Independent*,
   17 February 2008.
78 *Ibid*.
79 *Ibid*.
80 'The sting in the Scorpions tale', *politicsweb*, 24 April 2008.
   Available at: www.politicsweb.co.za.
81 'Country to lose its best crime-fighters', *Cape Times*, 5 February
   2008.
82 'Unit struck terror into long list of bad guys', *The Times*, 27 January
   2008.
83 'NPA hits back at ANC criticism of clearance for Scorpions',
   Business Day, 7 May 2008.
84 'Nyanda: "We will vet Scorpions"', *Mail & Guardian*, 15 February
   2008.

85 'Khampepe: Scorpions must stay', *Mail & Guardian*, 5 May 2008.

86 'Scorpions "still have a place in state law enforcement plan"', *Business Day*, 6 May 2008. Also see: 'Khampepe: Scorpions must stay', *Mail & Guardian*/SAPA, 5 May 2008.

87 'The sting in the Scorpions tale', *politicsweb*, 24 April 2008. Available at: www.politicsweb.co.za.

88 'Khampepe: Scorpions must stay', *Mail & Guardian*/SAPA, 5 May 2008. Also see: 'In the wake of the Scorpions', *Mail & Guardian*, 17 May 2008.

89 Feinstein, A. *After the Party*, p 177.

90 See: Squires, H. 'Judgment in the High Court of South Africa (Durban and Coastal Local Division) in the matter between the State and Schabir Shaik *et al.*', Case No: CC27/04, 31 May 2005. Available at: www.armsdeal-vpo.co.za.

91 '"My special bond with Zuma"', *The Star*, 22 February 2005.

92 *Ibid.*

93 *Ibid.*

94 When the auditor tasked with investigating Shaik's finances, Johan van der Walt, was asked about this matter, he noted that he could not find any record of payments being made from Floryn to the ANC reflected in Floryn's books. Under questioning, Van der Walt suggested that it was probable that the payments were made but not entered into the books. Van der Walt found this a strange tactic on the part of Floryn: 'The best way to donate money is to issue a cheque,' Van der Walt argued. See: 'No proof of payments to the ANC, says auditor', *Daily News*, 9 November 2004.

95 'Lynch-mob mentality does nothing for justice or clean government', ANCToday, Vol. 3, No. 34, 29 August 2003.

96 'Arms broker did give cash to the ANC', *Mail & Guardian*, 14 March 2008.

97 *Ibid.*

98 *Ibid.*

99 *Ibid.*

100 'State of the Organisation', ANC 49th National Conference, Bloemfontein 17–21 December 1994. Available at: www.anc.org.za.

101 Squires, H. 'Judgment in the High Court of South Africa (Durban and Coastal Local Division) in the matter between the State and Schabir Shaik *et al.*', Case No: CC27/04, 31 May 2005. Available at: www.armsdeal-vpo.co.za

102 Report of the Office of the Treasurer General to the 50th National
    Conference of the African National Congress, 16–20 December
    1997, Mafikeng. Available at: www.anc.org.za.
103 *Ibid.*
104 *Ibid.*
105 *Ibid.*

APPENDIX C

Extrapolated from: 'In the High Court of South Africa (Durban
    Coastal and Local Division) in the matter between the State and
    Schabir Shaik and Others: Summary of Substantial Facts in terms
    of Section 144(3)(a) of Act 51 of 1977' and 'Indictment: In the
    High Court of South Africa (Durban and Coastal Local Division)
    in the matter between the State and Jacob Zuma, Thint Holding
    and Thint (PTY)'; and 'Summary of Substantial Facts In Terms of
    Section 144(3)(a) of Act 51 of 1977 in the High Court of South
    Africa (Durban and Coastal Local Division) in the matter between
    the State and Jacob Zuma, Thint Holding and Thint (PTY)'.
    Available at: www.armsdeal-vpo.co.za.

RECOMMENDED READING

All of the sources referred to in this book are publicly available and easily accessible. So, if you feel the itch to investigate further, take the time to investigate the books and websites listed below.

BOOKS TO READ

So far, there have been three major works that have investigated the arms deal in considerable depth. The first is Andrew Feinstein's rip-roaring account of his time on Scopa and the travails he faced: *After the Party* (Jonathan Ball, 2007). The second is Mark Gevisser's unsurpassed biography of Thabo Mbeki, which includes some pretty startling revelations about the relationship between Mbeki, the arms deal and Jacob Zuma: *Thabo Mbeki: The Dream Deferred* (Jonathan Ball, 2007). The third book you have to read is Terry Crawford-Browne's devastating account of the arms deal, and his own attempts to have it declared unconstitutional: *Eye on the Money* (Umuzi, 2007)

BOOKMARK THESE PAGES

The internet truly is a gold mine for arms deal research. The following websites are ones that you should make every effort to visit and explore:

www.armsdeal-vpo.co.za

Perhaps the most important website related to the arms deal, this website, run by Richard Young, carries an archive of virtually every newspaper article run on the arms deal. Its 'special features' section is also vitally important: here, you can download all the legal documents referred to in this book, including the indictments served on Zuma and Shaik and various legal judgments.

www.pmg.org.za

The website of the Parliamentary Monitoring Group, which tracks and reports on all the happenings with Parliament's labyrinthine sub-committees. It is here that you will find all the minutes of the deliberations relating to the arms deal in the sub-committees.

www.parliament.gov.za

The website of SA's Parliament. Direct your browser here if you want to download *Hansard*, recording, word for word, the daily deeds of Parliament.

www.info.gov.za

A treasure trove of speeches and official reports. This website will provide you with the full text of almost all the speeches and important government correspondence quoted in this book. You can also download the full Joint Investigation Report from this website.

www.mg.co.za
The homepage of the *Mail & Guardian*. Refer to this website for daily updates of what's happening in the arms deal and for excellent commentary.

www.businessday.co.za
This is the homepage of *Business Day*. Again, click here if you want to a quick-fix of arms deal news reportage.

www.iol.co.za
Ideal if you want a quick and easy update on what's happening in the arms deal, Independent Online's site also offers a very useful and detailed archive search function.

www.news24.co.za
Another daily news update site, with similarly impressive archive search functions.

www.allafrica.com
This excellent website carries frequently updated news stories culled from a variety of South African and African newspapers.

www.ingramcontent.com/pod-product-compliance
Lightning Source LLC
Chambersburg PA
CBHW070841300326
41935CB00039B/1333